The Road to Teheran

THE STORY OF RUSSIA
AND AMERICA, 1781-1943

Foster Rhea Dulles

PRINCETON, NEW JERSEY
PRINCETON UNIVERSITY PRESS

1944

The Road to Teheran

THE STORY OF RUSSIA
AND AMERICA, 1781-1943

Dulles, Foster Rhea, 1900–

The road to Teheran; the story of Russia and America 1781–1943 ₁by₁ Foster Rhea Dulles. Princeton, N. J., Prince ton university press, 1944.

vi p., 1 l., 279 p. 20 cm.

"Bibliographical notes": p. 263–268.

PREFACE

THE purpose of this book is to trace the relations between the people of the United States and the people of Russia from the early days of our own independence to those of the common association of the two nations in the world struggle against Nazi Germany. It makes no claim whatsoever to being a definitive survey of the immensely broad subject with which it deals. It is rather an attempt to record the salient features in the past history of Russian-American relations as they may influence or affect the efforts that are being made today to discover an enduring basis for understanding and good will between Russia and America.

The account is necessarily written from an American point of view. It is based upon American sources. Whatever material was available on how Russia has interpreted her policy toward the United States, or on what the Russian people have thought of this country, was carefully used. But it must be admitted from the onset that our policy toward Russia, and the reaction of the American public to developments both in Czarist Russia and Communist Russia, provide the book's principal theme.

Bibliographical notes giving a chapter-by-chapter account of the sources will be found in the closing pages. It is sufficient at this point to note that they include the available official documents; the diaries, memoirs and other records of those who have played a significant role in Russian-American relations; contemporary comment on things Russian as found in newspapers and magazines during the nineteenth as well as the twentieth century, and a wealth of special monographic material.

The author would like to acknowledge his grateful indebtedness to Datus C. Smith, Jr., of the Princeton University Press upon whose suggestion the book was written; to Professor Allen Helms and Professor Henry R. Spencer, of Ohio State

London: Humphrey Milford: Oxford University Press

CONTENTS

PREFACE

University, for their helpful reading of the manuscript; to Mary Rhea Dulles for aid with the index, and to Marion Dulles, whose help and encouragement, as on previous occasions, has been virtually that of a collaborator.

FOSTER RHEA DULLES

Ohio State University

appears to be marked by the will of heaven to sway the destinies of half the globe."

Their similarities in background and character have caused the American and Russian people to have a marked interest in one another despite the fact that their countries are upon opposite sides of the world and direct contacts have always been extremely rare. From the days when Alexander I studied the American constitution to those in which the leaders of the Soviet Union have paid such flattering attention to our industrial development, the people of Russia have again and again looked across the Atlantic with wonder and admiration at what was happening in the United States. "We never forget that America is a capitalist country," Stalin has declared. "But we respect American efficiency in industry, technique, literature and life."

The American people have always been strangely fascinated by Russia. Even when we have understood her least, or have been appalled by developments that we could not reconcile with our own philosophy, the fascination has still been there. Henry Adams once wrote that "Russia was the most indigestible morsel he ever met." Many Americans have felt even more keenly that this vast country was an enigma they could never hope to fathom. But it nevertheless remains true that as a nation we have always had sympathy and friendship for a people with whom we have somehow felt strangely akin.

A land of snow and ice, of long cold winters, of limitless steppes, of frozen tundras—Holy Russia or Communist Russia, what has this great country really meant to Americans? It has meant many things, at different times and to different people. Napoleon's retreat from Moscow, the Crimean War, the Bear That Walks Like a Man, Port Arthur and the Japanese fleet, Ten Days That Shook the World, the Third International, the defense of Moscow and battle of Stalingrad are chapters in an historic drama whose long unfolding we have always watched with absorption. St. Petersburg—Petrograd—Leningrad; the Volga, mother of rivers; the forbidding walls of the Kremlin, the great industrial cities of the Urals, have each in turn stood

in
s.
e·
s.
1-
n
e
t

goal. Russia has had her expansive ambitions and the America people have not always restrained their acquisitive instinct. But more generally both countries have sought national se curity rather than foreign conquest or colonial possession. Thomas Jefferson once declared that Russia and America, essen tially pacific in character and practice, had a common cause in upholding the rights of all peaceable nations. His words were echoed by Franklin D. Roosevelt when he received the first ambassador of Soviet Russia to the United States. "A deep love of peace," he stated upon that occasion, "is the common heri tage of the people of both our countries."

The vast extent and great natural riches of the territories of the United States and Russia are the primary factor behind their emphasis upon national security rather than overseas empire. Boundless areas of plain and forest, fertile river valleys and broad prairies, are their common possession. No other country has such untold resources in arable lands, forest re serves, oil deposits and mineral wealth as have both Russia and America. The settling of these far-reaching expanses of territory and the development of these illimitable resources have been a constant challenge to their peoples and have in large part served to absorb their energies.

The frontier has played a major role in their respective his tories, placing its stamp upon national character, while in more recent years industrial development has served to open in each nation new vistas of national progress. Russia and America have always looked to the future, for it has always been big with promise, and their people have shared a sturdy confidence, a sense of inherent power, that have often impressed foreign visitors. "There are at present two great nations in the world," Tocqueville wrote a century ago, "which seem to tend towards the same end, although they start from different points. I allude to the Russians and the Americans. . . . Their starting point is different and their courses are not the same, yet each of them

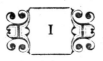

I

THE COMMON CAUSE

THE United States and Russia have been at peace throughout their common history of more than a century and a half. Even though there have been periods of marked friction between the two nations, and at the close of the first World War we found ourselves, however reluctantly, intervening in Russia's affairs, it is still true that over a long period of time Russian-American relations have been generally friendly. The United States has taken up arms against every other major power. If the record is carried back to the eighteenth century, we find that we became engaged in a flare-up of naval warfare against France in the late 1790's; something more than a decade later we fought England in the War of 1812, and more recently the great world struggles of the twentieth century have drawn us into conflict with Germany, Italy and Japan. So too has Russia at one time or another during these years been at war with each of these great powers. The peoples of Russia and America have fought together as allies; never as declared enemies.

Chance is not responsible for this long record of peaceful relations, nor is it entirely the fact of geographical separation. The objectives of trade and commerce, and the foreign policies of the two nations, have generally run along parallel lines. Their interests have been very much the same and threats to those interests have arisen in the same quarters. In the nineteenth century a common rivalry with Great Britain drew the United States and Russia together, and in the twentieth century the direct challenge of Germany and Japan has made them close allies.

The fundamental objective of their foreign policies, moreover, has been the maintenance of peace. There have been occasions when imperialism appeared to overshadow such

for Russia in the popular imagination. For some Americans Tolstoi's magnificent *War and Peace* has symbolized Russia, but for others it has been represented by the gigantic Dnieprostroy Dam, or perhaps the Red Terror and the extermination of the Kulaks. Again, the spirit of Russia has been found in the Moscow Art Theatre, hard-riding Cossacks, the knout and exile to Siberia, ikons, Nijinsky and the ballet, Dostoevsky, nihilism, the music of Tchaikovsky. . . .

The imagination of America has been caught by the great figures who have played their part on the Russian stage: the proud, imperious Catherine who kept our envoy waiting at her doorstep but commissioned John Paul Jones as an admiral in her fleet; Alexander I who corresponded with Jefferson, walked and talked with John Quincy Adams, and created the Holy Alliance to establish peace throughout the world; Alexander II who won the name of Liberator for freeing the serfs at the same time that Lincoln the Emancipator was freeing American slaves; and finally Nicholas II, paying the final penalty for the sins of autocracy, caught in the web of intrigue woven by the Czarina and the sinister Rasputin. Americans have also followed the dramatic careers of the more recent statesmen of Russia: the unlucky Kerensky, seeking to uphold democracy with endless and ineffectual talk; Lenin, ruthless, determined, inspired; the perennial revolutionary Trotsky; and Stalin . . . what may one say of Stalin? A symbol of cold, naked power; blunt and unemotional; harshly realistic. But as an individual? "A child would like to sit in his lap," we have read in the reports of former Ambassador Davies, "and a dog would sidle up to him."

For all our interest in the drama of Russia and our underlying sympathy for the Russian people, and despite our common goal of a peace that would enable us to work out our respective destinies, the political systems of the two countries have always been at opposite poles. Autocracy has been arrayed against Republicanism, Communism against Democracy. And this ideological conflict has led to periods of dangerous fric-

tion between the two governments. By the opening of the twentieth century, the oppressive tyranny of Czarist Russia as contrasted with the progressive liberalism of America threatened a serious breach in our official relations, but with the advent of Communism, the mutual antagonism between two even more opposing systems of government overlaid our traditional friendship with so tough a crust of mutual suspicion that for a time that friendship appeared to be doomed.

The interplay of these various factors in Russian-American history provides the framework for a story of compelling interest. As far back as the close of the eighteenth century, when the United States first sought Russian recognition, the contrast between the parallelism in our foreign policies and the conflict in political ideas was apparent. Catherine the Great would not lend her Cossacks for the suppression of American rebels since she welcomed any development that might reduce the power of Great Britain, but at the same time she could hardly look with favor upon republican revolt against monarchial authority. In the nineteenth century, the divergence between American and Russian political ideals did not deflect either nation from acting in concert to restrain, whenever possible, British maritime supremacy. The most autocratic of European governments and republican America together tried to uphold the freedom of the seas during the Napoleonic Wars. Jefferson declared that Russia was the most cordially friendly of all European powers, and Alexander gave proof of such an attitude by offering to mediate in our war with England in 1812. In their mutual desire to see each other strong and powerful as a counterpoise to Great Britain, the United States and Russia refused in the middle of the century to submit to European pressure for intervention in one another's internal affairs. America sympathized with Russia during the Crimean War; Russia stood stanchly by the Union in the crisis of our Civil War.

A solidarity firmly based upon national interest was apparently sealed with our purchase of Alaska. The two nation could hardly have been in closer accord. "Russia and the United States," we find the *New York Herald* confidently proclaiming in 1867, "must ever be friendly, the colossi having neither territorial nor maritime jealousies to excite the one against the other. The interests of both demand that they should go hand in hand in their march to empire."

The turn of the century nevertheless witnessed the first serious estrangement between the two nations. For a time their foreign policies clashed in a growing rivalry over trade and political interests in the Far East, while our underlying political antagonism flared up in American resentment at the reactionary program that was being pursued by Nicholas II. This outburst of hostility began to subside when Japan took up the challenge of Russian imperialism in eastern Asia. The rise of that new power in the Pacific, a far more ominous threat to American interests than Czarist Russia, once again brought our foreign policies in accord. Although there remained serious friction because of opposing political views, Japan began to take over the role that Great Britain had played in the nineteenth century as a catalytic agent in Russian-American relations.

The first World War created an even more important community of interests. Although the United States stood aloof for almost three years, we were eventually drawn into the struggle and found ourselves fighting side by side with Russia against the same foe. The challenge of Germany had sharply emphasized the common basis of our foreign policies. For a brief time too the old paradox of converging aims abroad and opposing political systems at home was resolved. With the overthrow of the Czar, Russia and the United States were aligned not only in support of their national security but in defense of democratic rights. "Here is a fit partner for a League of Honor," was President Wilson's enthusiastic welcome of Free Russia.

These days were short-lived. The Bolshevik revolution and establishment of the Soviet government renewed in far more virulent form the old ideological conflict. The political and

economic system that Russia now adopted was not only abhorrent to democratic America, but its threat of world revolution was a far more aggressive challenge to our social order than Czarist tyranny. Militant Communism could not be dismissed as in no way menacing American institutions. The possible bases of cooperation in the field of international affairs were undermined by contention far more bitter than anything Russia and America had experienced in the past. With emotions heightened by the hysteria of war, and under as complex and complicated a set of factors as ever bedeviled the relations between two countries, suspicion and mistrust wholly replaced the understanding of more than a century.

There were substantial grounds for this new hostility. Russia feared capitalistic encirclement; the United States feared the Communist propaganda of revolution. The Soviet Union could point to American intervention at Archangel and in Siberia, and the United States to the subversive interference in our affairs by spokesmen of the Third International. Diplomatic relations between the two countries remained severed for sixteen years as the United States obstinately refused to recognize the Soviet regime. The two great nations stood forth as champions of apparently irreconcilable social and political systems. The mutual antagonisms thus aroused set the pattern for Russian-American relations, even after we had at last recognized the Soviets in 1933, during a quarter-century of decisive world history.

Nevertheless the fundamental interests that had drawn Russia and America together in the past had not lost their validity. Both nations still needed above everything else national security in order to develop their great natural resources and to promote the economic progress upon which Russia as well as the United States had now embarked. Any threat to world peace was their common concern. The forces that had made for Russian-American friendship through the long years since they had together tried to uphold the freedom of the seas were still operating.

A renewed threat of Japanese imperialism in the Far East first brought this out. It was an important factor in our belated decision to recognize the Soviet government. But the still graver danger of Fascism failed to bring about any effective collaboration in restraining the aggression of Germany, even though events would soon prove it to be the really vital challenge to the peace and freedom of both nations. The two most powerful countries in the world were prevented by the mistrust and suspicion born of bitter ideological differences from acting in concert despite their ancient friendship and long record of mutual cooperation. The idea of collective security was thereby doomed. The United States and Soviet Russia retreated into isolation and war gradually engulfed the world.

It was only actual attack by the Axis powers, from which both the United States and Russia had sought to guard themselves by a policy of precarious neutrality, that finally brought the two nations together once again in defense of their liberties. A danger perhaps more urgent than either country had ever faced forced them to set aside their political controversies and seek to overcome a quarter of a century of discord in order that they might join forces, in common with other members of the United Nations, to repel the onslaught of totalitarian powers jeopardizing the freedom of the entire world.

The revival of their historic friendship could not fail to prove difficult. But the very fact that its roots were so deep in the past, and that it had developed through the years out of common interests transcending all other points of difference, marked the effort toward a new rapprochement as conforming not only to the immediate but also to the long-term interests of the two nations. Their leaders were in agreement that it was vital that the United States and Russia should remain in accord if the world was ever to know enduring peace. The conference at Teheran was both confirmation of the past and promise for the future.

AT THE COURT OF THE CZARS

On August 27, 1781, a young American, Francis Dana of Massachusetts, arrived at the Russian capital of St. Petersburg charged with the mission of seeking recognition of the United States from that "wise and virtuous Princess," the Empress Catherine II. It was a delicate task. Could the autocratic ruler of All-the-Russias be expected to receive the envoy of a handful of struggling colonies in rebellion against the might and authority of the British crown? To avoid the possibility of a humiliating rebuff, Dana was cautiously traveling "in the character of a private gentleman." Nevertheless he reached St. Petersburg fully impressed with the importance of his mission and hopeful of success.

The Continental Congress had considered the possibilities of this move as early as December 1776. Nothing had been done about it at that time, but by 1781 developments in Europe gave rise to the belief that for all her own devotion to autocratic principles of government, Catherine might be willing to welcome the United States into the family of nations. It was known that she had refused to loan any of her Cossacks to George III for the subjugation of the rebels against his rule. It was believed that she was sympathetic toward the Americans, not for their republicanism but because Anglo-Russian rivalry might be expected to make her favor any movement weakening the British Empire. Also she had a scheme on foot which the Continental Congress thought might provide a means for the United States to win her friendly support.

As a result of the constant interference with neutral shipping in the course of the general war raging among England, France and Spain, the Empress had taken the lead the year before in establishing a Maritime Confederacy for the protection of the rights of nonbelligerents. Sweden and Denmark had joined forces with Russia in an Armed Neutrality. In a sharp challenge to England's customary interference with neutral commerce, the Maritime Confederacy advanced the principles that free ships make free goods, that contraband should be expressly limited to arms and ammunition, and that no blockade is legal unless it is effectively enforced.

America, at war with Great Britain, was prepared to accept this interpretation of the rules of naval warfare. Our interests in this respect were identical with those of the Maritime Confederacy. Although Catherine's invitation to join the Armed Neutrality was extended to neutrals rather than belligerents, the Continental Congress hoped that by expressing a willingness to acknowledge its principles the United States might be admitted to membership. If Catherine could be prevailed upon to accept American adherence, it would constitute recognition of our independence and immensely strengthen our international position. The prize appeared well worth the effort of dispatching an envoy to St. Petersburg.

Against this background, but with no direct knowledge of what Russia's attitude might be, the Continental Congress had instructed Dana to seek recognition and possible support from Russia, to undertake negotiation of a treaty of amity and commerce, and to urge upon Catherine the advisability of the United States being "formally admitted as a party to the conventions of the neutral maritime powers." He was, however, to cooperate with the French government, our one ally in Europe, and to make no move in approaching Catherine which the French ambassador at St. Petersburg did not approve. To this extent at least our inexperience in the wiles of European diplomacy was recognized and the tutelage of France accepted for the proposed negotiations.

Dana was already abroad when the dispatches telling of his appointment reached him and it was after consultations in Paris with Benjamin Franklin and John Adams that he made the decision to travel privately rather than to storm St. Petersburg

in his official capacity. For these experienced diplomats were not as sanguine as the members of the Continental Congress about the American envoy's welcome. Russian foreign policy could hardly be predicted when it had to conform to the changing whims of an ambitious and self-willed autocrat. Soon Dana found these doubts more than confirmed. The French minister at St. Petersburg, the Marquis de Verac, strongly advised him to make no advances whatsoever to the court. He was certain they would be flatly rejected.

Dana was of a somewhat suspicious nature. He became convinced that the Marquis de Verac was attempting to block his path out of jealousy and a desire to prevent the United States from escaping French tutelage. There was perhaps some basis for this general charge. France did not like to see the Continental Congress make any diplomatic moves on its own initiative. The French minister on this occasion, however, was acting both in good faith and with far greater understanding of the European situation than Dana possessed. For by the time Dana reached St. Petersburg Catherine was playing with a new political ambition. She had almost forgotten the Maritime Confederacy. She would soon refer to it herself as the "Armed Nullity." In cooperation with the Emperor of Austria she had proposed mediation in the war between England and France and was casting herself in the magnificent role of the Pacificator of Europe.

Obviously under such circumstances there could be no recognition of the United States and no thought of admitting the young republic to any European League. Catherine could not afford to prejudice her neutrality in the eyes of Great Britain. "It is therefore clear," the Marquis de Verac sought to explain to Dana, "that their design is to avoid compromitting themselves by acknowledging the independence of the United States until England herself shall have taken the lead." The American could not deny this logic nor act against the informed advice of his mentor. There was nothing for him to do but wait a more propitious time for seeking an audience.

THE ROAD TO TEHERAN

Dana was doubly exiled in St. Petersburg. He was far from home and completely cut off from the social life of one of the most gay, colorful and sophisticated courts of all Europe. Catherine ruled in autocratic splendor and entertained lavishly amid surroundings that amazed all visitors. Her balls and receptions were dazzling, and no expense was spared to impress foreigners with the wealth and power of Russia. It was also a court honeycombed with intrigue and notorious for its "alcove politics." Throughout her entire reign Catherine took one lover after another only to cast him off as she grew bored with him, and the current favorite often exercised a greater influence over her than her ministers of state. His pleasure would be the pivot about which all other affairs revolved.

The lonely envoy of the Continental Congress had no part in all this, neither the social life nor the intrigue. As he walked the streets of the magnificent capital, "a superb monument to the immortal memory of Peter the Great" as he himself described it, he must have caught occasional glimpses of this world from which he was barred. Standing with the gaping crowd he may have seen Catherine moving in royal procession through the streets or reviewing her troops in the public square, but without being officially recognized he had no entree to the imperial palaces. Upon one occasion friends at The Hague sought to forward a portrait of Washington to him through a Russian courier. Catherine gave orders that the package addressed to "one Dina, an American agent here" should be at once returned: "This man is not known to her Imperial Majesty."

Dana was alone except for a single companion, his secretary, who was the fourteen-year-old John Quincy Adams. Time hung heavy on the hands of the restless diplomat and the precocious young boy. They had taken lodgings in a Russian inn, rather grandiloquently called L'Hotel de Paris, and except for occasional calls upon a few other foreigners they had virtually no social life. "Master Johnny" kept assiduously at the studies which were always a major interest for every member of the

· 12 ·

famous Adams family; Dana wrote injured letters to John Adams, Sr., and long complaining reports to the Continental Congress. He did not like the bitter Russian winter; he suffered grievously from colds and fever.

The instructions he received from Robert Livingston, Secretary of Foreign Affairs, did not add much to his comfort. His criticism of the attitude of the French minister, whom he continued to regard as unfriendly, was officially rebuked. He was told to follow the advice of the Marquis de Verac and make no attempt to present his letters of credence until he was assured they would be officially accepted. There should be no occasion for the least slight upon the honor of the United States.

During the winter of 1781-1782 Dana somehow became convinced that he might be able to overcome Catherine's dislike of republican rebels and her fear of offending England by demonstrating the commercial advantages to Russia of recognizing the United States. He carefully drew up certain "reflections" on the possibilities of American-Russian trade and succeeded in getting them into the hands of one of the Czarina's ministers. But he could make no further progress with his new project. Moreover his feeling of discouragement was increased when he learned that the signature of any treaty at the Russian court, according to well established custom, involved a gift of six thousand rubles to each of the four ministers empowered to sign such a document. He reported home that for him to accomplish anything at all "it would be indispensably necessary Congress should enable me to advance that sum," and it was quite apparent that he had slight hopes of any such extravagance.

Not until the receipt of news in December 1782 that preliminary peace terms had been concluded by Great Britain and the United States, were Dana's hopes of being officially received by Catherine revived. Now at last "the proper time" for him to appear at court seemed to be at hand. But obviously the situation had greatly changed since his arrival in Russia. Not only had Catherine largely lost interest in her Armed Neutrality; it was no longer to the benefit of the United States to join a foreign coalition. With independence in sight the Continental Congress was veering away from any European involvement, and Dana himself quite agreed that the young republic should adopt "a system of politics to ourselves." His strongest ground for seeking recognition, he believed, was his proposed commercial treaty. The French minister, whose advice Dana still felt obliged to follow, disagreed with him completely. Peace between the United States and Great Britain, he told the American envoy, did not sufficiently clear the air. It would be necessary to await as well peace among Great Britain, France and Spain before running the risk of a rebuff from the temperamental Catherine. The discouraged Dana retreated once more to the fastnesses of the Hotel de Paris and the tutoring of Master Johnny.

After nursing his impatience for another three months until preliminary peace terms were finally signed by the European belligerents, he made up his mind that he would wait no longer. Without consulting the Marquis de Verac he took the plunge and made formal announcement of his mission to the Imperial Vice-Chancellor. For long there was no response whatsoever to his official communication. When an answer finally came, it bluntly stated that recognition of the United States was not possible until a final and definitive peace was concluded. Dana was told that the Empress Catherine had no quarrel with the United States, and was quite satisfied with his own conduct and person, but her position as a mediatrix in the European conflict made it impossible for her to receive an American minister.

"I am sick, sick to the heart, of the delicacies and whims of European politics," Dana wrote despairingly, but he still felt obliged to wait upon Catherine's humor. It was hardly worthwhile. Her interest soon shifted from the affairs of western Europe to war with Turkey, and her desire for British support in this new venture made her all the less interested in recog-

nizing the United States. Dana was now told that entirely apart from the conclusion of peace, the fact that his letter of credence was dated before British recognition of American independence made an audience at court impossible.

It was the final blow. This latest objection to receiving him was an affront he refused to accept. He protested vigorously that it was a slur upon the dignity of the United States to make recognition dependent upon Great Britain. This spirited action caused a change of heart at court. Dana was now officially advised that he would be formally received by Catherine so soon as a peace treaty was formally signed, and that in the meantime American ships would be welcomed at Russian ports. If this were victory it came too late to assuage his ruffled feelings. The audience for which he had been waiting two weary years now appeared an "inexpedient and useless ceremony." He had failed to win Russia's moral support while his country was at war and it no longer appeared important. He would shake the inhospitable dust of St. Petersburg from his shoes and "quit this miserable existence."

Fortunately for Dana's peace of mind the Continental Congress had in the meantime arrived at very much the same conclusions. Adherence to the Maritime Confederacy had lost all point, the necessity of buying a commercial treaty made little appeal to an impoverished government, and even the possible advantage of maintaining a mission in St. Petersburg seemed hardly worth the cost. "The true interest of these states," Congress declared in a resolution directly foreshadowing our traditional national policy, "requires that they should be as little as possible entangled in the politics and controversies of European nations." Dana consequently received instructions that unless he was actually engaged in negotiations for a treaty, he should return to the United States. After making his peace with the Imperial Vice-Chancellor, he left St. Petersburg on August 24, 1783—just three days short of two years after his expectant arrival.

Russia had not recognized the United States and she would

not formally do so for another twenty-six years. Nevertheless the assurances of good will that Dana received before leaving the capital reveal that there was no real parallel here, as is so often stated, to our long delay in opening relations with Soviet Russia something over a century later. Catherine did not withhold recognition because of hostility toward the United States, or from concern over their establishment of a republican form of government. Her inaction was due to the changing political scene in Europe and a desire not to affront Great Britain whose friendship she then desired. As events were soon to prove, Russia actually favored the independence of the United States and the further delay in recognition was a consequence of American policy quite as much as Russian policy.

The next move toward establishing formal relations, indeed, came from St. Petersburg. At the close of the century European developments were drawing Russia and the United States together, as they would so many times down through the years, in common enmity toward a third power. Upon this first occasion it was France. Russia was actually at war with her upon land; America engaged in an undeclared war at sea. When the Russian envoy in London consequently suggested that the two nations establish diplomatic relations and conclude a trade treaty for the mutual protection of their commerce, the United States promptly responded by nominating Rufus King, our minister in London, to undertake such negotiations. But various difficulties soon arose and when this country prepared to make its peace with France, nullifying Russia's real interest in the project, the proposed negotiations were allowed to lapse.

A steady rapprochement nevertheless persisted during the next decade. American ships had become engaged in a thriving trade with the Baltic ports, and in 1803 Thomas Jefferson commissioned one Levett Harris as American consul at St. Petersburg. He was officially received at court, Alexander I now being on the throne, and in striking contrast to the indifferent attitude Catherine had maintained toward Francis Dana, the new Czar extended the courtesies he might have shown an accredited

minister. The vague and nebulous liberalism of Alexander at this stage of his career appears to have interested him in the republican experiment across the Atlantic, and through the medium of Harris a direct personal association developed between the Russian Czar and the American President. We find Jefferson warmly acknowledging the gift of a bust Alexander sent him, and in return forwarding to St. Petersburg a number of books on the American constitution. There was a lively correspondence between the two men, holding such different political positions, in which they professed a surprising admiration for each other. In a letter of April 18, 1806, Jefferson declared that one of the comforts of his life had been to see the elevation to the Russian throne of "a sovereign whose ruling passion is the advancement of the happiness and prosperity of his people; and not of his people only, but who can extend his eye and his good will to a distant and infant nation."

Nor was this effusion merely a diplomatic gesture. A year later, seeking to impress William Duane, the Pennsylvania editor, with what he had become convinced was the importance of Russian friendship for the United States, Jefferson enthusiastically characterized Alexander as one of the greatest men of his age. "A more virtuous man, I believe, does not exist," the President wrote, "nor one who is more enthusiastically devoted to better the condition of mankind." The Czar had "a peculiar affection" for the United States of which he had had both public and personal proof, Jefferson continued, and his sentiments were so closely in accord with the President's own that he was convinced America was assured of a real friend. "I am confident," he said in concluding this interesting letter, "that Russia (while her present sovereign lives) is the most cordially friendly to us of any power on earth, will go furthest to serve us, and is most worthy of conciliation."

There was, moreover, a stronger basis for Russian-American friendship than the mutual admiration of Alexander and Jefferson. It was founded upon the two nations' compelling interest in maintaining freedom of the seas during the Napoleonic

Wars. Whether herself neutral or belligerent, Russia sought to keep open the lanes of international trade. She opposed British control of the seas, as the Armed Neutrality first demonstrated, and even as an ally of Napoleon she refused to conform to his Continental System. Without either a navy or a merchant marine, Russia was dependent upon the commerce of neutrals and therefore did everything in her power to uphold their rights, whether against Great Britain or France. The United States of course resented to an even greater degree interference with its shipping on the part of either of the European belligerents. In the struggle to win economic as well as political independence, freedom of the seas had become the major goal of American foreign policy. Thomas Jefferson, busying himself with embargoes and nonintercourse acts in a vain attempt to win respect for American rights, consequently looked to St. Petersburg and to Czar Alexander for support. The common concern of the United States and Russia over this problem was the basis for his belief that the two nations were destined to be friends.

It was entirely natural that with such views Jefferson should undertake to strengthen the ties between Russia and the United States already established through his own correspondence with Alexander and seek to open formal diplomatic relations. When the apparent failure of the embargo as a means to compel either England or France to respect our rights heightened the need for the support of a friendly power in the armed camp of Europe, he consequently appointed William Short as minister to Russia. Moreover, without awaiting confirmation by the Senate he sent him abroad in October 1808 with instructions to explain to the Czar the position of the United States, to express our cordial feelings toward Russia, and to seek Alexander's aid in our efforts to assert and uphold neutral rights at sea.

The mounting dangers of the international situation caused Jefferson to look abroad for support on this occasion, but the Senate rebuffed this attempt of our traditional isolationist to tighten our European connections. It refused to confirm the

nomination of our new minister to Russia. It may have been in part political opposition to the man himself, but the surprised and annoyed President believed otherwise. The members of the Senate were fully sensible of both the influence and the friendship of Alexander, Jefferson wrote Short, "but riveted to the system of unentanglement with Europe, they declined the proposition."

This setback to opening relations with Russia proved to be only temporary. President Madison, coming into office the next year, took over this phase of Jefferson's foreign policy and one of his first acts was to submit the name of another minister to St. Petersburg. His candidate for the post was John Quincy Adams. A shift in domestic political alignments now led to senatorial approval and the former secretary of Francis Dana thereupon prepared to return to Russia in the official capacity of our first minister to the imperial court. In the meantime Alexander had appointed a consular representative authorized to serve as "chargé d'affaires near the Congress of the United States" and in May 1809 he named Count Pahlen as the first Russian minister in Washington. There was no longer any question whatsoever of the mutual desire of the two nations to enter into formal relations.

Adams reached St. Petersburg in October 1809 after a long and stormy voyage of eleven weeks on one of the vessels engaged in the Russian-American trade. His family accompanied him, and the party also included two secretaries of legation, a private secretary, a colored man-servant and his wife's maid. There was no need to creep quietly into the Russian capital and take up obscure lodgings in a Russian inn as upon the occasion of his earlier visit as Dana's secretary. Adams did not have to wait wearily—and unsuccessfully—for the Russian court to deign to notice his arrival. He was at once received by the Czar with the utmost cordiality and shown such evidence of imperial favor that his social status in the diplomatic society of St. Petersburg was immediately assured.

A highly serious and conscientious man, with conservative

instincts and a somewhat stern, forbidding manner, Adams found the gay life of the Russian court into which he was drawn little to his liking. "It is a life of such irregularity and dissipation," we find him noting in his diary on one occasion, "as I cannot and will not continue to lead." But it was clearly his duty, and for all his puritan misgivings and conscientious scruples, lead it he did. The American minister soon became a familiar figure at all court functions and at the balls, receptions and banquets of diplomatic society.

These were momentous days in the history of Russia. Throughout Adams' stay of four and a half years she was at war, first as an ally of France and then as her enemy. Alexander became the chief antagonist of Napoleon. The armies of the two nations were soon locked in a struggle which decided the fate of Europe. The American minister lived through days of deepening gloom as the Russian troops were rolled back before Napoleon's relentless advance; he heard the rumors of disaster which shook the capital as Moscow was burned; he rejoiced as the French Emperor fell back in his terrible retreat before the paralyzing grip of the Russian winter, and he attended the magnificent *Te Deums* which greeted the news of victories finally shattering Napoleon's dreams of European conquest. The affairs of America were for a time eclipsed in the shadow of these epic events. Adams often felt himself a spectator at a world drama in which his country's role had little significance.

His life in St. Petersburg nevertheless remained busy and active. It was not only receptions at the Winter Palace and levees at the foreign legations. Winter found him making expeditions to the ice hills in St. Petersburg, often returning, as he sadly confided to the diary, "with a hoarse cold and sore throat"; spring found him attending Easter Day services at the crowded churches, taking part in the holiday parades of carriages along the banks of the Neva, going on excursions into the country. He had an insatiable curiosity over every phase of Russian life. He visited schools and factories, went to the play at the Hermitage, watched the dancing bears in the market

place, and in long walks through "the city of princes" learned all he could about the country and people to which he was accredited. Sampling the liquors which the common folk drank as well as the champagne and vodka of society, he found they had "a taste of small beer, with an acid not unpalatable to me."

On one occasion the famous Madame de Staël was in St. Petersburg. She sought Adams out to get his advice on her American securities. He corresponded with Robert Fulton over a monopoly the American inventor was seeking to obtain for all steamboat transportation in Russia. There were conferences with the Czar's ministers over trade and commerce, and long hours of conversation with the diplomats of other governments. And over and beyond such activities Adams was continually seeking to improve his mind through his own studies. He read sermons, philosophic treatises and scientific works; every year went through the entire Bible in either French or German. He was never satisfied. "I have pursued no object steadily," he told his diary, "and the year has left no advantageous trace of itself in the annals of my life."

Perhaps the most interesting phase of his stay in St. Petersburg was his unusually friendly and close association with the Czar. Both Alexander and Adams had the habit of walking and they frequently met each other on these promenades and paused for conversation. "I took my usual morning's walk," reads one of the American minister's diary entries. "On the Fontanka, near the bridge through which the canal joins the river, I met the Emperor walking. As he approached he said, '*Monsieur Adams, il y a cent ans que je ne vous ai vu,*' and coming up, took and shook me cordially by the hand." There was an exchange of comments about the weather, inquiries about Adams' plans for the summer, some further conversation about news from America. Alexander then affably bid the minister good morning. "He made me his usual parting bow, or rather military salute, by raising his hand to his hat," Adams recorded, "and pursued his walk."

The principal concern of the American envoy during his

first years in St. Petersburg was to seek the protection of Russia against interference by Napoleon with our growing trade in the Baltic. The arrival at Riga of a ship flying the new flag of the United States had been proudly noted as early as 1783 by Francis Dana, and a year later the *Light Horse*, a 300-ton bark from Salem, put into the harbor of St. Petersburg. Following in the path of these pioneers more and more Yankee seamen braved the northern waters in their zealous pursuit of every possible opportunity for new commerce. By 1802 there were eighty-one American vessels, largely from Salem and Boston, engaged in this carrying trade, bringing to Russia both American goods and the products of the British West Indies. Valuable cargoes of pepper, coffee, tea, cotton, tobacco and especially sugar were exchanged for hemp, flax, cordage, sailcloth, linen sheeting and iron. It was highly profitable for the carriers. The ship *Catherine*, of Boston, cleared $115,000 on a single voyage the year of Adams' arrival at St. Petersburg. The wealth of New England during these years was derived from the Baltic trade as well as from even more distant voyages to China and the East Indies.

Commerce had naturally fallen off greatly during the days of the Jeffersonian embargo but by 1810 it had again risen to an annual value of some $4,000,000 and the next year it topped $6,000,000. Russia was quite as much interested in it as the United States, but as an ally of France at this time she was expected to conform to the provisions of Napoleon's Continental System, refusing entry to all neutral as well as English ships engaged in trade from the West Indies. For a time Alexander made a pretense of compliance and American ships were forbidden to unload in Russian ports or had their cargoes summarily confiscated. Upon Adams' energetic protests, however, these ships would generally be released. On at least one occasion the Czar even went so far as to intervene with the Swedish and Danish governments in behalf of American shipowners.

Adams was somewhat mystified by the success of his protests but he soon began to realize that Alexander had no intention

of accepting Napoleon's dictation on matters of trade. These imports were essential to Russia. As Jefferson had foreseen, the Czar was bound to befriend the neutral interests of the United States out of concern for his own commerce. In December 1810 his policy was brought clearly out into the open with official announcement that his ports were open to all colonial merchandise which was imported in other than British ships. Still without fully understanding the diplomatic maneuvers behind this move, Adams seized the opportunity to seek further concessions for American trade and revived Dana's old proposals for an American-Russian commercial treaty.

He had hopes it could be concluded. "Our attachment to the United States *is obstinate*," the Russian Foreign Minister told him on one occasion, "—more obstinate than you are aware of." At this point, however, dramatic developments upon the international stage suddenly interrupted the projected negotiations. Incensed at the Czar's violations of his Continental System, Napoleon declared war on Russia in June 1812 and Alexander thereupon joined forces with England in the grand coalition against the Corsican dictator. At almost exactly the same time America also became involved in war as continuing interference with our shipping led at last to the outbreak of hostilities with Great Britain.

These startling events naturally placed a different complexion on relations between Russia and the United States. We were at war with England, and Alexander was allied with England in war against France. It was at once very much to Russia's interest to bring the United States and Britain, her old friend and new ally, together and also to exert all possible pressure to prevent America from aligning herself with France in the complicated pattern of European hostilities. There was actually no likelihood of our joining forces with Napoleon. Our hostility toward France for her interference with our shipping was quite as pronounced as that toward England for her disregard of the rights of neutrals. But Russia could not be certain that the

United States might not be drawn within the orbit of Napoleon's influence.

Alexander consequently lost little time in offering his friendly mediation in our war with England. His proposals were relayed to the American government both through Adams and through his own minister in Washington. Secretary of State Monroe at once declared they would be accepted. Without waiting to know England's reaction, a special peace mission was appointed to undertake negotiations in St. Petersburg. Adams was to be joined by Albert Gallatin, Secretary of the Treasury, and James A. Bayard, senator from Delaware, as special envoys for this purpose.

The United States fully realized that Russia was pursuing her own aims in proposing mediation, but it was nonetheless felt that Alexander remained sincerely friendly to this country and would also be anxious to promote a peace that would uphold American maritime interests. "Since 1780," Secretary Monroe reminded the peace envoys in his instructions, "Russia has been the pivot on which all questions of neutral rights have essentially turned." There was complete confidence in Washington that under the Czar's auspices these questions could be favorably settled. The mission dispatched to St. Petersburg was therefore authorized not only to conclude peace between the United States and Great Britain, but also to negotiate commercial treaties with both England and Russia. The only thing that President Madison and Secretary Monroe overlooked was that, because of these very circumstances, England might not be as willing as the United States to accept the Czar's mediation.

Gallatin and Bayard arrived in St. Petersburg in July 1813. The war had not been going too well for the United States. Peace was all the more desirable with the failure of our arms. The American envoys were consequently doubly discomfited and disappointed to discover that England had in fact refused Alexander's proposals. Even though he was an ally, the Czar was held suspect by Great Britain because of his known sym-

pathy with our views upon neutral rights. The formal reason given for this attitude by Lord Castlereagh, the British Foreign Secretary, was that the war with the United States had arisen out of questions of "internal government," as he described the impressment issue, and that the whole controversy was in the nature of a family quarrel which should not be brought into the arena of European politics. As the British minister at St. Petersburg exclaimed to Adams: "Maritime law submitted to a Congress! What can there be upon earth more absurd?"

The bewildered American envoys found themselves at a complete loss. They learned only indirectly of England's refusal to accept mediation and they could not discover from the Russian government whether or not the whole project had been definitely abandoned. Alexander was with his troops in Bohemia, in what would prove to be the final stages of the allies' victorious campaign against Napoleon. His ministers appeared to be working at cross purposes in alternatively encouraging the Americans to believe that there was still a chance for mediation, and telling them that England's stand had caused the complete collapse of the Czar's plans. Gallatin and Bayard were also uncertain as to their own position. They had no authority to conduct direct negotiations with England. And finally to make confusion worse confounded, Gallatin received belated news that the Senate had refused to confirm his nomination as an envoy because he still held the post of Secretary of the Treasury.

If communications with the United States had not been so infrequent and long delayed, Gallatin and Bayard would have known that confusion also reigned in the councils of the government at Washington. Opposition to Madison's policies was making itself strongly felt, and his acceptance of the mediation of the Czar was vigorously attacked in some quarters as a hypocritical gesture. The role of Russia in European affairs appeared to be as paradoxical as it proved to be something more than a century later. Could the United States accept in good faith the aid of a tyrannical autocracy? Could we have any confidence in a government which had first allied itself with Napoleon, and then belatedly entered into a coalition against him only when Russia herself was attacked by France?

Niles' Register, among other contemporary journals, disregarded any possible parallelism in our foreign policies to raise the issue of what a later age would term the ideological conflict between American and Russian systems of government. It satirically attacked popular enthusiasm for "Alexander the Deliverer" and the current vogue of Cossack festivals because the Czar had momentarily found it to be to his interest to make war on Napoleon. The history of the Russian throne was one of murder and outlawry, *Niles' Register* declared. The great Catherine had been "an infamous strumpet" who had commanded the services of "a regiment of male prostitutes to gratify her lusts," while even the "amiable Alexander" had not escaped "the suspicions of moral parricide." His rule was a "government of horror" and the mighty empire over which he held sway was "immediately composed of *conquered* countries, *usurped* provinces, and *ravaged* territories."

The policy of the government was not changed by these attacks. Any hopes for Russian mediation were fast fading away but it was because of the stubborn refusal of England to accept it rather than any reluctance on our part. The American people remained generally convinced of Alexander's friendship. The popularity of Cossack festivals continued, and there were many toasts at public banquets to Alexander the Mediator. As for the issue of peace or war, a first step toward settlement of the conflict came from another quarter. Partly to mollify the Czar, Great Britain proposed to the United States direct negotiations between the two governments in lieu of Russian mediation. The offer was at once accepted.

In the meantime the disappointed delegates in St. Petersburg were having a miserable time. Gallatin and Bayard, accepting the failure of their mission, were anxious to get away from what they considered "the prison" of St. Petersburg. Although the attitude of the Russian government remained entirely

friendly, the Czar even offering to defray the envoys' expenses, there was nothing whatsover for them to do but await official word of the collapse of mediation. It was not, however, until January 1814, having finally learned of England's new proposals, that Gallatin and Bayard felt free to leave St. Petersburg and proceed to Gothenburg, the Swedish city where it had been suggested the new negotiations might be held. Three months later Adams, who had stayed on at the Czar's court, received instructions to join his former colleagues at these parleys. Eventually the conference was transferred to Ghent and peace terms agreed upon between the United States and England without the good offices of the Czar.

Despite the failure of mediation the interest shown by the Czar in American affairs had far-reaching consequences. It was during these years when John Quincy Adams served as our first minister to St. Petersburg that the tradition of Russian-American friendship, to which the correspondence of Thomas Jefferson and Alexander I had pointed the way, was firmly established. Our common concern over neutral rights provided its practical basis. In addition, the Czar had given Adams many proofs of his cordial feelings toward the United States and they were reciprocated in a general sympathy for Russia on the part of the American people. The two countries knew little of each other. They had no other contacts than a relatively small trade and the tenuous ties of diplomacy. Nevertheless Alexander's offer of his services in our quarrel with Great Britain marked an amity that would characterize our relations throughout the remainder of the century.

III

RUSSIA AND THE AMERICAS

IN THE years following the War of 1812 two new issues entered into Russian-American relations. What was believed to be a threatening Russian advance in the Pacific Northwest and the possibility of intervention by the Holy Alliance in the affairs of Latin America for a time caused deep concern in Washington. There was little actual danger to the interests of the United States in either area. Both questions were settled by negotiation and caused no rift in the cordial friendship established during the Napoleonic Wars. A final consequence of the two widely separate developments, however, was the declaration of the Monroe Doctrine. With Russia very much in mind the United States took the position that the American continents should no longer be looked upon as subject to colonization, and that any attempt on the part of European powers to intervene in the Western Hemisphere would be considered dangerous to our peace and safety.

The issue of conflicting rights and rival claims on the Northwest coast first came up officially when John Quincy Adams was minister at St. Petersburg. By that time both nations had substantial interests on the bleak, barren stretch of rocky shoreline which stretches from the Aleutian Islands to the more inviting reaches of what was then the Spanish province of California. They were rivals in a thriving trade in sea otter furs, during these years when Europe was shaken by the Napoleonic Wars, and each was seeking to plant colonial establishments to promote this valuable commerce.

Russia's interests were derived from the eighteenth century voyages of Vitus Bering, who set up certain somewhat shadowy claims on the American continent from the Aleutians to as far south as the forty-ninth parallel, and from the later overseas

ventures of Siberian traders and fur hunters on the Alaskan coast. Catherine the Great had showed little concern over these developments. She had no intention of involving the government in protection of merchants operating in so distant a part of the world. But the interests of all Russians engaged in the American fur trade were merged in 1799 with the chartering of the Russian American Company, and upon his accession to the throne Alexander confirmed the monopoly granted this company and placed it under his official protection. It was given full control over all Russian settlements from Bering Straits to the fifty-fifth parallel—all of what is now Alaska—and the further authority to enter into treaties with the Indians and to establish colonies south of this line wherever the territory was not already occupied by another power. The Czar sought to establish an organization comparable to the British East India Company or Hudson's Bay Company. It was virtually an independent branch of government designed to promote Russian interests in the New World.

The capital of this outpost of possible empire was New Archangel, or Sitka, founded in 1804. After incredible difficulties the Russians succeeded in establishing a strong hold upon the adjacent coast and in substantially developing their little colony. The bastion of the governor's palace, known through the Northwest as "the Castle," commanded the harbor with a force of sixty guns, while a strong palisade surrounded the homes, storehouses, shops and gardens of a community which grew to almost a thousand persons. The Russians had to contend with a rigorous and inhospitable climate, with the hostility of cruel and treacherous natives who on at least one occasion staged a bloody massacre, and with a lack of resources which kept them almost on the verge of starvation each long and cold winter. Communications with Russia through the Siberian port of Okhotsk were impossible except during the summer months, and even then only a few vessels made the voyage across the North Pacific. Russian America was almost entirely cut off from the outside world. Its merchants and hunters were solitary exiles in a vast expanse of cold, gray sea and dark, forbidding coastline.

The fur trade nevertheless reaped rewards which compensated for the exile and hardships of these pioneers. The Russians contracted with the Aleuts, more friendly than the Indian tribes of the Northwest coast, to hunt for them on shares. Each season hundreds of these natives would put out in fleets of tiny bidarkas—similar to the kayaks of the Eskimos—to capture the sea otters whose fine, glossy pelts fetched fantastically high prices in Europe and China. Every autumn the Russian ships would then take back to Siberia valuable cargoes for the enrichment of the stockholders of the Russian American Company. In the first decade of the nineteenth century furs to the value of more than twenty million rubles were shipped from Sitka. Whatever the sufferings and dangers endured by the company's servants in Alaska and on the Northwest coast, its books showed during this period net earnings which increased the value of its stock fivefold.

The life and soul of the Russian American Company throughout the entire period from 1790 to 1819 was its manager and territorial governor—Alexander Baranov. This indomitable, courageous, stubbornly persevering Russian became an almost legendary figure on the Northwest coast. He ruled his domain with a rod of iron, commanding the stanch loyalty of both native and Russian employees, inspiring a fearful dread among the unfriendly Indians and winning the respect of all Americans who came in contact with him. "A rough, rugged, hard-drinking old Russian," is the description given in Washington Irving's *Astoria*; "somewhat of a soldier, somewhat of a trader; above all a boon companion of the old roystering school, with a strong cross of the bear. . . ." Throughout the entire territory he was known as "the little Czar" and enforced a strict and unrelenting discipline. But it was tempered by occasions at which Baranov joined with his men in wild, unrestrained carousing. The timbered bunkhouses of Sitka often rang with shouts and bursts of song, and

the stamping of heavy-booted feet, as the exiles forgot the rigors of their life in magnificent drinking bouts where vodka, brandy and good New England rum flowed freely for everyone. They danced with the amazed but willing Aleut girls, flinging their shrieking partners high in the air, while Baranov roared out his applause.

For all such occasional revelry the biting cold of the northern winter, the lack of fresh food, the resultant disease and scurvy caused the Russians to think longingly of the more temperate climate and kinder land which lay to the south. The idea of planting other colonies was a natural one, and its possibilities were first explored in 1806 when Nikolai Rezanov, Court Chamberlain to the Czar Alexander, wintered in Sitka in the course of an official survey of Russian America. It was a year in which actual starvation threatened the colonists even more dangerously than usual and Rezanov consequently undertook a voyage to California with the ostensible purpose of seeking supplies. He might have headed toward the Hawaiian Islands—and here somewhat later the Russians would also consider colonization—but the valley of the Columbia River, and possibly also San Francisco Bay, were the territories of which he dreamed as possible Russian outposts.

After skirting along the coast in a ship which had been bought from one of the Yankee traders who had visited Sitka, Rezanov finally put into San Francisco Bay and sought permission from the Spanish authorities to obtain the supplies so necessary to the Russian colony. There were strict regulations against any such commerce. Spain rigidly enforced a monopoly of all trade. Had it not been for a budding romance Rezanov might have found his voyage entirely futile. But the beautiful daughter of the Spanish commandant fell in love with the handsome, polished chamberlain of the Czar's court, and doors were opened which might otherwise have remained closely barred. Moreover Rezanov succumbed to the charms of the lovely Dona Concepción and the two became affianced with the blessings of her family. Did diplomacy dictate the course of true love? It may well have, but contemporary descriptions of the Spanish beauty allow the presumption that Rezanov really lost his heart. "Her love-inspiring and brilliant eyes, her excellent and beautiful teeth, her smiling expression and beautiful features, her shapeliness of figure," we are told, made Doña Concepción the toast of California.

After obtaining his supplies in brisk and profitable trade with the Spaniards, Rezanov set sail again for Russian America. But he pledged his early return and Doña Concepción promised to wait for him. Their hopes for a quick reunion, and whatever ambitions Rezanov may have harbored for Russian settlement in California, were alike doomed to disappointment. Rezanov planned to return to St. Petersburg to seek the Czar's permission for his marriage and while making the long, arduous journey across Siberia fell ill and died. For many years no word of his fate reached Doña Concepción. When at last the sad news arrived through some later Russian visitors, she entered a convent, and until her own death remained faithful to the memory of her dashing Russian lover.

Back at Sitka, Baranov forgot neither the tales which Rezanov had told of California nor his idea of establishing a Russian colony somewhere in the south. Three years later another Russian vessel was sent out to look over the land and it carefully explored the reaches of Bodega Bay, lying some forty-eight miles above San Francisco Bay. The reports were favorable and in 1812 the ambitious project of attempting actual settlement was launched. A party of one hundred Russians, together with some eighty Aleuts, landed on the California coast just north of Bodega Bay itself and there founded the colony of Fort Ross. The Spanish authorities strongly protested against this Russian advance into their territories, but California was too weakly held to allow them to drive the invaders out. The Russians stayed on at Fort Ross with the idea of developing it as a new outpost of Pacific trade and a source of supplies for their more northern colony.

But what of American interests on the Northwest coast while

the Russians were extending a long finger southward to California? The first Yankee traders had appeared off its somber shores in the 1790's. After the discovery of the Columbia River in the memorable round-the-world voyage of Captain Robert Gray in the ship *Columbia*, their vessels could be found every season threading their perilous way among the bays and inlets scattered along the entire coastline. Like the Russians they were in pursuit of sea otter furs. Their trade, however, was directly with the Indians. Little vessels of at best one hundred or two hundred tons, almost invariably hailing from Boston, anchored offshore while the natives swarmed out in their long canoes to trade for cloth, blankets, molasses, ironware, rum and firearms. Their holds deeply laden with the glossy otter skins, the Yankee vessels would then sail for Canton and exchange their new cargoes for teas and silks and chinaware. Between 1790 and 1818 there were well over one hundred American vessels on the Northwest coast. The trade brought in immense profits, those of a single voyage in some instances ranging anywhere from $100,000 to $300,000.

It was also venturesome, exciting and highly dangerous. Many vessels foundered on the treacherous, rocky coastline; many were ambushed by even more treacherous savages, their crews cut down in fierce, bloody fighting. The Indians who burned Baranov's first settlement at Sitka were no more friendly to the Boston men. Every vessel went heavily armed against attack, cannon mounted on the deck and the seamen armed with muskets and cutlasses, while the most careful precautions were taken when the Indians came out to trade. Only three or four would be allowed aboard ship at one time and the others held off with the cannon trained on their canoes. But once a vessel was caught off guard, or found itself impaled on some sharp, protruding reef, the savages would attack with blood-curdling yells. The crew might well find themselves overwhelmed before they could muster their defenses.

The Americans soon had the idea, following the example of the Russians, of establishing settlements to promote the fur trade. The Winship brothers of Boston undertook to build a fort at the mouth of the Columbia in 1810, but their sanguine hopes "to have planted a Garden of Eden on the shores of the Pacific, and made that wilderness to blossom like a rose," came to nothing because of the hostility of the Indians. A year later John Jacob Astor, fur merchant extraordinary, backed a more ambitious and successful project, sending out both overseas and overland expeditions to found Astoria. It became the first American settlement in Oregon, an important way station in the China trade. Its establishment was linked with our earlier discovery of the Columbia River itself to substantiate American territorial claims in the Northwest.

Americans and Russians first came into direct contact as the former extended their trading operations along the Alaskan coast and their ships put into Sitka for safe anchorage or to exchange supplies. Relations were generally friendly. Baranov welcomed the Yankee sailors. Occasionally they cooperated in their trade, the Russians chartering American ships or the Americans hiring Aleuts in the service of the Russian American Company to hunt on shares. Sometimes the Boston traders carried Baranov's furs to Canton, the chief market for otter skins, as the Russians were not allowed by the Chinese to trade directly with this port.

Controversy eventually arose between Russians and Americans over charges by Baranov that the Yankees were selling firearms to the Indians and endangering the safety of the Russian settlements. Soon the growing dispute had been carried to the Russian government and the formal complaints to which we have already alluded were lodged with John Quincy Adams at St. Petersburg. In taking the issue up with the American minister, however, the Russian chancellor proposed in 1810 not only an agreement outlawing the trade in firearms but also definite determination of the Russian and American spheres of influence in the Northwest. The boundary, he suggested, might be the Columbia River. Sensing that there might be more at stake than he realized and unwilling to make any move

which would restrict the field of possible American expansion in the Pacific, Adams refused to make any commitments as to our policy.

The question slumbered for some time. On the basis of contemporary claims, control of the Pacific coast was disputed by four powers. The Russian settlements in the north were admitted to give her title to Alaska, in the south Spain held California, and the area between was sought by both the United States and Great Britain. In no case was interest in this still largely unsettled land sufficient to make the drawing of boundaries a problem of great immediate importance. The fur trade involved comparatively few persons and public opinion in the United States had not yet been aroused to any great concern over possible overland expansion to the Pacific coast. Nevertheless with the almost simultaneous settlement of an American outpost at Astoria and of a Russian colony at Fort Ross, the claims of these two nations were overlapping. By 1816 we find Secretary of State Monroe calling the attention of Adams' successor at St. Petersburg to the problems this might create. "In looking forward even to a distant period," he wrote, "the only circumstance in which a difference of interest is anticipated between the United States and Russia relates to their respective claims on the Pacific Ocean. . . . Remote however as the danger of collision is it had better be provided against."

Further point was given to this decision to safeguard our interests when two years later detailed reports were received at Washington as to just what the Russians were doing in California. J. B. Prevost, a naval officer who had gained first-hand information about the colony at Fort Ross, informed the State Department that in his opinion Russia's southern advance was distinctly alarming. "The growth of a race on these shores, scarcely emerged from the savage state, guided by a chief who seeks not to emancipate but to enthrall," he wrote, "is an event to be deprecated—an event, the mere apprehension of which ought to excite the jealousies of the United States, so far at least as to induce the cautionary measure of preserving a station which may serve as a southern barrier to northern aggrandizement."

However apathetic the general public, John Quincy Adams, now Secretary of State, was in full agreement on the need to safeguard all our rights on the Pacific coast. Soon after this report was received he sought through negotiations with the powers concerned to delimit the boundaries of Oregon. That territory itself, the scene of greatest activity on the part of American and British fur traders, should be held jointly by the United States and Great Britain for a period of ten years. This was agreed upon in an Anglo-American convention signed in 1818. Its southern limits were California. The United States and Spain signed a treaty the next year whereby the line between Spanish and American possessions was extended to the Pacific along the forty-second parallel. As for Oregon's northern boundary, Secretary Adams instructed our minister at St. Petersburg to sound out the Russian government, intimating a willingness on our part to accept the forty-ninth parallel, which would have extended Russian territory to the present Canadian border.

No immediate action was taken on the suggested Russian-American agreement, and in the meantime various rumors began to be heard to the effect that Russia was contemplating a marked extension of her Pacific holdings despite the treaties among the United States, Great Britain and Spain. There were reports that she was seeking to acquire eight hundred miles of coastline in California. At least one newspaper caught the note of alarm first sounded in Prevost's report. "Looking to the east for everything," the St. Louis *Enquirer* warned in 1819, "Americans have failed to notice the advance of the Russians on the Pacific coast until they have succeeded in pushing their settlements as far south as Bodega. Their policy is merely the extension of the policy of Peter the Great and Catherine. Alexander is occupied with a scheme worthy of his vast ambition . . . the acquisition of the gulf and peninsula of California and the Spanish claim to North America."

Two years later, in reporting upon American occupation of the Columbia River Valley, Representative John Floyd also drew attention to the Russian position on the Pacific. He stressed the growing importance of both Sitka and Fort Ross, declaring that it was the Russians' evident intention, with "their disgusting notions of monarchy," to seek control of the entire Pacific.

Such alarms suddenly appeared to be substantiated when in 1821 the Czar Alexander, without any forewarning, issued an official ukase declaring that the entire North Pacific, from Bering Straits to the fifty-first parallel, would henceforth be closed to the trade or navigation of every foreign power. No vessels other than those operating under the Russian flag, it was decreed, would be allowed to approach within one hundred Italian miles (the equivalent of about 115 English miles) of the shore of any island or part of the coast belonging to the Czar.

Adams was at once stung into action. The country as a whole may not even yet have been widely aroused, but the Secretary of State viewed such pretensions as wholly unwarranted and a direct infringement of American rights. He was willing to reach a generous settlement of the boundary of Russian America, but the Czar's new ukase threatened our carrying trade in the Pacific, in which as a New Englander he had a lively interest. It also violated those principles of freedom of navigation which he had so often championed. After vigorously protesting against Alexander's action, he again instructed our minister to take up the whole question of conflicting American and Russian territorial claims on the Northwest coast. His proposal now was that the United States would accept a definite boundary for Russian America no further south than the fifty-fifth parallel, but that the remaining coastline as far south as California should be left open to settlement by either nation upon a basis comparable to that already agreed upon by England and the United States.

Russia at once declared her willingness to enter into negotiations. There was actually slight warrant for any fears of her imperialistic encroachment on the American continent. Alexander had no great interest in Sitka or Fort Ross, and no intention of seeking territory along the California coast. Nor did his ukase have the far-reaching significance which Adams had read into it, for in response to our protests he at once made it clear that it would be enforced only against ships engaged in contrabrand trade. Russia still considered the United States a potential ally in her rivalry with Great Britain. Nothing was further from Alexander's mind, as events proved, than prejudicing our good will by a quarrel over the relatively unimportant question of the trade and boundaries of Russian America. Whatever ambitious dreams Baranov, Rezanov and some few other imperialistic-minded Russians may have had, Alexander was not seeking further colonies in North America.

John Quincy Adams, however, wished to make assurance doubly certain. Pending negotiation of the proposed territorial treaty, he obtained President Monroe's consent to a positive statement of American policy which might check any possible renewal of Russian activity in the Western Hemisphere. In a forthright note to Baron de Tuyll, the Russian minister at Washington, in July 1823, he made clear the position of the American government. The United States would contest the right of Russia, the Secretary of State declared, to any territorial establishments on this continent and it distinctly assumed the principle "that the American continents are no longer subjects for any new European colonial establishments."

Within a few months this principle would be given added weight by its incorporation into the annual message of President Monroe, but in the meantime Russia's attitude toward the independence of Latin America had brought to the forefront of public interest that second issue which entered into Russian-American relations following the War of 1812. Here too our answer to the supposed threat of Russian intervention in the New World, as already stated, would be publicly an-

nounced in the Monroe Doctrine. But there were important preliminary negotiations.

Upon the general pacification of Europe following the Napoleonic Wars, Alexander had formed the Holy Alliance as a means to guarantee international peace and uphold the principle of monarchial government in the interests of Europe's sovereign powers. Firmly convinced of the liberal instincts and high idealism of the Czar, the American people were at first inclined to look upon the Holy Alliance with great sympathy. It was accepted as a token of that devotion to peace which had early won Thomas Jefferson's confidence in Alexander's policies. There was a widespread pacifist movement in this country and its adherents enthusiastically hailed the Holy Alliance as harbinger of a better day in international society. Sixteen peace organizations in various states gave the Czar's program their formal endorsement and Noah Webster, secretary of a Massachusetts society, wrote Alexander directly that the objective of New England pacifists was "to disseminate the very principles avowed in the wonderful alliance."

Possibly encouraged by such manifestations of support, Alexander instructed his minister in Washington to sound out the American government upon the possibility of the United States itself joining the Holy Alliance. Secretary Adams, however, had a somewhat more realistic understanding of European politics than the enthusiastic devotees of peace. He fully realized that the Czar had other strings to his bow than an idealistic promotion of brotherly love. Although he retained the respect and personal affection he had felt for Alexander when they had met on their daily walks along the Neva, he knew that the Czar had outlived the liberal phase of his career and that even greater than his interest in peace was his determination to make Europe safe for autocracy. In a letter written in 1817 Adams sardonically pointed out that at the very time Alexander was exchanging peaceful platitudes with the enthusiastic Webster, he was making other moves not so easily reconcilable with the declared objectives of his alliance. "The venerable founder of the Holy League is sending five or six ships of the line," the Secretary of State informed his correspondent, "and several thousand promoters of peace armed with bayonets, to Cadiz, and then to promote good will to men elsewhere."

Adams also had the shrewd idea that the Czar's apparent anxiety to have the United States join the Holy Alliance might have an ulterior motive. It was inspired more by a desire to separate us from England, he believed, than to win our allegiance to any general principles of peace. Great Britain had refused to be drawn into an alliance* which was already demonstrating its opposition to all liberalism and she stood outside the new concert of powers. American adherence would consequently have had the effect of drawing the United States within the orbit of Russian influence, thereby emphasizing still more strongly England's isolation.

Adams could not rebuff Alexander's overtures by the expression of such views. When the Russian minister brought up the question, trying to point out that the United States would inevitably come under the influence of the European political system sooner or later, he diplomatically temporized and put off any definite answer. For the time being the matter was dropped. But when the Czar indicated in 1819 that he was still hopeful of American support, the Secretary of State felt called upon to make our position clear. The United States fully subscribed to the peaceful principles of the Holy Alliance and would be "among the most earnest and conscientious" in observing them, our minister in St. Petersburg was instructed, but he was to make clear our policy of avoiding any foreign entanglements. "The political system of the United States," Adams stated for Alexander's benefit, "is . . . essentially extra-European. . . . To stand in firm and cautious independence of all entanglements in the European system has been a car-

* A new quadruple alliance actually replaced the Holy Alliance, but contemporary American opinion did not recognize this distinction.

dinal point of their policy under every administration of their government."

Apart from the inconsistency with our traditional policy, American membership in the Holy Alliance had now become all the more impossible because its real nature was growing increasingly clear. Adams' original suspicions were fully justified. Alexander had revealed the repressive policy of the League in the forceful measures he advocated to uphold the divine right of kings and the sanctity of established authority. As under the cover of its professed peaceful principles Austria intervened to suppress a liberal revolt in Italy in 1821, and France crossed the Pyrenees two years later to put down a Spanish uprising and restore the reactionary Ferdinand VII to the throne, popular sympathy for the Holy Alliance was wholly alienated.

"The Holy Alliance and the Devil," ran a popular toast. "May the friends of liberty check their career, and compel them to dissolve their partnership." The Russian minister did not dare accept an invitation to a Fourth of July banquet for fear of having to listen to attacks upon his sovereign. "In the perfection of the scheme of the 'holy alliance,'" the editor of *Niles' Weekly Register* wrote, "we must anticipate the extinction of civil and religious liberty."

The attacks upon the Holy Alliance were not primarily inspired by its activities in Europe, however. The intervention of France in Spain had raised the issue of possible intervention in the Spanish colonies in the Western Hemisphere. Latin America had thrown off the yoke of Bourbon rule and proclaimed its independence. If the Holy Alliance was prepared to send its armies to suppress revolt throughout Europe, it might attempt to reach out across the seas to put down rebellion on this side of the Atlantic. There were various intimations, official and otherwise, of the mounting annoyance of the Czar over the spread of republicanism in Latin America. A note of alarm was sounded throughout the country: the New

World must be jealous of its liberties against the possible threat of Old World intervention.

The American people were naturally wholly in sympathy with the movement for independence on the part of Spain's colonies in Latin America and they had welcomed the rise of these young republics, following our own example in throwing off the control of a mother country. Our official policy was also one of friendship, but we had delayed recognition because we were engaged in negotiating a treaty with Spain for the annexation of Florida. We did not wish to prevent its ratification by too directly offending the Spanish government. But by the time of the French invasion of Spain—that is, in 1823—this issue had been settled and the United States had formally recognized the new republics. We were directly interested in seeing that they successfully maintained their independence. The fear of interference by the Holy Alliance consequently invaded the official circles of Washington as well as enlivening Fourth of July banquets.

The belief that Alexander was the driving force behind the policies of the Holy Alliance, and the European monarch who was most likely to attempt to extend its malevolent influence to the New World, appeared to be confirmed by two notes delivered to Secretary Adams in the autumn of 1823 by Baron de Tuyll. The Czar would not under any circumstances recognize the independence of the Latin American republics, the United States was officially informed in the first of these documents, and he explicitly refused to welcome the ministers of any of the *de facto* governments. The second note was even more outspoken in its opposition to all such political experiments. The policy of the Holy Alliance, it categorically stated, was "to crush all revolutionary movements, and thereby to preserve order in the civilized world."

There is no evidence that Alexander actually contemplated intervention in Latin America. In this instance at least his bark was worse than his bite. But these notes awoke immediate and serious concern in Monroe's cabinet. The President

himself was certain that "some project against the new govern-ments is contemplated," and Secretary of War Calhoun ap-peared to fear imminent invasion. Adams was not such an alarmist. "I no more believe that the Holy Alliance will restore the Spanish dominion upon the American continent," a diary entry dated November 15, 1823, reads, "than that the Chim-borazo will sink beneath the ocean." Nevertheless he felt that Czarist Russia was "bearding us to our faces upon the monar-chial principles of the Holy Alliance," and that the challenge of the Czar should not be ignored—"it was time to tender them an issue."

It was while these discussions were taking place in the Cabi-net at Washington that word was received from Richard Rush, the American minister in London, of proposals made by the British Foreign Secretary, George Canning, for joint action on the part of the United States and Great Britain to ward off any intervention in Latin America by the Holy Alliance. The end-result of these negotiations and of the discussions upon Amer-ican policy in the Cabinet is well known: the United States decided that whatever action it would take, would be taken independently. Various considerations influenced this decision but one factor, emphasized among others by Secretary Adams, was the effect which Anglo-American cooperation on the issue would have upon our relations with Russia. It was fully re-alized that Alexander's friendship for the United States was in large part based upon the idea of counteracting too close an accord between Washington and London. We find President Monroe writing Thomas Jefferson, in their memorable corre-spondence on this crisis facing American policy, of Russia's dread of "a connection between the U. States and G. Britain." Consequently the argument was advanced that America could better safeguard her interests, and at the same time avoid un-necessarily irritating Alexander whose friendship we wished to maintain, by staying clear of any entanglement with England.

In any event it was decided that the answer to the problem raised both by Baron de Tuyll's notes expressing the anti-republican views of the Czar, and by the suggestion for joint action in defense of Latin America made by Foreign Secretary Canning, should be an independent announcement of American policy in the President's annual message to Congress. At the same time Adams insisted that entirely apart from this general statement of our attitude there should be an immediate reply—"firm, spirited and yet conciliatory"—to the pretentious views of Alexander and the Holy Alliance. He agreed that it should correspond to the pertinent paragraphs in the forthcoming presidential message, but he felt it to be of utmost importance that it should be directly addressed to Russia.

President Monroe somewhat reluctantly agreed, and on November 27 the Secretary of State thereupon informed the Russian minister that the United States could not see with indifference the intervention of any power other than Spain in the affairs of Latin America. Our objections embraced any attempt, Adams stated emphatically, to restore Spanish dominion over the emancipated colonies, to establish monarchial governments in those countries, or to transfer any possessions subject to Spain in the American hemisphere to any other European power.

Within less than a week President Monroe declared the general doctrine which publicly reaffirmed these principles and also reiterated the parallel policy that the United States could not countenance any attempt at future colonization by the European powers upon the American continents. Both sections of the famous message had thus been largely inspired by the fear of Russian encroachments in the New World. In the one instance it was Russia as the driving force behind the Holy Alliance, and in the other Russia as a colonizing power on the Northwest coast. And also in the case of both phases of our newly declared policy, we had already officially stated our position in notes directly addressed to the Russian government. It had been forewarned, before the Monroe Doctrine was publicly announced, just where the United States stood on the general issues at stake.

It remains to be seen how Russia reacted to the American policy. It has already been stated that Alexander had no real desire to expand his colonial holdings on the American continent and that he had expressed his willingness to negotiate a treaty for the settlement of any conflicting claims on the Northwest coast. Nor was there any conclusive evidence that he actually intended to intervene in Latin America. It is true that the Russian government on one occasion—and that was actually after declaration of the Monroe Doctrine—sounded out the French government upon the possibility of such a move. Nothing whatsoever came of it. The strong position that the United States took in 1823, both in its notes to the Russian government and in the declaration of the Monroe Doctrine, was directed against largely imaginary fears. Its future significance, nevertheless, was of the utmost importance. President Monroe had laid down the principles of what has ever since been the most consistently supported feature of our foreign policy.

While there is little evidence of any important repercussions to the Monroe Doctrine in St. Petersburg—our minister reported that its "decided tone" had been duly noted in official circles—two of the Czar's foreign emissaries were aroused by the sweeping nature of the American claims. "Here, then, is the Government of the United States," Baron de Tuyll reported, "making common cause with the insurgents of America: loftily announcing itself their protector, and constituting itself the head of a democratic league of the New World. . . ." And in London the Russian minister wrote with even more obvious distaste that the United States was attempting to constitute itself "the sovereign arbiter of the destinies of the whole world."

These views reflected the ever-present conflict between Russian autocracy and American republicanism, but the friendly relations between the two governments were in no way marred. They had agreed to negotiate the one definite issue outstanding between them; that is, the boundary line between their possessions on the Pacific coast, and these negotiations now proceeded in an atmosphere of complete cordiality. Both nations were conciliatory; both nations were anxious to come to an understanding "most conformable to their mutual interests."

On April 17, 1824, the United States and Russia consequently reached a final agreement in regard to the Northwest in a treaty which marked the first formal accord to be concluded by the two powers. The southern boundary of Russian America was fixed at the parallel of 54° 40'—the present territorial line of Alaska—and it was expressly stipulated that there should be complete freedom of the seas in the North Pacific. It was further agreed that on the still unsettled parts of the coast Russian and American citizens should not encroach upon one another's preserves; a strict ban was imposed upon the sale of firearms and liquor to the Indians, and American vessels were granted fishing and trading privileges in Russian territorial waters for a period of ten years.

Although there had been no real warrant for fears of Russian imperialism, the treaty nevertheless was a distinct diplomatic triumph for the United States. The boundaries of Russian America did not extend as far south as we had at one time been willing to concede; title to the whole Oregon territory was definitely left to ultimate settlement between the United States and Great Britain, and the way had been opened up for the further development of our political and commercial interests in the Pacific. While the complete expulsion of Russia from the North American continent was to wait upon our purchase of Alaska forty-three years later, the Treaty of 1824 obviated any danger of a future Russian barrier to American continental expansion.

. . . WHEN THE WORLD WAS OUR FOE

HAVING successfully weathered controversy over the Northwest coast and the independence of Latin America, relations between the United States and Russia remained for some time quiet and uneventful. In 1832 the commercial treaty which Dana had first suggested and Adams vainly sought to conclude during the Napoleonic Wars was finally negotiated. Our trade with Russia, however, was no longer as important as it had been when American ships were playing such an extensive role as carriers for the belligerent nations of Europe. While the treaty was important in that it established the basis for Russian-American commercial relations for almost a century, and also defined the rights of American nationals in Russia and Russian nationals in the United States, it had no special political significance. With the Czarist government abandoning any idea of interference in the affairs of the New World and showing only the mildest interest in its distant territories in Russian America, and the United States committed to its policy of no entanglements with the political system of Europe, the spheres of interest of the two powers were so distinct and widely separated that Russian and American paths hardly crossed.

A rapid succession of ministers represented the United States at the court of the Czars. The relative unimportance of the post and its great distance from home, the rigors of a St. Petersburg winter, and the heavy expense of maintaining a diplomatic establishment at the most extravagant court in Europe combined to make it one of the least desirable of diplomatic appointments. The correspondence of our envoys during these years was filled with complaints about financial difficulties in meeting the social demands made upon the American legation and the endless "drudgery of etiquette." It was incumbent upon the minister to maintain a considerable staff of servants and to keep a coach and four, with postilion and chasseur, for driving to all formal functions. "How absurd," one of our envoys sharply commented, "all this appears to a Republican!"

The shortest stay in the capital of all American ministers was that of John Randolph of Roanoke. Appointed by President Jackson in 1829, he reached St. Petersburg early in August of that year and left just a month later. This most erratic of all American statesmen, whose mind hovered so closely on the narrow line which separates genius from insanity, was already given over to what a friendly biographer describes as "occasional flightiness." Vainly fighting his chronic ill-health with both alcohol and drugs, he found St. Petersburg too much for him.

"Heat, dust impalpable, pervading every part and pore, and actually sealing the last up, annoying the eyes especially, which are further distressed by the glare of the white houses," Randolph wrote in frantic exasperation. "Insects of all nauseous descriptions, bugs, fleas, mosquitos, flies innumerable, gigantic as the empire they inhabit, who will take no denial. . . . This is the land of Pharaoh and his plagues—Egypt and its ophthalmia and vermin, without its fertility—Holland without its wealth, improvements, or cleanliness. Nevertheless it is beyond all comparison the most magnificent city I ever beheld."

Short as was his stay, Randolph apparently made a deep impression upon St. Petersburg for his successor found diplomatic society humming with fantastic stories of his eccentric behavior. "How are you, Emperor? How is Madame?" he was reputed to have addressed the Czar at his official audience. Refusing to wear formal dress, he appeared at court according to his own account in a full suit of finest black cloth, carrying a steel-capped sword. His scorn for the gold braid, lace and feathers of diplomacy was shared by other envoys of democratic America. Some years later George Bancroft, our minister in Berlin, was asked why it was that American diplomats appeared

at court "all dressed in black, like so many undertakers." His reply reflected the flamboyant republicanism of young America. "We could not be more appropriately dressed than we are —at European courts," Bancroft answered. ". . . what we represent is the Burial of Monarchy." In marked contrast to the tales of his insistence upon democratic privilege, however, Randolph was also said to have fallen upon his knees before the Empress to the great amusement of her ladies-in-waiting. This tale he indignantly denied and Washington Irving, meeting the discomfited envoy sometime later in London, came valiantly to his defense. The proud Virginian was "too lofty a fellow to have made such a blunder," Irving wrote, but thereupon added that he had no doubt that upon quitting the Russian capital, Randolph had "left behind the character of a rare bird."

James Buchanan, following the path of political preferment that would eventually lead him to the White House, was our next minister. He arrived in St. Petersburg in 1832 with a retinue of three slaves and fortified for his stay—as Ambassador Davies would be a century later—with ample provisions to meet the expected deficiencies of a Russian diet. Several bags of ham, a barrel of bread, a coffee pot and mill were listed among the various articles of his baggage. Perhaps because of these precautions he managed to stay out a term of almost two years, and it was during his mission that the long-sought commercial treaty was finally signed.

Buchanan apparently enjoyed St. Petersburg and entered into the social life of the capital even more than had Adams. At first he was highly scornful of the Russian nobility. He felt that they had all the vices and none of the virtues of the French aristocracy. They knew little and cared less about the United States because they feared the contamination of liberty. But as they accepted him socially, Buchanan gradually came to like them. Happily he went the round of imperial balls, diplomatic receptions and military reviews and found himself very much in demand at all manner of other social functions. In his letters to his friends he repeatedly declared how "really astonished" he was at his own success.

Russia could hardly have presented a more striking contrast to the United States, Buchanan wrote President Jackson. There was no freedom of the press, no public opinion—"in short, we live in the calm of despotism." There was no intermediate class, except a handful of merchants, between the nobility and the great mass of "ignorant and barbarous" peasantry. He found the new Czar, Nicholas I, a man of fine-looking appearance, great energy and ability, and without a moral blemish. He compared him very favorably to his predecessors. Alexander had been a mild and amiable ruler, Buchanan reported, but he had completely abandoned his early liberalism to die a fanatic. Catherine the Great had also been amiable and kindhearted, even lighting her own stove in the morning to save her servants trouble, but at the same time she had been, as our minister delicately wrote an inquiring Mrs. Slaymaker, "destitute of religion—the sweet guard of female virtue."

Buchanan further found that while America might be "a sealed book in regard to the Russians," both Nicholas and his ministers were wholly faithful to the tradition of friendliness toward the United States. The two nations were at the political antipodes, but the autocratic Czar was nevertheless anxious to remain at all times upon good terms with "the most free people upon earth." The American minister intimated that as previous experience had already shown, this cordiality was perhaps derived not so much from love of the United States as from fear of the political ambitions of France and England. But in any event Nicholas looked across the Atlantic, as had Alexander, for friendship and sympathy.

Buchanan spent almost all his time in St. Petersburg but he made one trip to Moscow and duly reported his experiences and impressions in his dispatches and letters home. Driving through the country on what he described as excellent macadam roads, he observed with special interest "the mousiques." They were jolly, good-natured and all rogues; they

appeared perfectly content with their lot and were far too
ignorant to be fit for liberty. At every stop for changing horses,
driven four abreast at a furious pace, these heavily bearded
peasants, invariably dressed in tanned sheepskin coats, crowded
about to gaze in awe at the strange spectacle of a foreigner.
Moscow itself, entirely rebuilt since Napoleon's invasion, Buchanan discovered to be an impressive city of broad, imposing
streets and innumerable churches, dominated by the walls of
the Kremlin. He went sight-seeing assiduously. At a school for
the children of nobles the pupils were asked for his benefit who
was the greatest American. When they dutifully answered
"Washington," his good republican soul felt a "thrill of
delight."

After signature of the commercial treaty Buchanan grew
restless. His attempts to negotiate a treaty upon maritime
rights—again the old objective of both Dana and Adams—
made no headway. The Czar was no longer greatly interested
in this question and the American himself had some doubts
as to whether it would prove of any great value to the United
States. Under these circumstances he persuaded President Jackson to accept his resignation, and after diplomatically assuring
the Czar that he was leaving for personal rather than official
reasons, returned to the United States late in 1833.

Even the slight interest in Russian-American relations occasioned by the missions of Randolph and Buchanan tended
to subside in subsequent years. The post at St. Petersburg was
at times left vacant, and such envoys as were appointed were
neither very important in themselves nor left any worthwhile
record of their experiences in Russia. The one or two minor
diplomatic questions which came up were handled in routine
fashion. By the middle of the century, however, new interests
developed between the two nations. First Russia and then the
United States found itself involved in war, and each country
looked across the Atlantic for some practical expression of the
friendship so often expressed in official circles.

The first of these wars was the Crimean, breaking out in

1854 when England and France came to the aid of Turkey to forestall possible Russian expansion in the Near East and Balkans. The American people knew little of either the causes of this conflict or of the issues at stake, but they sided almost instinctively with Russia. The tradition of friendship stemming from Alexander's offer to mediate in the War of 1812 played some part in creating this pro-Russian sentiment, but it was more largely derived from a strong anti-British feeling. Controversy with England in Central America and over fishing privileges in Canadian waters made twisting the lion's tail a popular sport in this period. Politicians appealing to the Anglophobe vote, especially among Irish immigrants, made the most of every opportunity coming their way. It was a natural reaction that when England went to war popular sympathy should be extended to her enemy. Our distrust of the mother country, in Secretary of State Marcy's phrase, tended "to Russify us."

The Russian government sought to take full advantage of this feeling. Our official attitude was one of neutrality, but as in every European conflict we tried to persuade the belligerents to observe our maritime rights. The principles which we had adopted during the Revolutionary War and attempted to uphold during the Napoleonic era were again put forward. Russia was fully prepared to accept them and hoped that England would refuse to do so, thereby further intensifying American hostility toward the British. In this she was disappointed. In striking contrast to her attitude forty-odd years earlier, Great Britain recognized our maritime rights. Foreign Secretary Clarendon informed James Buchanan, now Secretary of State, that the neutral flag would protect all cargo except contraband, and that the property of neutrals captured aboard enemy ships would be restored to its owners. England may well have been influenced in following this conciliatory policy by the fear that interference with our shipping might have driven us into Russia's arms. It was a marked concession to our viewpoint. Even though the Czar might have preferred to have us

become embroiled with Great Britain, it was also a boon to Russia. Freedom of the seas for neutral shipping meant that she could keep open her trade and commerce with the outside world.

The Russian minister in Washington at this time, Edward Stoeckl, hoped to profit more directly from our sympathy. He played with the idea of outfitting privateers in American harbors to prey upon British commerce. There appeared to be every reason to believe that Americans could be recruited for such a purpose—at one time some three hundred Kentucky riflemen were reported to have volunteered for service at Sebastopol under the Russian flag—and the enthusiastic envoy had high hopes of being able to strike an effective blow at England's shipping. His government, however, definitely vetoed his plans. The Czar feared that the suggestion of any such infringement of our neutrality might alienate American good will and do Russia more harm than good. His cautious policy soon bore fruit. For when England now tried to enlist American volunteers for her army, the United States protested at once and forcefully. Moreover public opinion compelled the government to dismiss the British minister and three consuls on the charge that despite our remonstrances they failed to cease their recruiting activities.

A final move indicating our sympathy for Russia was an offer to mediate in her struggle against England and France made in July 1854 by Secretary Marcy. We were prepared to repay in kind the favors done us in 1812. But while the question was discussed in Washington during the following winter, Russia hesitated to accept the offer of our good offices. The Czar was afraid that England, recognizing the sympathy of the United States for Russia, would interpret any willingness on his part to accept American mediation as a confession of weakness. Nothing consequently came of Marcy's gesture and the war was fought on to Russia's ultimate defeat.

The friendship the United States showed Russia at this time was within a decade more than reciprocated by that Russia

exhibited for the Union in the course of our Civil War. In the early years of that conflict there was no more haunting fear in the minds of President Lincoln and Secretary of State Seward than the possibility that the European powers would recognize the Confederate States. The sympathy of both the British and French governments for the South was clearly evident, and while other factors played their part in forestalling the intervention which for a time appeared imminent, the stanch support rendered the Union cause by Russia was of material aid during a highly critical period.

A first warning to England and France that they could not expect the cooperation of Russia in any move to intervene in the American war appeared in an article, known to be inspired by the Russian Foreign Office, which was published in the *Journal de Saint Petersbourg* in August 1862. "Russia entertains for the United States," this semi-official newspaper declared, "a lively sympathy founded on sentiments of mutual friendship and on common interests. She considers their prosperity necessary to the general equilibrium. She is convinced that the American nation can only find in the preservation of the Union the conditions of power and prosperity which she wishes to see it enjoy."

There was no question of the motive behind Russia's policy. Alexander II, who had succeeded to the throne in 1855, favored the maintenance of the Union, as Catherine had in fact welcomed our independence and Alexander I upheld our rights during the Napoleonic Wars, because a powerful America offset the maritime supremacy of the British Empire. His policy was nationalistic, and realistic. It had little to do with sentiment. As Stoeckl, still minister in Washington, bluntly expressed it, the United States in rivalry with Great Britain was "the best guarantee against the ambitious projects and political egotism of the Anglo-Saxon race."

Direct assurances of Russian sympathy were repeatedly made to the American representatives at St. Petersburg during these years. Upon one occasion Foreign Minister Gorchakov made

a full and frank exposition of his country's policy to Bayard Taylor, serving at the time as chargé d'affaires. Russia's desire above everything else, Gorchakov declared, was "the maintenance of the American Union, as one indivisible nation." Under no circumstances would she take part in any program of intervention or depart from the policy of friendship that had been consistently followed since the opening of Russian-American relations. "Russia alone has stood by you from the first, and will continue to stand by you," he stated in what Taylor described as an impassioned manner that gave every indication he was speaking from the heart. "We are very, very anxious that some means should be adopted, that any course should be pursued, which will prevent the division that now seems inevitable." At an imperial audience in January 1863, Taylor also received comparable assurances from the Czar himself. Upon our envoy's declaring that the American people considered him their best friend, Alexander solemnly answered: "I shall remain so."

The diplomatic correspondence of the period between St. Petersburg, London and Paris reveals that Russia made good these pledges. When England was seriously considering mediation on the basis of a separation between the North and South in September 1862, Russia's objections had an important restraining influence upon the British Foreign Office. "My only doubt is whether we and France should stir if Russia holds back," Lord John Russell wrote Palmerston. "Her separation from our move would insure the rejection of our proposals." And a little later he again wrote that "we ought not to move at present without Russia." While the British Foreign Secretary may have continued to hope that the Czar might be won over to support an interventionist policy, the French Foreign Minister had no such illusions. He told the British ambassador in Paris about this time that his soundings at St. Petersburg upon the possibility of cooperation had been met "by an almost scornful refusal."

The victory of the Union armies at Antietam, and clear

intimations from the United States that intervention from abroad would be countered by war, soon began to dampen British ardor for mediation. Nevertheless France took up the issue again, during the next month, and put forward the specific proposal that Great Britain, France and Russia undertake to persuade the Americans to conclude a six-months armistice. And once again the Czar made clear his unwillingness to participate in any move that might embarrass the United States. The furthest Russia would go, the official reply to France's overtures stated, would be to lend her moral support to the new proposal, and then only if she were first convinced that "it would not cause irritation." With Great Britain also rejecting the French plan, Napoleon III's ambitious project made no further headway.

The attitude of Russia toward intervention was paralleled by her consistent refusal to afford any encouragement whatsoever to the missions sent abroad by the Confederacy to seek foreign recognition. At one time there were vague rumors that a Southern envoy might be received at St. Petersburg, but upon official inquiry by our envoy the Russian Foreign Minister emphatically stated: "No, he dare not come here." The knowledge that he could hardly hope to be received at court, indeed, discouraged L. Q. C. Lamar, who had been appointed minister to Russia by the Confederacy, from even attempting to carry out his mission. "I became convinced," he wrote his government in April 1863, "that the state of things supposed to promise useful results from diplomatic representation at the Court of St. Petersburg has been essentially changed."

The United States was able to make a return gesture of friendliness along strangely parallel lines shortly after the collapse of the French program of intervention in the United States. Russia too was confronted with domestic strife, and an uprising in Poland led the Czar to impose severe retaliatory measures. England and France protested in behalf of the Poles, and just as they had asked the support of Russia for their proposed mediation in our Civil War, they now sought American

endorsement of their action in Central Europe. Secretary Seward, however, declared that the United States could not associate itself with England and France in their protests because of its traditional policy of noninterference in European affairs. To the gratification of the Czar's government, he also took occasion to indicate American sympathy for Russia and to reaffirm the strong bonds of solidarity between the two countries. There was no question then or at any time during the Civil War of Seward's lively appreciation of Russian services. "In regard to Russia," he wrote on another occasion for the benefit of the Czar, "the case is a plain one. She has our friendship, in preference to any other European power, simply because she always wishes us well, and leaves us to conduct our affairs as we think best."

Apart from the diplomatic support the two governments accorded one another, there was a further feeling that their interests were running along parallel lines in the almost simultaneous action taken in both countries to meet the great problem of human bondage. Alexander II freed the serfs in 1861; Lincoln emancipated the slaves in 1862. In view of the intense feeling stirred up in the North by the slavery issue, nothing Russia could have done would have created more sympathy among the American people for the Czarist government. Alexander II was hailed, as for a time Alexander I had been hailed, as a champion of liberal views, leading his country along the same path as that being followed by the United States. From Cassius M. Clay, the American minister in St. Petersburg who returned to his post early in 1863 after the year in which Bayard Taylor had represented our interests there, came the most glowing accounts of the progressive character of the Czarist government.

This fiery Kentuckian, who bettered all the previous diplomatic records with a six-year term in St. Petersburg, was a popular envoy. His penchant for the ladies led to several challenges to duels, which he invariably parried by choosing bowie knives as the prescribed weapon, but even the nobles who objected to his flirtations with their wives apparently accepted him as one of themselves. No American minister more zealously promoted Russian-American relations. "Let us be careful for our own sakes and the cause of humanity," he wrote home after expansively prophesying a great future for Russia, "to reciprocate her friendly feelings toward us."

Popular pro-Russian sentiment in this country was also strengthened by the fact that a number of Russian officers volunteered in the Northern armies. Among them were Prince Alexander Eristov and Colonel Charles de Arnaud, but the most spectacular career was that of Colonel John B. Turchin. Known throughout the army as "the Mad Cossack," Turchin fought valiantly and well. He commanded an Illinois regiment, found himself in hot water and was court-martialled after his troops sacked the town of Athens, was then promoted by Lincoln to brigadier-general, marched with General Sherman to the sea, and finally returned to Chicago a conquering hero and symbol of Russian sympathy for the Union cause.

The climax of this reign of good will took place in the autumn of 1863 when detachments of the Russian fleet unexpectedly put into the ports of San Francisco and New York. Their arrival was immediately and enthusiastically hailed as still further evidence of Russian sympathy for the Union, the American people jumping to the conclusion that their appearance was a promise of active aid should there be any further attempt at foreign intervention in the war. The real purpose behind this spectacular visit was quite different. The protests of England and France on the Polish question had created a tense situation in European politics and Russia feared that it might lead to war. Her navy was too weak to offer effective resistance to the British fleet and in the event of hostilities would in all probability have been so completely bottled up as never to get to sea. Upon the suggestion of Admiral Milikhov, the Czar consequently ordered it to move secretly to neutral ports before war broke out in order that it might then be free to wreak such damage as it could upon British shipping before

its inevitable defeat. The ports of New York and San Francisco were a natural choice for such a maneuver, both because of their geographic position and the assurance of a friendly welcome. There was in fact nowhere else the Russian vessels could go.

Neither the American public nor apparently the American government, knew the real explanation for the Russians' presence in our harbors. A contemporary article in *Harper's Weekly* shrewdly interpreted it as somehow related to the European situation, recalling that the Russian fleet had been bottled up at Kronstadt and in the Black Sea during the Crimean War. The country as a whole, however, did not stop to reason why. A legend grew up of Russia's gallant gesture to uphold the Union which would persist for more than half a a century, and only be completely demolished when historic research in the Russian archives finally brought to light the Czar's secret orders to the fleet.

In New York delegates from every neighboring state came to the city to visit the Russian vessels lying at anchor in the bay; their officers were invited to cities throughout the East for memorial banquets. Secretary Seward received the Russian admiral at Washington and the Navy Department offered him the full facilities of the Brooklyn Navy Yard. On the West coast too there were gala receptions for the officers. Everywhere the American people were drinking enthusiastic toasts to Lincoln the Emancipator and Alexander the Liberator. A "thrill of joy pervaded America" at what was universally accepted as a symbol of faith in the Union cause, and a promise of support for Union arms, on the part of the great, friendly power of eastern Europe. The nation echoed Secretary of Navy Welles' heartfelt "God bless the Russians."

On October 1 New York itself prepared to pay its tribute to the visitors in the expansive manner with which the city has always honored its heroes. A special committee of the Common Council set off down the bay in the early morning aboard a revenue cutter. As it approached the *Alexander Nevski*, flagship of the

Russian fleet, a salute of twenty-one guns was fired from each
of the five vessels and the Stars and Stripes were dramaticall·
unfurled at their forepeaks. The cutter then drew alongsid·
the *Alexander Nevski* and the staid councilmen, weighed
down with official dignity, clambered over her sides to be of
ficially received by the Russian admiral and his lieutenants ir
full dress uniforms "tastefully decorated with gold lace anc
embroidery about the collars and cuffs." After speeches anc
toasts the Russian officers accompanied the councilmen aboarc
the cutter to be taken back to the city. The band aboard the
frigate broke out into "Yankee Doodle," which the Russian·
fondly believed was America's national anthem, and the cutter
sped off to the pier at the foot of Twenty-Third Street. There
an honorary escort of one thousand police and the first division
of the New York National Guard awaited the distinguished
guests, and they proceeded to the City Hall amid cheers and
huzzas, the fluttering of handkerchiefs and the salute of guns.

"The moving pageant," wrote a rhapsodic reporter of the
New York Times, "rolled in a glittering stream down the
broad thoroughfare between banks of upturned faces, the
trappings of the equipages, the gold and silver epaulettes of
the Muscovite guests and the sabres, helmets and bayonets of
the escort reflecting back in unnumbered dazzling lines the
glory of the evening sun." One of the Russian officers was heard
to utter "in sonorous Russ" his astonishment and admiration
at "the grace, loveliness and animation . . . of our fair dames
and damsels." It inspired the reporter to new flights. "On the
chill banks of the Neva," he wrote, "perhaps when far away
on the boisterous billows of the Black Sea or the Caspian, he
will recall, in his lonely midnight vigil, while he paces the
storm-beaten deck, the sunny smiles that brightened the au-
tumnal sunshine on the borders of the Hudson."

So much for the moving spectacle, but in its comment the
next day the *New York Tribune* declared that it did not believe this immense and enthusiastic concourse of thirty thousand people had been drawn to the scene by idle curiosity.

"Hardly one but understands," it stated editorially, "that while the great Protestant power of England, and the great Catholic power of France, had intrenched themselves behind the brittling abatis of diplomacy, ready to quarrel, to grumble, and to contend for the ninth part of a hair, Russia, far distant from us, but, in her turn, intent in an opposite quarter of the globe, upon the extension of popular civilization, has preserved those relations of friendship, which, when they become ancient, may also become indissoluble."

There had always been cordial relations between Russia and the United States, the *Tribune* continued, but the secret of this feeling was not to be found in their trade or in the wide distances which separated them. It was in the two great nations' common experience in the political emancipation of great masses of their people from bondage. There were also further ties. Both nations faced a glowing future "in which great tracts of territory are to be rescued from barrenness," while Russia had a unique and special interest in the United States because she "finds here mechanical and manufacturing ingenuity of which she has need." With a final tribute to Russia, the editorial then concluded with a fervent expression of American appreciation of the friendship of the Czar—"obligations like this, abstract as they are, are never forgotten."

If possible, *Harper's Weekly* was even more fervent than the enthusiastic editors of New York's daily press in applauding Russian good will for the United States. It proposed a Russian-American alliance. Our isolationist policy had outlived its usefulness in a day in which more rapid means of transportation and communication were bringing us every year closer to Europe, *Harper's Weekly* declared. Under these new circumstances England and France were a potentially hostile combination to which the only answer was a combination of Russia and America. There was a natural affinity between the two nations: "Russia, like the United States, is a nation of the future." When both the serfs and slaves were freed and educated, there would be nothing impossible for the Russian and

American people. "Certainly the least of the purposes which they could achieve," the editorial concluded, "would be to keep the peace of the world, and prevent the ambition of despots or the slavery of shop-keepers from embroiling nations in useless wars."

At the time of this exuberant outburst of pro-Russian feeling Northern victories on the field of battle had largely averted all danger of foreign intervention in the Civil War. There was a new feeling of confidence everywhere in the preservation of the Union. Nevertheless the visit of the Russian fleets, whatever the Czar's motive in sending them to American ports, quickened the responses of the American people to what they felt was Russia's steadfast sympathy in an hour of national trial. This feeling lived on for many years. Oliver Wendell Holmes gave it lyrical expression upon the occasion of the visit to America of the Grand Duke Alexis in 1871:

> *Bleak are our shores with the blasts of December,*
> *Fettered and chill is the rivulet's flow;*
> *Throbbing and warm are the hearts that remember*
> *Who was our friend when the world was our foe.*

V

SEWARD'S FOLLY

FOUR years after the Civil War visit of the Russian fleets to American waters, a momentous deal was concluded between the governments at Washington and St. Petersburg. Russian America was purchased by the United States for $7,200,000. That cold, forbidding country, where Baranov had once ruled with an iron hand and offered at his "Castle" at Sitka such a roistering welcome to American visitors, became the territory of Alaska. And had it not been for the close bonds that were forged as Russia proved herself "our friend when the world was our foe," it is highly improbable that the American people would have approved this transfer of territory.

For the United States did not really want to buy Alaska. It was Russia that wanted to sell. Among American statesmen and political leaders, only Secretary of State Seward showed any enthusiasm over the transaction. He engineered it single-handed. It was his ambitious imperialism, his soaring vision of the future importance of the Pacific, that was primarily responsible for this new addition to American territory. Few of his countrymen recognized either Alaska's economic potentialities or its highly strategic geographic location. Before the congressional and public debate upon the treaty he negotiated with Russia was concluded, Seward had been able to convince the country that Alaska was possibly worth the $7,200,000 we had agreed to pay for it, but this alone could not clinch the bargain in view of the public apathy at this time toward expansion. Popular friendship for Russia played a decisive part in securing both ratification of the treaty and the appropriation of the necessary money. We were repaying a debt of gratitude.

If today it appears surprising that there should have been

any hesitation over taking Alaska off Russia's hands on such relatively easy terms, it must be remembered that in the 1860's little was known of its material wealth. Prevalent ideas of its climate had convinced the few Americans who had ever heard of Alaska that such a frigid, barren country could hardly have any real value for the United States. It was also believed to lie too far north to have any commercial or strategic importance. After all it is only the airplane that has given validity to Seward's conception of Alaska as a drawbridge linking America and Asia, and in 1867 our modern conquest of the air was not even a gleam in the eye of statesmanship. Not until well into the twentieth century, perhaps not until the 1940's, could the American people appreciate the tremendous significance of what at the time they derisively called "Seward's Folly."

After the death of Baranov in 1819 there had been a steady decline in the fortunes of the Russian American Company. Alexander I had not responded to the occasional urgings of those who tried to revive the dream of imperial expansion on the American continent, and the Russo-American treaty of 1824 had marked the abandonment of all idea of acquiring new territory. Russians remained in control of the settlement at Fort Ross for some time, not withdrawing from this outpost until the eve of our own acquisition of California, but this colony dwindled in importance even more than that at Sitka. The gradual extermination of the sea otter was in large part responsible for the hard times that fell upon the Russian American Company. As the century advanced it was no longer possible for it to send home an annual fleet laden with a cargo of priceless skins, and other ventures undertaken to compensate for these losses did not greatly prosper. Alaska was becoming a liability rather than an asset. The Czarist government lost what slight interest it had ever had in the territory, and the officials at St. Petersburg began to feel that the difficulties in holding it and providing for its protection outweighed its possible value.

Suggestions for the transfer of Alaska to the United States were in the air around the middle of the century. Cassius M. Clay, our minister to St. Petersburg in the 1860's, was the doubtful authority for a report that Russia would have been willing to cede the territory without compensation at the time when the United States and Great Britain were involved in controversy over the division of Oregon. During the Crimean War there were rumors that Russia was anxious to sell. These reports were denied by Minister Stoeckl but they had at least some slight foundation. A fictitious sale to a San Francisco company had been proposed with the idea of averting possible attack by Great Britain. This plan was soon dropped and Alaska's neutrality during the Anglo-Russian hostilities had then been assured through an agreement with the Hudson's Bay Company, to which the Russian American Company had leased certain of its property.

The Crimean War, however, brought home to St. Petersburg the exposed situation of Alaska, and the idea of selling it was given serious consideration in 1857. The Grand Duke Constantine now took the lead in urging cession of territory which Russia could not hope to hold in the event of another war. He was strongly supported in these views by Stoeckl. The Russian minister agreed that Alaska was virtually defenseless, and he also pointed out that it represented a possible source of needless friction with the United States which might well jeopardize Russian-American friendship. There had been continuing controversies over American fishing rights in Alaskan waters since the expiration of the clause in the treaty of 1824 granting us such privileges, but—far more important—Stoeckl was convinced that some day the United States would seek to absorb Alaska as it had already absorbed Oregon and California. He reported to his government in some alarm that there were rumors that the Mormons under Brigham Young planned a northern emigration. Alexander wrote on the top of his minister's dispatch that this fresh complication provided additional support for the views of those who were urging that Alaska be sold.

As a result of these developments Stoeckl was instructed to be ready to take advantage of any suggestion that the United States might be interested in acquiring the territory. Early in 1860 he reported that the idea had been broached in conversations with Senator Gwin of California and Assistant Secretary of State Appleton. He was informed that President Buchanan favored purchase and a price of $5,000,000 was mentioned. Neither government, however, was prepared to commit itself definitely on the proposition. Secretary of State Cass was apparently not even informed of what was going on, and Foreign Minister Gorchakov advised Stoeckl to proceed with extreme caution. Meanwhile the shadow of impending Civil War crept over the horizon and the negotiations lapsed under the stress of far more important problems.

Six years later the issue came up again at St. Petersburg. Affairs had been going from bad to worse in Alaska. The charter of the Russian American Company had expired and its tangled finances left it on the verge of bankruptcy. If Alaska were to be maintained as a Russian colony, the government had either to subsidize the company heavily or itself take over administration of the territory. All the arguments advanced a decade earlier in favor of its possible transfer to the United States appeared now to be more valid than ever. Stoeckl, home on leave, was still certain that the time would come when Americans would overrun the territory and he strongly felt that it would not be to Russia's interest to become involved in a hopeless struggle to retain something she did not really want. It was now known in Russian official circles that there was gold in Alaska. But ironically enough this served only to make Stoeckl more anxious to sell the territory because he feared that once the fact became known there would be no resisting the American onrush whatever Russia sought to do. His position was that Russia was bound to lose Alaska sooner or later,

either to Great Britain or to the United States, and that it should be sold before it was too late.

The whole matter was threshed over at a council of ministers at St. Petersburg in December 1866 and, in the face of some opposition from those who felt that Russia should preserve "every clod of earth along the coast of an ocean which has world-wide importance," the proponents of sale won the day. The United States was of course the logical customer, for Russia as always sought to strengthen this country at the expense of Great Britain, and the decision was now definitely reached that the transfer should be urged upon the American government at the earliest opportunity. Stoeckl was commissioned to return to Washington and to carry out the agreed-upon policy to the best of his ability. The minimum price he was authorized to accept was $5,000,000.

The moment of his return was unexpectedly propitious. Secretary Seward was looking about for new territories the United States might acquire, ready to give free rein to his expansionist ambitions. He wanted to annex Santo Domingo and to purchase the Danish West Indies; he hoped to negotiate a treaty of either annexation or reciprocity with the Hawaiian Islands, and he had quietly appropriated Midway Island. With his main interest centered upon the Pacific, which he so confidently believed to be "the chief theatre of events in the world's great hereafter," nothing could have fitted more neatly into his plans than the purchase of Alaska.

There were not many other Americans who felt as did Seward. The public was far too much absorbed in domestic questions arising out of the Civil War, as the Secretary of State himself wrote somewhat despairingly, to entertain "the higher, but more remote, questions of national extension." As for Alaska itself, it was so far away that the American people not only had no direct contacts with it whatsoever but hardly knew of its existence. There were only two slender threads which might be considered as linking the United States with the Russian colony now on the market. One involved the project of a telegraph line to Europe by way of Alaska and Siberia, and the other was the question of fishing privileges on the Alaskan coast. Here were the sum and total of American interests in Alaska outside the fertile and imaginative mind of Secretary Seward.

In connection with the proposed telegraph line the Western Union Company had obtained from the Russian government, with the enthusiastic cooperation of Cassius Clay, the necessary charter and privileges. It had conducted extensive surveys throughout Alaska. The whole project nevertheless fell through in 1866 when an Atlantic cable was at last successfully laid and a telegraph line across Alaska consequently no longer justified the great expense of its construction. The old issue of fishing privileges, however, had been revived with the presentation to President Johnson of a memorial from the legislature of Washington Territory urging conclusion of a new treaty with Russia to obtain for American vessels the right to fish off the Alaskan coast and visit Alaskan ports. The memorial did not reflect any wide popular demand, even on the West coast. It was largely the work of one Joseph Lane MacDonald who had organized the Puget Sound Steam Navigation Company and hoped to extend its operations to the north.

Secretary Seward knew of these developments and the memorial concerning fishing privileges, presented early in 1866, appeared to him to afford an opportunity for which he had long been looking. Why not use it as an opening wedge to persuade the Russian government to sell Alaska to the United States? Without any knowledge of the instructions which Stoeckl was actually bringing back with him from St. Petersburg, the ambitious Secretary of State decided on just this step. He made the memorial so conveniently adopted by the Washington legislature the occasion for communicating to Stoeckl, in his own words, "the importance of some early and comprehensive arrangement between the two countries, to prevent the growth of difficulties arising out of the fisheries in the Russian possessions."

One may easily imagine the surprise and gratification with which the shrewd and skillful Russian diplomat, upon reaching Washington in March 1867, listened to the impulsive Seward's suggestion. Nothing could have more directly played into his hands. Negotiations for the transfer of Alaska were consequently taken up at once between two such willing partners and carried forward with both haste and complete secrecy.

Seward offered $5,000,000 as a purchase price; Stoeckl asked $7,000,000. A compromise between these two figures appeared logical and the Russian minister actually reported to his government that he was ready to accept anything from $6,000,000 to $6,500,000. But he soon realized that there was no need to reduce the price for so eager a purchaser. He stood by his original demand. After some half-hearted haggling on Seward's part, the final price of $7,000,000 was agreed upon. Moreover, when the question arose of various franchises and concessions leased by the Russian American Company, the Secretary of State went even further in declaring that he would add $200,000 to the price if Alaska came to the United States free of all encumbrances. The bargain was quickly sealed under these happy circumstances. Seward obtained the somewhat sceptical approval of President Johnson and Stoeckl telegraphed his government by means of the new Atlantic cable for final authorization to sign a treaty.

"On Friday evening, March 29," as the next step in this remarkable transaction has been recorded by the Secretary of State's son, "Seward was playing whist in his parlor with some of his family, when the Russian minister was announced.

"'I have a dispatch, Mr. Seward, from my Government by cable. The Emperor gives his consent to the cession. Tomorrow if you like, I will come to the department, and we can enter upon the treaty.'

"Seward, with a smile of satisfaction at the news, pushed away the whist table, saying:

"'Why wait till tomorrow, Mr. Stoeckl? Let us make the treaty tonight.'"

Startled secretaries were at once routed out; Charles Sumner, chairman of the Senate Foreign Relations Committee, hastily summoned, and the two men repaired to the State Department. By four o'clock the next morning the treaty had been drawn up and signed. Passers-by, wondering why the Secretary of State's office should be so brilliantly lighted at such an unlikely hour in the morning, little suspected that it signified their country's acquisition of new territory totaling some 591,000 square miles, an area more than twice the size of Texas and equal to nearly one-fifth of continental United States. Nor could any legislative body have been more surprised than was the Senate when later that same day it received a special message from President Johnson, laconically submitting for its approval "a treaty for the cession of Russian America."

So secretly had the brief negotiations been conducted that outside of a handful of people in Washington, no one had even suspected that the United States was seriously considering the purchase of Alaska. The announcement of Seward's dramatic coup was at first greeted with stunned surprise. Newspaper editors throughout the country hurried to their atlases and encyclopedias to discover what they could of Russian America, and in some cases launched into descriptions of the territory even without the benefit of such hastily acquired information. An even more ignorant public was treated to some amazing descriptive material. It was confidently stated that the ground in Alaska was frozen throughout the year to a depth of some six feet, that the streams were all glaciers, and that the territory's only products were icebergs and polar bears. While "Seward's Folly" became the most popular name for our prospective new possession, it was also joyously termed "Walrussia," "Johnson's Polar Bear Garden," and "Seward's Icebox." Although it would later support the cession, the *New York Herald* took its fling at the Secertary of State by advising him to purchase Patagonia "to make both ends meet," publishing a fictitious advertisement:

> CASH! CASH! CASH!—Cash paid for cast-off terri-
> tory. Best price given for old colonies, North or South.
> Any impoverished monarchs retiring from the coloni-
> zation business may find a good purchaser by address-
> ing W. H. S., Post Office, Washington, D.C.

The anti-administration papers, bitter against President
Johnson on the eve of the impeachment proceedings resulting
from his conflict with Congress over reconstruction in the
South, automatically condemned anything for which he could
directly or indirectly be held responsible. His Secretary of State
was consequently denounced for his "bad bargain" and the
"egregious folly" of the whole affair. It was a "dark deed done
in the night."

Although this outburst was somewhat dismaying, and Senator Sumner actually advised Stoeckl to withdraw the treaty
rather than risk its rejection by the Senate, Seward believed he
could win sufficient popular support to ensure favorable action.
He launched a nationwide propaganda campaign to convince
the country that Alaska was well worth the $7,200,000 being
paid for it. Friendly newspapers were furnished with abundant
copy emphasizing the reasons why we should acquire the territory. The argument was put forward that opposition to this
purchase was based upon the same shortsightedness and pro-
vincialism that had sought to block that of Louisiana. The
known resources of Alaska in fish, furs and lumber, and its
commercial and strategic importance in the Pacific area, were
carefully elaborated upon as wholly justifying the cession. The
final and supposedly conclusive reason advanced for ratifying
the treaty, however, was that since the Czar desired to sell, and
an agreement had actually been reached, our debt to Russia for
support during the Civil War did not permit us to rebuff her
overtures.

The backing of Senator Sumner proved to be Seward's most
powerful asset in securing approval by the Senate. The treaty
could hardly have been ratified without it. The Massachusetts

statesman did not share Seward's glowing dream of Pacific expansion. He had doubts upon the advisability of the purchase. But he was won over to its support, despite his opposition to the Johnson administration on so many other counts, because of his desire to have the United States retain the friendship of Russia. "The Russian treaty tried me severely," Sumner later wrote; "abstractly I am against further acquisitions of territory, unless by the free choice of their inhabitants. But this question was perplexed by considerations of politics and comity and the engagements already entered into by the Government. I hesitated to take the responsibility of defeating it." Having once made up his mind, however, the influential senator from Massachusetts threw himself wholeheartedly into the fight to secure prompt ratification.

In a memorable speech before the Senate which is still a mine of information about Alaska, Sumner declared that possession of the Russian territory would immensely strengthen our naval and commercial position in the Pacific. It was essential, he said, that we should take advantage of this opportunity to acquire it. Otherwise it might well fall some day into the hands of Great Britain and afford her control over an ocean which should be kept free for American trade and commerce. Describing the Aleutian Islands as "extending a friendly hand to Asia," he further emphasized Alaska's role as a link with the people of China and Japan. But the argument upon which he laid the greatest stress and to which he repeatedly returned, as had the newspaper articles inspired by Seward, was our international obligation. "It is difficult to see," he stated emphatically, "how we can refuse to complete the purchase without putting to hazard the friendly relations which happily subsist between the United States and Russia."

So decisive was Sumner's attitude that he persuaded his fellow senators to accept the agreement, whatever their feelings as to its wisdom, rather than affront Russia by rejecting it. The treaty was ratified on April 9, 1867, by a majority of 27 to 12. A motion was then introduced to make the vote unanimous as

a gesture of cordiality toward Russia, "the old and faithful friend of the United States," but two ballots were still cast in the negative.

It was now necessary to secure House approval for the appropriation of the $7,200,000 purchase price. Consideration of the necessary bill was long delayed by the absorption of Congress in the impeachment proceedings against President Johnson, and for a time it appeared highly doubtful if favorable action would ever be taken. The political situation stacked all cards against the administration. Stoeckl grew so despairing that he even suggested to his government that it offer to forego all payment for Alaska in the hope of shaming Congress into making the funds available. Foreign Minister Gorchakov vetoed this idea. Possibly he feared the Congress would take advantage of it.

Justification for such cynicism existed in the fact that certain private claims had been brought against the Russian government and there was at least some congressional support for demanding their settlement as a condition of paying for Alaska. These claims were shown to be fraudulent and the proposition rejected. Nevertheless even their discussion introduced an unsavory element into the transaction foreshadowing the scandals which would soon become so notorious in Washington during the Grant administration. Rumors were also spread about somewhat later which hinted at bribery and corruption as a means of winning support for the treaty. There was no question that Seward and Stoeckl spent large sums for propaganda, but how much further their agents may have gone cannot be definitely answered. A memorandum subsequently discovered among the papers of President Johnson quoted Seward as having told the President that the Russian envoy had actually paid considerable sums to certain important Washington figures to win their support. Thaddeus Stevens was said to have received $10,000, N. P. Banks, chairman of the House Foreign Relations Committee, $8,000, John W. Forney $30,000, and R. J. Walker and F. P. Stanton $20,000 apiece.

This hearsay evidence is not in itself proof of corruption, but the testimony given at the time by the principals in the transaction is not altogether reassuring. While Seward stated before a congressional committee investigating the "Alaska Swindle" that "no engagement was ever made with anybody for any part of the purchase-money, or any fund," he was not altogether candid in certain of his other statements. For his part Stoeckl reported to the Russian government that the greater part of the $200,000 added to the purchase price had been used for "secret expenses," and he finally asked that he be transferred to some other post where he could "breathe an atmosphere purer than that of Washington."

The debate in the House upon the appropriation bill, apart from these aspects of the question, reflected the public attitude toward Alaska's purchase. Partisan opposition to the Johnson administration, the constitutional issue involved in the right of the Senate to ratify a treaty dependent upon a congressional appropriation, the value of Alaska to the United States and our obligations to Russia all played their part in the discussion. There were those who followed Seward's lead in declaring that acquisition of the territory would give us control of the Pacific, and bitter opponents of the transfer who saw in Alaska nothing at all but a useless and expensive burden. The argument stressing our debt to Russia was brought up repeatedly, to be answered in one instance with the statement that if it involved the payment of $7,200,000, we should meet it promptly but not accept Alaska even as a free gift.

"Alaska, with the Aleutian Islands," Ferris of New York caustically remarked, "is an inhospitable, wretched, and God-forsaken region, worth nothing, but a positive injury and incumbrance as a colony of the United States." Washburn of Wisconsin blandly suggested that if we were determined upon acquiring a white elephant, we could get a much superior one "in Siam or Bombay for one-hundredth part of the money, with not one ten-thousandth part of the expense in keeping the animal in proper condition." Let Russia keep Alaska was the

burden of these critics' song. "Have the people desired it?" Williams of Pennsylvania demanded. "Not a sensible man among them ever suggested it. The whole country exclaimed at once, when it was made known to them, against the ineffable folly, if not the wanton profligacy, of the whole transaction."

Proponents of the purchase stood their ground against all such attacks. There was strong support for purchasing the territory from the West coast, where the value of the Alaskan fisheries was better known, and a number of representatives dwelt upon the importance of our trade in the Pacific. Maynard of Tennessee echoed Seward's views in stating that possession of Alaska would give the United States "commercial and naval supremacy on the Pacific as complete as Great Britain has for two centuries enjoyed on the Atlantic Ocean." N. P. Banks shared—or perhaps borrowed—the Secretary of State's prophetic visions of the Pacific. "That ocean will be the theatre of the triumphs of civilization in the future," he grandiloquently proclaimed. "It is on that line that are to be fought the great battles of the hereafter. It is there that the institutions of the world will be fashioned and its destinies decided. If this transfer is successful, it will no longer be an European civilization or an European destiny that controls us. It will be a higher civilization and a nobler destiny. It may be an American civilization, an American destiny of six hundred million souls."

Long before these floods of impassioned oratory inundated the halls of Congress, Seward had gone ahead with the formal process of taking possession of Alaska, and the American flag had been impressively raised at Sitka on October 18, 1867. By the time the House got around to taking final action, in the summer of 1868, it was actually confronted with a *fait accompli*. Refusal of the necessary appropriation had become more than ever difficult. "Shall that flag which waves so proudly there now be taken down?" cried Representative Orth of Indiana. "Palsied be the hand that would dare to remove it. Our flag is there, and there it will remain." This was a decisive argument.

And four days later, on July 23, the House at last acted. The appropriation was approved by a vote of 113 to 43.

It is clearly evident both in this vote and in the newspaper comment of the period that there was no overwhelming popular demand for Alaska. Seward had fought an uphill battle in winning public support for his treaty. It would also appear that despite such converts as he may have made to his own expansionist doctrines, there might have been no purchase of Alaska if it had been owned by any other nation than Russia. The Secretary of State did not succeed in any of his other attempts to acquire new possessions. "I doubt that there was any member of either house of Congress," John Bigelow, a friend of Seward, later wrote on the basis of contemporary conversations, "who supposed the Government then had any other motive in the purchase of Alaska than to recognize the obligations to the Czar. . . ." While this was most certainly not true of Seward himself, it was an attitude widely held and probably decisive in the final acceptance of the transfer.

Not many years were to pass before the value of Alaska would be proved far beyond the most optimistic predictions of Seward and his supporters. Taxes upon Alaskan industries poured back into the Treasury within a few decades a sum greater than the territory's total purchase price. Even before the Klondike Rush in 1896, gold production had far surpassed this figure of $7,200,000, while the mounting profits of the fisheries and fur seal industry completely dwarfed a sum which had loomed so large in the minds of timid congressmen. The "ineffable folly, if not wanton profligacy" of our deal with Russia turned out to be one of the shrewdest bargains the country ever concluded.

While the fisheries, fur sealing industry and gold mining early revealed Alaska's economic significance, its role as a base for air transport has more recently demonstrated many times over its tremendous strategic value to the United States. "Alaska is the most central place in the world for aircraft," Brigadier General William Mitchell even went so far as to write

in 1935. "And that is true either of Europe, Asia or North America, for in the future I think whoever holds Alaska will hold the world, and I think it is the most important strategic place in the world."

With the outbreak of the Pacific war in 1941, this aspect of the territory was doubly emphasized. Whatever might have been the role of Alaska in the hands of a foreign power, its possession by the United States provided a northern anchor for a vital defensive line which stretched from the Aleutian Islands through Hawaii to the Panama Canal. Perhaps even more important, the rocky and fog-girt Aleutians had fulfilled Seward's nineteenth century prophecy. They were at last becoming "this drawbridge between America and Asia, these stepping stones across the Pacific Ocean."

THE BEAR THAT WALKS LIKE A MAN

WHILE there was a period of almost thirty years of continuing cordiality in Russian-American relations following the purchase of Alaska, a marked change began to take place in our attitude toward the Czarist government by the close of the nineteenth century. It was not altogether apparent upon the surface. The visit of the Grand Duke Alexis in 1871 had awakened a new popular interest in Russia, and upon the death of Alexander the Liberator ten years later newspapers throughout the country gratefully recalled his services to the Union during the Civil War. When Russia was stricken in the early 1890's by a severe famine taking a toll of millions of lives, the American people came to her aid by raising $77,000,000 in relief funds and sending abroad five steamers loaded with flour. Russia in turn reciprocated these gestures of good will in standing by the United States when we became involved in war with Spain, refusing to take part in the proposed mediation of the Continental powers. Nevertheless, America was beginning to grow both suspicious and even fearful of the direction in which Russian foreign policy appeared to be heading. St. Petersburg in turn would soon resent what it regarded as our obstructive and interfering attitude. A heavy cloud gathered over the historic friendship.

In the background of these developments was the ideological conflict between autocracy and democracy. This was nothing new but it was heightened by an ever-widening divergence in the trends of domestic policy. Nicholas II, who became Czar in 1894, was personally mild and unassuming in character, but he lent himself as a weak ruler often does to an arbitrary exercise of power that sought to stamp out all reform tendencies. His government was despotic and reactionary; there was little

evidence of the liberalism which had occasionally flowered among the weeds of tyranny in Czarist Russia. And during the years of his rule the United States was entering upon the Progressive era, seeking to strengthen in every possible way the bases for both political and economic freedom. It was natural that the American people should judge what they regarded as retrogression in Russia all the more severely because of their own liberal, forward-looking advance.

Evidence both of what was happening in Russia and of the American reaction to it may be found before the close of the century in the writings of Andrew D. White, minister at St. Petersburg in the early 1890's. He wrote feelingly of the deadening influence of the whole Russian system and of the atmosphere of repression evident everywhere, declaring it to be impossible to have any trust or confidence in the Russian government. Its cruel treatment of the Jews, subjecting them to restrictive laws reminiscent of the Middle Ages, and its brutal suppression of the liberties of Finland were especially singled out for condemnation. The Russian dynasty, White somberly and prophetically stated, would in time be punished for following a policy that was both wicked and certain to be disastrous.

Such antagonism to the Czarist regime was further intensified in this country because the Russian government meted out to Russian-born American citizens who returned to their home the same treatment accorded its own subjects. Those who were Jews were refused the privileges supposedly guaranteed by the old treaty of 1832, their passports withheld and their property made subject to seizure, while other naturalized Americans were arrested and held for military service. The anti-Semitism of the Czar's government added to popular distrust of Russia already aroused by travelers' reports of cruel suppression, political arrests and exile to Siberia under incredible conditions of hardship and suffering.

These feelings were fanned to a new intensity by a tragic incident occurring in 1903. On Easter Sunday of that year, anti-Jewish riots broke out in the city of Kishinev. Homes were

THE ROAD TO TEHERAN

wantonly looted and put to the torch; brutal attacks made upon defenseless men, women and children. When order was finally restored, 8,000 people had been rendered homeless, 500 injured and 50 killed. A wave of horror at this bloody pogrom swept over the United States, all the more intense because it was believed that the attack upon the Jews had actually been encouraged by the Minister of the Interior. No protection had been afforded by either the police or the military, and nothing said after the event could disguise the bigoted anti-Semitism of the Czar's government.

"Russia, indeed, today stands before the world," the *New York Commercial Advertiser* declared, "not as one of the great Powers of Christendom, but as a gigantic force which makes for barbarism." The *Philadelphia Public Ledger* and the *New York Times* agreed that her government could no longer be called civilized, having lost all title to the respect of decent nations. William Randolph Hearst, probably more interested in a popular issue than the plight of Russian Jews, was even more vehement in the denunciations he contributed to the papers under his control. He demanded an immediate protest by the State Department, declaring that if it should hesitate to express what the American people really thought, the rulers of Russia would learn of it even more directly. "They will know when they hear from Congress," Hearst wrote combatively, "that they are hearing FROM THE POWER THAT MAKES TREATIES AND DECLARES WAR. Let Mr. Hay bow as politely as he chooses to the bear with the bloody paws. That bear knows that there is a power over Hay, and from that power Russia will hear."

The Secretary of State did not submit to Mr. Hearst's dictation. However much he might himself have liked to protest to St. Petersburg, for John Hay was no friend to the Czarist government, there were no grounds upon which the United States would have been justified in intervening in what was a wholly domestic affair. For a time he considered forwarding a popular protest, but even this project was dropped when the Czar let

it be known that under no circumstances would he receive it. Nicholas' arrogant attitude naturally did nothing to allay public hostility toward Russia. Autocracy—bigotry—absolutism—intolerance—bureaucracy—corruption—tyranny—cruelty: these became the stereotypes associated with the Czarist regime in the American mind.

More important than this wave of popular resentment toward the Czar's domestic policies, however, a direct conflict in foreign policies had for the first time developed between Russia and America. The scene was the Far East. Nothing could have been further from the public mind upon the sale of Alaska, or at any time during the 1870's and 1880's, than alarms and excursions over conflicting claims in Manchuria and China. Port Arthur, Mukden and Antung were not found on the political map in 1867. But some thirty years later the United States and Russia appeared to be reaching out toward control of the Pacific, and they unexpectedly found themselves facing each other as rivals in eastern Asia. We had arrived on these distant shores by way of Hawaii, Guam and the Philippine Islands; the Russians had pushed east and south through Siberia, Korea and Manchuria.

Russia had at first welcomed the extension of American influence in this part of the world. The old desire to uphold the United States as a commercial and naval rival of the British Empire was the real motive behind the Czar's approval of our acquisition of the Philippines, but throughout the Spanish War his ministers repeatedly emphasized their good will for the American people. "We were friends, we are friends, and we intend to remain friends," Foreign Minister Mouraviev told our envoy at St. Petersburg in June 1898. Nicholas himself echoed the very phrases used by his predecessors in 1812 and 1863. "We are always in agreement with the United States," he stated emphatically, "and I hope we shall always remain so."

When America undertook to promote her interests on the Asiatic mainland, however, there was a different story to tell. This meant possible interference with Russia's plans. Furthermore, our developing Far Eastern policy was marked by a new rapprochement with Great Britain which undermined the bases for Russia's traditional support of America. With the shifting political alignments of this period, the two nations no longer stood together against England. It was more likely to be the United States and Great Britain presenting a common front against Russia. In time these tangled threads of national interest would be unraveled. The three great powers would be drawn together in actual war against Germany. But the turn of the century found the Anglo-Saxon nations more immediately concerned over what was regarded as the menacing danger of Russian imperialism in Asia.

What were the objectives of the United States and Russia in these faraway parts? Russia sought the warm water outlets to the sea which were denied her in western Europe. Perhaps her ambitions flared even higher. "The throne of the future of the Orient," Senator Albert Beveridge excitedly told the American public through the pages of the *Saturday Evening Post* in 1902, "appears now to be planted upon the eminence that lifts above the waters of Port Arthur, and above it already floats the Russian flag." There was no popular support in Russia for this program of expansion. But urged on by an imperialist clique among his ministers, Nicholas was plunging ahead in his ambition to dominate eastern Asia.

As for America, the call of manifest destiny in the heyday of flamboyant imperialism following the war with Spain beckoned us to further overseas adventures. The expansionists of 1900 caught a glimpse of Seward's old dreams. The Pacific was the ocean of the future and they believed it was destined for control by America. "The inevitable march of events," Theodore Roosevelt declared, "gave us control of the Philippines at a time so opportune that it may without irreverence be held Providential. Unless we show ourselves weak, unless we show ourselves degenerate sons of the sires from whose loins we sprung, we must go on with the work we have begun."

The extent to which these expansive drives of Russia and

America conformed to their real national interests, or could count upon the public support which would make them effective, is highly questionable in the case of both nations, especially in that of the United States. Moreover, our policy never contemplated the seizure of additional territory. On the contrary, our primary interest was maintenance of the independence of the great country of China as the most effective means of promoting our Far Eastern trade and commerce. But as the Czar's soldiers pushed on into Manchuria and his diplomats maneuvered for control over the Chinese government, we nonetheless stood squarely athwart Russia's path.

Secretary of State Hay had taken the first step to protect our interests in dispatching his well-known Open Door notes to the several powers in 1899. The complete dismemberment of China appeared imminent. "The various powers cast upon us looks of tigerlike voracity," exclaimed the redoubtable old Empress Dowager who sat upon the Dragon Throne, "hustling each other in their endeavors to be the first to seize upon our innermost territories." Using our newly won possession of the Philippine Islands as a springboard to make American influence felt in this critical situation, Hay sought to obtain at least a promise on the part of the powers that they would not discriminate against American trade in their respective spheres of influence.

Russia's advance in Manchuria, where she already held important railway concessions and leaseholds at Port Arthur and Talienwan, caused the greatest apprehension on Hay's part. From the American minister at Peking came repeated warnings that the Czar's grasp upon North China was continually tightening. Other observers emphasized his alarm. "The Russification of Peking and of North China will proceed as rapidly as has that of Manchuria," wrote A. E. Hippisley, one of the prime movers in the whole project of writing the Open Door notes. Here was the most immediate threat to our trade. Should Russia exclude American goods from Manchuria and North

China, the full promise of our penetration into the Far East could hardly be realized.

The replies of the powers to Secretary Hay's notes were in each instance qualified and grudging, but that of the Russian government was so evasive as to have no real binding force whatsoever. The Czar would make no definite commitments of policy within the Russian sphere of influence. "The truth is," Ambassador Tower wrote Hay from St. Petersburg, "that the Russian Government did not wish to answer your proposition at all. It did so finally with great reluctance. . . ." Nevertheless the Secretary of State decided to accept the replies of all the powers, however ambiguous, as indicating agreement with his policy in an attempt to win popular support for the Open Door policy both at home and abroad.

It was soon put to the test. Within a few months, in the summer of 1900, the Boxer Rebellion broke out in China. Antiforeign fanatics, convinced that China's troubles were due to Western influence, tried to drive the "foreign devils" into the sea and at Peking besieged the legations with the secret support of the Empress Dowager herself. The powers sent an allied expedition to the relief of the legations and succeeded in lifting the siege in time, but Hay became immediately fearful that the incident would be made the excuse for further intervention in China's affairs. The breakup of China and consequent collapse of the Open Door policy seemed more likely than ever. To meet this issue the Secretary of State decided to dispatch a second circular to the powers further clarifying the attitude of the United States. On July 3 they were informed that the American policy was to seek a solution of the crisis that would both uphold the Open Door and also preserve China's territorial and administrative entity.

Although no replies were received to this new overture, Hay's objective was secured in the subsequent negotiations among the powers for settlement of the Boxer controversy. There was no dismemberment of China. It soon became all too apparent, however, that Russia at least had no intention of

observing the Open Door policy. She had taken advantage of the situation in 1900 to strengthen the hold she already had upon Manchuria. Additional Russian troops poured into the Chinese provinces north of the Great Wall and there was every indication that the Czar intended to keep them there. His apparent goal, according to reports from the Far East, was to establish protectorates over Manchuria, Mongolia and Turkestan, throwing "the treaty rights of other nations into the dustbin." There was increasing discrimination against American trade; the Open Door was slowly swinging shut.

Secretary Hay vigorously protested against such discrimination. Foreign Minister Mouraviev suavely replied that he did not know what he could be talking about. Russia was in no way infringing upon the principles of the Open Door policy, she had no aggressive designs whatsoever upon China, and she was about to withdraw all her troops from Manchuria. But nothing whatsoever was done to carry out these conciliatory pledges. Still further concessions were exacted from the helpless Chinese government and the Russian grip upon Manchuria steadily closed. Our trade was more severely restricted than ever. Hay fumed with impotent rage at Russia's cavalier disregard of all promises. "Her vows," he exclaimed wrathfully, "are false as dicers' oaths when treachery is profitable." He could get no satisfaction from the Russian ambassador in Washington. Arrogant, shifty, unscrupulous, Count Cassini resented American interference in what he considered were affairs of no concern to this country. When Hay protested at one meeting that if Russia persisted in her course in Manchuria, there would be nothing for the other powers to do except take over other Chinese provinces, Count Cassini broke in angrily: "This is already done. China is dismembered, and we are entitled to our share."

Henry Adams, always a shrewd observer of international affairs, wrote at this time that "the wall of Russian inertia that barred Europe across the Baltic would bar America across the Pacific; and Hay's policy of the open door would infallibly fail." The Secretary of State finally realized that this was probably true. He succeeded in persuading China to open two new ports for American trade, Mukden and Antung, but he was compelled to recognize that Manchuria as a whole remained effectively under Russian control. Events forced him to modify the policy he had so confidently proclaimed in 1900. In April 1903 we find him writing despondently that Russia knew America was not prepared to go to war over the issue and under such circumstances there was nothing we could do. "What's the use?" he commented. "Russia is too big, too crafty, too cruel for us to fight. She will conquer in the end. Why not give up now and be friendly?"

Theodore Roosevelt, who had become President on the death of McKinley in 1901, shared Hay's scorn for Russia. He fulminated against the Czar—"a preposterous little creature"—and grew indignant as only Roosevelt could against "the brazen and contemptuous effrontery" with which the Russian diplomats lied while busily organizing China against American interests. For a time he favored putting up a stiff resistance to the Czar's advance. "I have not the slightest objection," he belligerently wrote Hay in July 1903, "to the Russians knowing that I feel thoroughly aroused and irritated at their conduct in Manchuria; that I don't intend to give way and that I am year by year growing more confident that this country would back me up in going to an extreme in the matter."

If Roosevelt had any idea of challenging Russia with war, he was wrong in thinking the American people would have backed him up. The public was only mildly aroused. The periodical press was featuring such articles as "Is Russia to Establish a Universal Empire?" "Russia's Conquest of Asia," "Shall Russia Dominate the World?" Editorial writers and public speakers warned that the Muscovite Peril rather than the Yellow Peril was the real menace to Western civilization. But for all these bellicose hints, the American people did not feel any vital interests of theirs were at stake in Manchuria. They knew too little about it; it was too far away. They were heartily in

favor of the Open Door policy, but they had no idea of upholding it by force. The President would have found little popular
support for "going to an extreme in the matter."

In the meantime events in the Far East were moving toward
a dramatic climax. The United States was not in a position to
oppose Russia by force in Manchuria, but another nation, far
more directly threatened by her advance, was ready to do so.
This was of course Japan. Her national security was gravely
endangered as the Czar extended his control over territories so
near to Japanese shores. When Russia paid no heed to her
protests, Japan's answer was consequently war. Without waiting for a declaration of hostilities, she struck suddenly and
unexpectedly at the Russian fleet at Port Arthur in February
1904.

The United States at once declared its official neutrality. But
there was no question where our sympathies lay. President
Roosevelt believed that Japan was fighting to uphold the Open
Door policy and that a Japanese victory would therefore safeguard American interests throughout the Far East. Two days
after Port Arthur he wrote his son how thoroughly pleased he
was with this first Japanese victory—"Japan is playing our
game." While he tried to persuade Russia and Japan to observe
the neutrality of China, which would have had the effect of
preventing Russia from fighting in Manchuria, he did not
hesitate to accept Japan's claims in Korea. His attitude lent
encouragement to American loans which largely financed
Japan's war effort. Roosevelt, indeed, indicated that he was
ready to go even further in implementing his pro-Japanese
feelings.

"As soon as this war broke out," he wrote on July 24, 1905,
to Cecil Spring-Rice, then Secretary of the British Embassy at
St. Petersburg, "I notified Germany and France, in the most
polite and discreet fashion, that in the event of a combination
against Japan to try to do what Russia, Germany and France
did to her in 1894, I should promptly side with Japan and
proceed to whatever length was necessary on her behalf. I of

course knew that your government would act in the same way, and I thought it best that I should have no consultation with your people before announcing my own purpose."

The President was referring to pressure Russia, Germany and France had brought to bear upon Japan in 1894 in order to compel her to forego the fruits of her victory in the Sino-Japanese War of that year, and to the fact that England was already bound by the Anglo-Japanese alliance to come to Japan's assistance should any third power intervene in the war with Russia. In other words, he was stating an attitude which would have made the United States virtually a silent partner in the Anglo-Japanese alliance. There is, however, no evidence other than this letter that Roosevelt took any such action as he mentioned. His statement is significant only in that it clearly demonstrates the strength of his sympathies for Japan. His attitude toward Russia, moreover, was no less clearly revealed. "I should have liked to be friendly with her," he wrote during the war, "but she simply would not permit it, and those responsible for managing her foreign policy betrayed a brutality and ignorance, an arrogance and shortsightedness, which are not often combined."

The American public almost universally shared the President's views. A survey of newspaper opinion conducted by the *Literary Digest* upon the outbreak of the war did not find a single paper favoring any policy other than neutrality, but an overwhelming majority openly expressed their full sympathy for Japan. Both conservative and liberal organs were in agreement. "Japan is not only fighting the battle of progress and civilization," the *Journal of Commerce* stated. ". . . She is standing as the champion of commercial rights in whose maintenance no nation is so vitally interested as the United States." "In this war Russia stands for reaction and Japan for progress," the *Arena* declared. "The organization and control of the millions of China by Russia is far more dangerous to the rest of the world than would be their control by the Japanese." The press generally hailed every Japanese victory and did not

disguise its hopes that Russia would be quickly and decisively defeated.

Russian resentment of the attitude of the United States was quite as pronounced as the anti-Russian feeling expressed in American newspapers. Count Cassini tried to resurrect the tradition of Russian-American friendship, patriotically recalling the visit of the Czar's fleet during the perilous days of the Civil War. He declared the sole purpose of the expedition had been to give aid and comfort to the Union cause, and expressed his "bitter disappointment" and "pained surprise" at American ingratitude. There was in some quarters support for his pleas for a more sympathetic attitude toward Russia. A few writers elaborated upon the fleet story with alleged proof that the Russian admiral's sealed orders called for his reporting immediately to President Lincoln and offering his services should any other European power seek to intervene. But the press more generally ridiculed the idea that the United States owed any debt to Russia. Whatever her services in the past, it was repeatedly said, her recent behavior in Manchuria and her treatment of the Jews had wiped the slate clean. A very moderate editorial in the *New York Sun* declared that while it had to be recognized that Russia had been "the one unwavering friend we have had since the birth-throes of the nation," the time had come when the American people "were constrained to say to Russia that they could no longer trust her."

The Russian press was not content with charging America with ingratitude. The more chauvinistic papers held this country directly responsible for the war in the Far East. "The whole activity of the United States," the St. Petersburg *Novoye Vremya* stated, "is directed toward making China an industrial center ruled by American directors and viceroys in the form of trusts. . . . The policy of Washington is to push Japan on to make war." The Port Arthur *Novy Krai* was even more explicit. "Japan is not the real opponent," it declared. ". . . Her whole strength lies in the support of the United States." This country was said to have made Japan its cat's-paw in carrying out "the well-known policy of President Roosevelt, who has repeatedly claimed that the Pacific Ocean, with all its islands and coasts, is the proper sphere of American domination."

While this newspaper war was still being waged, however, events in the Far East suddenly caused a striking shift in both official and unofficial opinion in the United States. As Japan went from one spectacular victory to another, crushing the force of Russian arms on both land and sea to the amazed surprise of the Western World, doubts began to arise in the United States as to whether such a decisive Japanese victory would really be to American interests. Would Japan remain the champion of the Open Door when she was in control of Manchuria? Would she continue to respect American interests in China when she was in a position to dominate that country? It was gradually borne in upon both President Roosevelt and the American people that the defeat of Russian imperialism might well be paving the way for the rise of an even more dangerous Japanese imperialism. As 1904 gave way to 1905 we were perhaps not loving Russia more, but we were decidedly beginning to love Japan less.

American national interest clearly pointed to something like a balance of power between Russia and Japan which would prevent either nation from wholly dominating China. If Russia were crushed and completely expelled from the Far East, there would be no effective restraints upon future Japanese expansion. Roosevelt recognized this. He did not lose his sympathy for Japan, but his original policy of unquestioning support was modified by his desire to limit the scope of her victories in order to prevent the rise of too powerful a rival to the United States. For all our antagonism to the Czar's government, circumstances were thus driving us once again to uphold Russia. The self-interest which in the past had caused Russia to support the United States as opposed to Great Britain, now belatedly led us to feel more friendly toward Russia as we recognized the aggressive power of Japan.

The opportunity for the President to exercise his influence

in favor of a peace that he hoped would preserve a Far Eastern balance of power occurred in May 1905. Japan asked him to mediate. Despite her victories she was nearing the end of her financial resources and the prospect of a long drawn-out war, with her armies advancing farther and farther from their bases, was hardly encouraging. At the same time Russia was in no position to continue the conflict. Despite her greater potential resources, she had met with successive defeats on land and sea, the strain of transporting troops and supplies over the long, single-track Siberian railway had become overwhelming, and the unpopularity of the war and loss of governmental prestige had led to increasing popular discontent that was headed toward open revolt. Although it was known that Nicholas was strongly opposed to admitting a Japanese victory, the conclusion of an early peace appeared highly logical for both countries.

Assured that Japan was ready for negotiations, Roosevelt's first task was consequently to win over the Czar. He brought all possible pressure to bear upon him through diplomatic channels and instructed George Meyer, our ambassador at St. Petersburg, to seek an immediate audience to try to convince him that peace was altogether in Russia's interests. Nicholas received Meyer in private and the two men sat down together to talk the situation over. The Czar at first seemed very cool to Roosevelt's proposals but as the ambassador elaborated upon the futility of continuing the struggle, Nicholas finally agreed. Having reached a decision he then insisted upon immediate action.

"You have come at the psychological moment," he said to Meyer. "As yet no foot has been placed upon Russian soil; but I realize that any moment they can make an attack upon Sakhalin. Therefore it is important that the meeting should take place before that occurs." The ambassador now prepared to take his leave but Nicholas had a further statement to make. "Say to your President," he said with great earnestness, warmly shaking Meyer's hand, "I certainly hope that the old friendship which has previously existed and united the two nations for so

long a period will be renewed. I realize that whatever difference has arisen is due to the press, and in no way to your government."

With the consent of Russia obtained, public invitations for
a peace conference were issued to the two nations on June 8,
1905, and two months later negotiations were commenced at
Portsmouth, New Hampshire. The principal terms were easily
agreed upon. Japan fell heir to the concessions and special
privileges formerly held by Russia in both Korea and southern
Manchuria. The immediate issue of the war was settled wholly
in her favor. The stumbling block to a full accord, however,
was Japan's further demand for cession of the island of Sakhalin and a huge indemnity. Russia was willing to compromise
on the territorial question but her envoys obdurately refused
to consider any indemnity. The conference hung in the balance.

At this point Roosevelt took a direct hand in the situation.
He was not certain of the consequences of renewal of the war.
If Japan should succeed in driving Russia wholly out of the
Far East, he feared that she might threaten American interests.
On the other hand, should her staying power prove unequal to
the strain and the situation reverse itself through a Russian
victory, the menace of Russian imperialism would be revived.
Maintenance of something like the *status quo* insofar as the
relative strength of the two nations was concerned was a far
more favorable alternative than the complete triumph of either
power. Roosevelt consequently undertook to persuade Japan to
forego her demand for an indemnity and to accept an immediate peace settlement. It is again necessary to emphasize that he
did not seek modification of the Japanese terms out of friendship for the Czarist government. Although the swing in public
opinion had greatly lessened both our original sympathy for
Japan and our hostility toward Russia, Roosevelt's personal
ideas had not greatly changed. Russia still remained in his
opinion "so corrupt, so treacherous and shifty, so incompetent,
that she might break off negotiations any moment." In inter-

vening in the impasse at Portsmouth, he sought to promote the interests of the United States.

The issue still remained in doubt when the delegates of Russia and Japan met for a concluding conference. Count Witte, able and popular spokesman for the Russians, presented his final terms. His government would cede the southern half of the island of Sakhalin to Japan, but it again refused to consider payment of an indemnity. Baron Komura, head of the Japanese delegation, remained impassively silent for a few minutes and then quietly announced his decision. The Japanese government accepted the Russian proposals.

The peace treaty was signed on September 5, 1905. In view of the military and naval history of the war, it was a diplomatic triumph for Russia. And it had been won with American assistance. Nevertheless the real victory, obscured though it was at the time, was Japan's. Roosevelt had in reality failed to uphold a balance of power in the Far East. Japan had replaced Russia as the most powerful nation in eastern Asia. She had taken an immense forward stride on her destined course of imperialistic expansion. Time was to prove that she was a far more formidable rival to American interests in the Pacific than ever Czarist Russia had been.

VII

ALLIES FOR DEMOCRACY

THE Russo-Japanese War brought to an end the conflict of interests between Russia and the United States in the Far East. When the Taft administration somewhat later sought to implement the Open Door policy by proposing the neutralization of Manchurian railroads, key to both economic and political control of the Chinese provinces north of the Great Wall, it was sharply rebuffed by both Japan and Russia. The two former antagonists joined forces to inform our State Department that there was no warrant for changing existing arrangements. They had agreed upon a division of their respective spheres of influence, now that Russia had been compelled to relinquish her rights in southern Manchuria, and would brook no outside interference.

Going even further, they concluded a series of treaties, culminating in a secret pact signed in 1916, which appeared to be directly aimed at possible American intervention in the Far East. As subsequently revealed, the two nations agreed that in the event of a declaration of war against either one of them, the other would come to the attacked country's aid. But this temporary rapprochement did not affect any vital American interests. The United States did not again press the issue raised by the proposed neutralization of Manchurian railways. Whatever danger there had ever been of an actual clash between Russia and America in this distant sphere had been averted, as a possible contest over the two nations' conflicting claims on the Northwest coast had been, by the abandonment of any ambitions the Czar may have had for aggrandizement in the Pacific.

Nevertheless there was no full restoration of the accepted friendship of the nineteenth century. It was more than ever

difficult to reconcile autocracy and democracy as the ferment of the Progressive era intensified the striking contrast between American liberalism and Russian reaction. After having been compelled to make a conciliatory gesture toward reform by promising his people a liberal constitution, Nicholas II took advantage of the restoration of peace with Japan to punish ruthlessly all who had defied his authority. The new Duma was largely stifled. Absolutism was again enthroned. The arrest, exile or execution of all political agitators became the mark of an autocracy that evasively ignored the promised democratic reforms.

Moreover the Russian government continued its persecution of the Jews and American sympathies were once again enlisted, as they had been at the time of the Kishinev massacre, for these unfortunate victims of Czarist bigotry. Thousands of them fled Russia to seek asylum in the United States. Poor and ignorant, many of them anarchists or nihilists in bitter reaction to Russian absolutism, they were not an entirely welcome class of immigrants. For all its sympathy for them while they stayed at home, the United States did not particularly want them as citizens. Its resentment consequently rose all the more against a government which bred such rebels and then drove them forth to create new and difficult problems for the American "melting pot."

How the Russian government treated its own subjects was its own affair, but there was one instance of anti-Semitism which directly affected the United States. Russian consular officials in this country continued to refuse passport visas to Russian Jews who had become naturalized American citizens and de- sired to return to their homeland. Against such discrimination we had every right to protest, and as the Russian government blatantly ignored the rights of these American citizens, pub- lic opinion became thoroughly aroused. There was a wide- spread demand for retaliatory action and in 1911 Congress prepared to take matters into its own hands. A resolution was introduced for abrogation of the treaty which James Buchanan had negotiated in 1832, still the only one governing commercial relations between Russia and the United States, as a frank avowal of American antagonism to the Czar's policies. Alarmed over the possible repercussions of such a step, the State Department hurriedly moved to terminate the treaty itself as a less pointed rebuke than summary action by Congress.

Foreign Minister Sazonov considered our attitude, as well he might, distinctly unfriendly, and tried to defend Russia's policy. His government could not surrender the right to bar undesirables, even though they might nominally be American citizens, he heatedly told our ambassador at St. Petersburg. And Jews were distinctly undesirable. They were a perpetual menace to the integrity of the Russian Empire; they were a threat to law and order. If Americans felt so strongly about the anti-Semitic policy of his government, Sazonov declared, he was prepared to consider an arrangement whereby all the Jews in Russia might be transferred to the United States. To this suggestion the American ambassador made no reply.

The undercurrent of friction created by this controversy had hardly abated when events upon the international stage directed public attention to far more important developments than the abrogation of a century-old Russian-American commercial treaty. The first World War broke out. A stunned American public watched the conflagration spread from the marshes of Poland to the battlefields of Belgium. Our first reaction, that the war was nothing more than a new chapter in the interminable clash of European imperialisms, was in no small part due to the role of Russia. A natural sympathy for England, largely born of ties of race and language, and a sentimental attachment to France, found no counterpart in our feelings for Russia in 1914. There could be no real conviction that the struggle against Germany had any significance for democratic America when the autocratic government of the Czars was enrolled among the Allies.

We were willing to trade with Russia, however, for all our scepticism of her part in the war. While no such flood of sup-

plies made its way across the Pacific to her port of entry at Vladivostok as crossed the Atlantic to England and France, there was a tremendous increase in our exports to Russia between 1914 and 1916. They were valued in the latter year at almost half a billion dollars, in comparison with only some twenty-eight millions annually before the outbreak of the war. Russian bonds were also sold in moderate amounts in the American market. A $10,000,000 issue offered in May 1915 paved the way for successive loans finally totaling some $86,000,000. Although our wartime ambassador, David R. Francis, failed to negotiate a new trade treaty, the exigencies of war made for stronger financial and economic bonds than had ever before existed between the two nations.

As the United States drew closer and closer to intervention, it was still despite Russia rather than because of any friendship for her that we gradually became convinced that the Allies were fighting our battle. Germany had become the enemy—the enemy which had first brought together such traditional rivals as England and Russia, and was now to bring us within the common fold. Nothing else mattered. But when the Kaiser's declaration of unrestricted submarine warfare at the end of January 1917 made American participation in the war almost inevitable, the idea of a prospective partnership with Czarist Russia remained an important barrier to our complete acceptance of the Allied cause. How could a struggle for freedom and democracy, it was asked, be fought alongside the conscript armies of the Czar?

It was just at this point—the most critical juncture in our relations with Germany—that the world was suddenly electrified by the startling news that revolution had overthrown the Czarist government. The American press exultantly announced that the people had finally risen against the corrupt, despotic regime which had for so long stifled their liberties. It had actually collapsed more of its own weight than through any concerted revolutionary program, but the belief was nevertheless widespread that liberal forces had swept Nicholas II off his throne, asserted their right to self-rule and were prepared to establish a constitutional government with full recognition of democratic rights. "The six days between last Sunday and this," Ambassador Francis exultantly cabled from the Russian capital, now renamed Petrograd, on March 18, 1917, "have witnessed the most amazing revolution . . . the practical realization of that principle of government which we have championed and advocated. I mean government by the consent of the governed." A provisional administration of twelve ministers, headed by Prince Lvov, a Constitutional Democrat, had been appointed by members of the Duma to take over power from the abdicated Emperor, he went on to report, and there were plans for the immediate summoning of a constituent assembly. In the meantime the war against Germany would be prosecuted with the renewed vigor of a triumphant democracy.

These dramatic developments were hailed in the United States with immense enthusiasm. It was the answer to all our remaining doubts as to the justice of the Allied cause. There is little question that we would have overlooked ideological differences and taken our place alongside Russia in war against Germany even if the Czarist government had remained in power. The parallelism in international objectives, as a quarter of a century later, overshadowed the divergence in our political systems. But with the Russian Revolution the way was made easy for us in 1917.

"American editors rejoice," the *Literary Digest* stated in its summary of newspaper opinion on March 31, "that instead of reluctantly taking the corrupt despotism of the Romanoffs as an ally, we may proudly join hands with the self-governing people of Russia in a war of peoples against kings." While the *Boston Transcript* declared that "a nightmare had been taken from the breast of the whole liberal world," the *New Orleans Item* expressed its deep relief that we would now not have to align ourselves with "the most cruel and despotic government in the world." The American people could uphold the principles in which they believed, the *Springfield Republican* hap-

pily stated, "without the taint of a decadent and besotted Caesarism defiling their consciences and mocking their faith in democracy's final triumph throughout the world." There was not a single dissenting voice in the chorus of approval that greeted the Russian Revolution. To most of the papers throughout the country it simply illuminated more clearly than ever before our duty to participate in a war against the powers of darkness and evil, now so clearly symbolized by German tyranny.

Government officials in Washington were no less gratified than the public in the changed aspect of Russian affairs. Secretary of State Lansing immediately impressed upon Wilson how greatly the democratic cause had been strengthened. But the President hardly needed to be persuaded. The Russian Revolution, and the possibility that it might spread beyond Russia's borders, appeared to him to transcend in importance almost everything else that had happened in the war. If our intervention could now serve to "hasten and fix the movements in Russia and Germany," Wilson stated, "it would be a marked gain to the world and would tend to give additional justification for the whole struggle." When cables were received from Ambassador Francis asking for authority to recognize the new régime without delay in order to give the Russian people all possible moral support, it was at once granted. There was no waiting any test of the Provisional Government's stability. The instructions to Francis to extend official recognition were cabled on March 20—just five days after the abdication of the Czar.

Upon receiving them, Francis immediately informed Foreign Minister Miliukov of our policy, the United States thereby becoming the first country to recognize the revolution, and on the afternoon of March 22 the Council of Ministers, headed by Prince Lvov, formally received the American ambassador and his staff. The old cordiality between the two nations was miraculously re-established. Russia and America were not only friends. They were allies against the Central Powers. "This recognition," as Francis later commented with justice, "undoubtedly had a powerful influence in placing America in a position to enter the war backed by a practically unanimous public opinion."

Events were now moving rapidly on the international stage. Germany had given substance to her threat of unrestricted submarine warfare by the successive sinking of several American ships. On April 2 President Wilson went before Congress to ask a declaration of war as the only possible answer to the German challenge. His message strongly emphasized the new validity given to the Allied cause by the Russian Revolution.

"Does not every American," he asked, "feel that assurance has been added to our hope for the future peace of the world by the wonderful and heartening things that have been happening within the last few weeks in Russia? Russia was known by those who knew it best to have been always in fact democratic at heart. . . . The autocracy that crowned the summit of her political structure, long as it had stood and terrible as was the reality of its power, was not in fact Russian in origin, character or purpose; and now it has been shaken off and the great, generous Russian people have been added in all their naïve majesty and might to the forces that are fighting for freedom in the world, for justice, and for peace. Here is a fit partner for a League of Honor."

There was already, as perhaps this section of the President's message illustrates, a note of unreality, of wishful thinking, about both the official and the popular interpretation of events in Russia. We had adopted a conception of the democratic impulses of the great masses of the Russian people that would continue to blind us to the significance of every happening that ran counter to our own preconceptions of how the course of revolution should develop. The factors making for the disintegration of the Russian state after the glowing promise of the March revolution, the inherent weakness of the Provisional Government, the slight likelihood of the disorganized and confused Russian armies remaining in the field against Germany,

and the gathering strength of the extreme socialists represented in the Petrograd Soviet of Workers' and Soldiers' Deputies were all ignored in the confident belief that Russian democracy would somehow shape its new institutions in the image of America.

No one was more optimistic and confident of Russia's future during the ominous developments of the summer of 1917 than our well-meaning, visionary and kindly ambassador. "Extreme socialist or anarchist named Lenin," Francis cabled Washington on April 21, "making violent speeches and thereby strengthening government; designedly giving him leeway and will deport opportunely." Possibly he should not be blamed for this casual dismissal of Lenin's role at so early a stage of the revolution, but there would never be any real awakening on the part of the American ambassador from the blind complacency which this cable typified.

The principal task facing American diplomacy in our relations with the new Russia was to assure her continuance in the war. The Revolution had been precipitated by the increasing war weariness of the Russian people and popular resentment toward a government responsible for bringing things to such a pass. Defeat on the field of battle, the collapse of the transportation system, resultant hunger and suffering in the large cities provided the grim and tragic background for the strikes, riots and mutinies which had finally culminated in the overthrow of the Czar. When the new government reaffirmed its determination to reorganize the fighting front, it was soon realized that this was a stupendous task blocked at every turn by the overwhelming desire of the Russian people for peace. The Petrograd Soviet took the lead in demanding a reorientation of foreign policy to bring to an end what it asserted was an imperialistic war promising nothing but suffering and death. It called upon the peoples of Europe for concerted, decisive action in the interests of immediate peace. "Proletarians of all countries, unite" was its challenging summons to friend and foe. If the great influence of this propaganda was to be combatted, the United States had somehow to convince Russia that vigorous prosecution of the war was really to her interest and that Germany's military defeat was a necessary requisite for the kind of peace the Russian people wanted.

To this end every effort was made to strengthen the Provisional Government and re-enforce its decision to keep on fighting. The cables hummed with messages of congratulation to the country's new leaders and expressions of sympathy and support for the people. The American Federation of Labor, among many other organizations, sent its fraternal greetings to its new companions in liberty among the Russian workers. Our government was prepared to extend definite assistance to the Provisional Government in the form of military equipment and supplies; it undertook to grant loans for the purchase of war material in the United States. Were these gestures of good will effective? Ambassador Francis reported from Petrograd that they were. There had been a friendly demonstration of 50,000 persons in front of the American embassy, he cabled on April 29, and he had had to make five speeches. A few days later came another message telling of mass meetings whose keynote had been the new solidarity between a Free America and a Free Russia joined in war against a common foe.

Nevertheless the hard-pressed Provisional Government found it almost impossible to re-create a will for war among the weary Russian masses. Speeches by Ambassador Francis were hardly enough. In an effort to find a more effective answer to the reiterated demand of the socialists for an immediate negotiated peace, Foreign Minister Miliukov asked President Wilson for a clearer definition of the Allies' war aims. Those who were urging an end to the war at once could fall back upon the high authority of the President's own peace-without-victory speech. How could the principles Wilson had enunciated in January 1917, the Provisional Government sought to discover, be reconciled with his new insistence that Germany must be fully and completely defeated?

Wilson tried to answer the unanswerable. The war aims of

the United States, he declared in a special message to Russia published June 10, were freedom and self-government for all peoples, and their liberation everywhere from the aggressions of autocratic force. Wrongs must be righted and adequate safeguards erected to prevent them being committed again. These aims could not be achieved without first overthrowing German tyranny, but there should be no transfer of territory except with the free consent of the inhabitants, and no exaction of indemnities from a defeated foe. "The brotherhood of mankind," the President concluded, "must no longer be a fair but empty phrase; it must be a structure of force and reality. The nations must realize their common life and effect a workable partnership to secure that life against the aggressions of autocratic and self-seeking power."

Was this statement of policy, however eloquent, anything more than "a fair but empty phrase"? The Provisional Government, anxious as it was to continue the war and have Russia live up to her international engagements, found little in the note to combat successfully the propaganda of the extreme socialists. It sought something more definite, vainly asking for a conference among the Allies to blueprint the objectives of the war in more precise terms and at least sound out the possibilities of peace. In other than official circles disappointment was expressed more violently. The socialist press attacked the message as wholly unsatisfactory, while the Petrograd Soviet, in response to Lenin's impassioned pleas, passed a fiery resolution appealing to the democracies of the world to overthrow the war governments and force action. It proposed an international socialist convention to unite the proletariat of all nations "in an energetic and stubborn struggle against the world butchery."

Could Wilson have made any more effective move to encourage the waning spirit of the Russian people and win over the socialists to continue the war? He was already caught up in the conflict between his own idealistic war aims and the practical objectives of the Allies. Any more definite discussion of possible peace terms, he felt, would only weaken the united front against Germany. Since his primary goal, and that of the American people, had become Germany's total defeat despite his earlier statements upon a negotiated peace, there was no way in which he could give Russia the assurances she sought. And it must also remain extremely doubtful whether anything the President might have said or done, whether any reconsideration of war aims, could have actually stayed the course of events in Russia.

The most ambitious attempt to bolster up Russian morale and aid the Provisional Government was the dispatch of a special mission, headed by Elihu Root, which reached Petrograd in the middle of June. It was widely hoped that it could somehow draw tighter the bonds between Russia and the United States, and upon its embarkation the press had generally characterized it as a vitally important effort "to save Russia to the Entente cause." But the whole project reflected the blindness of our government to the realities of the situation in Russia. Occasional dispatches reached Washington from our consuls in Petrograd and Moscow which should have given some insight into the growing influence of the Bolsheviki under the leadership of Lenin and Trotsky. The State Department, however, built its policy upon the interpretation of events given by Ambassador Francis.

Throughout these critical months, Francis continued to dismiss the grave threat to the stability of the Provisional Government marked by the Bolsheviki's assumption of more and more power in the Petrograd Soviet. He failed to realize that while Lenin and Trotsky received German aid in getting to Russia, they were not dupes of the Kaiser's General Staff but determined men with ambitious plans of their own. To his conservative mind the doctrines they preached were so fantastic as to be nothing but the veneer of treachery. He saw the Bolshevik leaders as German agents whose treasonable activities would soon be exposed and who would reap their well-merited reward in arrest and execution.

The personnel of the Root mission was poorly chosen for the

purpose of strengthening the ties between capitalist America and what was rapidly becoming socialistic Russia. As an elder statesman Root was an important figure in American public life, but his background and associations were thoroughly conservative. No one could have been further removed from the proletariat. "I am a firm believer in democracy," he said revealingly upon visiting a Russian village, "but I do not like filth." The other members of his commission, supposedly chosen to represent all elements of American life (except women, despite the bitter protests of Carrie Chapman Catt) were only less well equipped to meet and understand the masses of Russian people whose support would determine the fate of the Provisional Government and its policy toward the war. They included Major General Scott and Rear Admiral Glennon, representatives of the army and navy; John R. Mott, outstanding leader of the Y.M.C.A.; Charles R. Crane, Cyrus H. McCormick and Samuel R. Bertron, industrialists and bankers; Charles Edward Russell, a socialist, and James Duncan, first vice-president of the American Federation of Labor. While the last two men had been chosen to promote confidence among Russian workers, the former represented the pro-war faction of his party and was expelled from socialist ranks for accepting his appointment, and the latter was as conservative in his views as the spokesmen of industry. There was no one on the commission who was really acceptable to the Social Democrats in the Russian government, let alone able to talk the language of the Petrograd Soviet. "Root in revolutionary Russia," Raymond Robins, who was in Petrograd that same summer with the American Red Cross, later wrote Theodore Roosevelt, "was as welcome as the small pox, and occasioned as much enthusiasm as would be aroused by an Orangeman leading a popular parade in Dublin."

Again the question may be raised whether a commission less blatantly bourgeois in its composition could have been any more successful in influencing future developments in Russia. It is extremely doubtful. The undercurrents of radical revolt were too strong to be deflected by diplomatic intervention on the part of the United States. Our confident belief in the influence of the Root mission, and our persistent disregard of the strong hold of radical socialism among the elements shaping Russia's future were completely unrealistic.

The Root mission was cordially received by official Petrograd. It was wined and dined. The air at these formal functions was heavy with the exchange of glowing platitudes upon Russian-American friendship. They put to shame the expressions of good will when Russia was ruled by a Czar. At other meetings the commission members talked with those elements in Russian society which they themselves represented at home. The military and naval officers held long conversations with Russian staff members; there were innumerable conferences among businessmen and bankers. Groups of intellectuals received the other American delegates. Confused and uncertain over what was happening in this alien world, Root remarked upon one occasion that "the entire people seem to be talking at once—making up for lost time." His mission contributed its quota to these interminable discussions. But there was almost no contact with the Russian masses, with the workers and soldiers. Only the most casual encounters were had with a few lesser Bolshevik leaders. The mission moved in a rarefied atmosphere of bourgeois liberalism in which its members saw only their own kind, exchanging views solely among those who already thought as they did.

The burden of Root's many speeches was a reaffirmation of American faith and confidence in Russia's democratic future, modified by his reiterated insistence that her newly won freedom could be assured only by the military defeat of Germany. Here was the real threat to Free Russia, he told his audiences. And the United States was in the war to fight for the liberties of other nations as well as for its own. Russia too must continue to play its great part in the struggle. "Freedom all over the world," Root again and again declared, "cannot live beside German power." These sentiments found a ready response

among those to whom he talked. The elder statesman became convinced that his mission was accomplishing its purpose more successfully than he had dared to hope. He did not know that for all the official attention it was receiving, it was almost completely ignored in more important nonofficial quarters. While Ambassador Francis duly reported to Washington how well Root's speeches were being received, our consul at Petrograd made the far more significant statement that the socialists were paying practically no attention whatsoever to the United States.

For all the complacency which enabled Root to follow the lead of Francis in reporting that he saw no visible agitation against the Provisional Government, he at least realized that the question whether Russia would remain in the war would be decided by the Russian people and that they showed no great enthusiasm for continuing the struggle. "We have to get at them some way," he declared. His own suggestion was active measures to combat German propaganda, which he found to have great influence, and he proposed the immediate allotment of $100,000 and the eventual appropriation of $5,000,000 for a pro-Ally campaign of news, pamphlets, advertising and motion pictures. It was essential, he believed, to impress upon the Russian masses the importance of the war and the extent to which the Allies, especially the United States, were cooperating with Russia to overthrow German tyranny. "These poor fellows," he said in a statement which would be echoed a quarter of a century later by another American ambassador under somewhat analogous circumstances, "have been told that no one is really fighting except Russian soldiers and they believe it."

To these practical suggestions—virtually the only recommendations the Root mission made—the response in Washington was somewhat apathetic. An expenditure of $30,000 made from funds advanced by the members of the commission themselves, was approved by President Wilson. The Y.M.C.A. extended its activities to Russia and the Red Cross sent a commission, first under the direction of William B. Thompson and Raymond Robins, in the interest of good will. Edgar G. Sisson arrived in Petrograd representing the Committee on Public Information. But otherwise little importance was done during the summer of 1917 to promote Allied cause among the Russian people. Root would express himself with outspoken bitterness upon what he considered a pronounced lack of official support. "Wilson didn't want to accomplish anything," he wrote his biographer, Philip C. Jessup, in 1930. "It was a grandstand play. He wanted to show his sympathy for the Russian Revolution. When we delivered his message and made our speeches, he was satisfied; that's all he wanted."

One far more practical undertaking, however, should be mentioned at this point. A railroad commission was sent to Russia to aid the Provisional Government in working out the problems resulting from the breakdown in the country's transportation system. Under the direction of John F. Stevens, formerly chief engineer of the Panama Canal, it at once undertook to relieve congestion at Vladivostok and its plans contemplated taking over the tremendous task of reorganizing the entire Trans-Siberian Railroad. In July, Premier Lvov expressed his government's gratitude for this assistance and his hope that it would be supplemented by further help. Russia had in one jump reached America's condition of freedom, he declared, and now depended on her aid in the "slower but not impossible task to overtake her in education, material progress, culture and respect for order."

While the Root and Stevens missions were carrying on these activities in Russia, the Provisional Government sent a mission to the United States. It was headed by Professor Boris Bakhmetev, who was to stay on as permanent ambassador, and it had as its objective not only the exchange of diplomatic amenities but further loans to Russia. It was welcomed with enthusiasm in this country and there were again warm expressions of the mutual sympathy now so happily existing between the

American and Russian governments. Bakhmetev was formally received by both the House and the Senate, eloquently expressing his confident views of the future of democratic Russia amid congressional cheers. The Provisional Government was reorganizing Russia on the basis of freedom, equality and self-government, he declared, and it had the support of all classes except a few reactionaries and certain small groups of extremists and internationalists. It had firmly rejected all ideas of a separate peace with Germany. Upon the presentation of his credentials to President Wilson, Bakhmetev was assured of the wholehearted cooperation of the American government and the friendly sympathy of the American people.

Negotiations for the extension of credits to Russia provided substantial expression of this support. A first loan of $100,000,-000 had been granted to the Provisional Government in May, and additional credits were now advanced which by November brought the total up to $325,000,000. From this sum there were actual cash disbursements of $188,000,000 largely utilized by the Russian mission for the purchase of war supplies in the American market.

While the statements of Bakhmetev conformed to the generally optimistic picture of Russian developments drawn by both Francis and Root from the vantage point of Petrograd, midsummer nevertheless witnessed many disturbing developments. Root had no sooner left Russia in early July, apparently convinced that both the army and the government had been strengthened in morale and effectiveness, than demonstrations of soldiers and armed workingmen in Petrograd shouting the Bolshevik slogan of "All power to the Soviet" led to clashes with Cossack troops. The government succeeded in putting down this incipient revolt. Lenin went into hiding; Trotsky for a time was held under arrest. But it caused a shift in the Council of Ministers in which Prince Lvov was replaced by the Minister of War, Alexander Kerensky. The new premier was a member of the Social Revolutionaries, a radical agrarian party, and the change in government marked a moderate swing to the left. Foreign observers were confident that this reorganization constituted a final answer to the menace of Bolshevism. As a supposed "strong man" (although Francis considered him weak and blundering), Kerensky was in a position to exercise the dictatorial powers which it was believed would carry Russia through its domestic crisis and enable it to play its full part in the war. "No difficulties," Kerensky told our ambassador, "will cause Russia to give up her steadfast determination to carry on the war until the complete triumph of the ideals proclaimed by the Russian Revolution."

An earlier attempt to launch a new offensive against Germany, however, had already revealed the rapid disintegration of both the military and home front. Disorder, doubt and dissensions more and more characterized the Russian scene. "We have tasted liberty and it has made us drunk," the new Premier declared. The Bolsheviki's power in Petrograd was growing day by day. They were insistently demanding the adoption of a threefold policy: distribution of the land to the peasants, handing over of the factories to the workingmen and an immediate peace based upon no annexations and no indemnities. Strikes, revolts, mutinies were once again reported throughout the land. Insofar as effective frontline operations were concerned, Russia was already out of the war. The imminent danger of Germany completely overrunning the country was added to the growing threat of domestic strife.

The United States hopefully continued to try to bolster up the tottering Kerensky regime. President Gompers of the American Federation of Labor declared that "the soul of American labor and democracy beats in unison with the spirits and aspirations of Russia's people." The United States Chamber of Commerce sought to prove our sympathy with socialism by grandiloquently informing Russia that half a million American businessmen had agreed to limit war profits. These inspiring messages were duly forwarded to Petrograd by Secretary

Lansing. The disconcerting answer of the Bolsheviki was to protest against our arrest of Alexander Berkman and Emma Goldman, Russian anarchists, and to launch a campaign of violent abuse against "Free America."

Ambassador Francis was in no way disheartened. He continued to inform Washington of his confidence that the crisis would be surmounted both in domestic and foreign policy. He was certain that a revulsion against the obstreperous Bolsheviki, whose leaders he still insisted were nothing more than treasonable German agents, would soon make itself felt and force them into hiding. "My sympathy with Russia deep, sincere," he cabled on October 4, "and my conviction strong that the country will survive the ordeal and be safe for democracy if we and the Allies are patient and helpful."

At the close of the month he was disappointed that a threatened Bolsheviki demonstration had failed to materialize. He was positive that the Kerensky government would have been easily able to suppress it, and the arrest of the ringleaders would then have cleared the air for placing the government on a still stronger footing. When a few days later discouraging stories based upon an interview with Kerensky appeared in the American press, headlined in at least one instance under the startling caption "Russia Quits the War," he cabled such reassuring reports to the State Department that Secretary Lansing issued a soothing statement to calm American fears. "Our own advices," this announcement read, "show that the Provisional Government in Petrograd is attacking with great energy the problems confronting it. . . . Premier Kerensky and his Government, far from yielding to discouragement, are still animated by a strong determination to organize all Russia's resources in a wholehearted resistance and carry the war through to a victorious conclusion. At the same time this Government, like those of the Allies, is rendering all possible assistance."

But the sands were running out for the Provisional Government. The final crisis was approaching. One may easily imagine the outraged bewilderment with which Ambassador Francis cabled, and Secretary Lansing read, the momentous dispatches of November 7, 1917:

"Bolsheviki appear to have control of everything here. Cannot learn whereabouts of any Minister. . . ."

VIII

THE BOLSHEVIKI MAKE PEACE

"Lenin and the Petrograd workers had decided on insurrection, the Petrograd Soviet had overthrown the Provisional Government, and thrust the coup d'etat upon the Congress of Soviets. Now there was all great Russia to win—and then the world! Would Russia follow and rise? And the world, what of it? Would the peoples answer and rise, a red world-tide?

"Although it was six in the morning, night was yet heavy and chill. There was only a faint unearthly pallor stealing over the silent streets, dimming watch-fires, the shadow of a terrible dawn grey-rising over Russia. . . ."

So John Reed wrote in his vivid *Ten Days that Shook the World* of an event that was to have the most momentous consequences not only for Russia but for all Europe, all Asia and all America. Its significance could hardly be foreseen. The Bolshevik revolution of November 1917 ushered in years of the utmost confusion. The economic collapse of a nation, foreign war and bitter civil strife, blockade and famine, the Red Terror, widespread suffering, misery and death would all be endured before great Russia again achieved anything like stability. And throughout these critical years foreign nations, including the United States, watched in uncertainty and with divided counsels, in appalling ignorance of what was really happening, the unfolding of a terrible drama.

The immediate reaction to the Bolsheviki's assumption of power was everywhere one of stunned and horrified surprise. For the American ambassador at Petrograd these feelings were mitigated only by the reassuring conviction, which he never lost, that the Reds could not possibly remain in control of the government. Francis wrote Consul General Summers in Moscow on November 8 that it was reported that the Petrograd

Soviet had named a new cabinet with Lenin as Premier and Trotsky as Foreign Minister—"Disgusting!—but I hope such effort will be made as the more ridiculous the situation, the sooner the remedy."

His reports to Washington constantly reiterated his view that the new regime would not last and that the forces of democracy, so much more representative of the Russian people, would quickly reassert themselves. When the Bolsheviki did create a Council of People's Commissars, with Lenin as Premier and Trotsky as Commissar of Foreign Affairs, he dismissed it as an aberration. In striking contrast to his plea for immediate recognition of the government set up during the March revolution, Francis urgently advised that no action whatsoever be taken until the situation righted itself and the Bolsheviki were driven out of office.

The United States followed this advice—it continued to follow it for sixteen years. Reports poured in from every quarter which tended to confirm the impressions of the American envoy. The Russian ambassador in Washington promptly repudiated the new Soviet government, and the ill-starred Admiral Kolchak, on a visit to the Pacific coast, added his voice to the chorus predicting Lenin's speedy downfall. And apart from the supposed instability of the new regime, there was every other reason why America should hesitate to extend recognition. The Bolsheviki had seized power to carry out a revolutionary program of expropriating the land, turning the factories over to the workingmen and concluding an immediate peace. How could the capitalist world, the nations engaged in war against Germany, accept the implications of this declared policy? Little wonder that Secretary Lansing cabled Francis—"This Government awaits further developments."

Public opinion in the United States was thoroughly bewildered. Here and there was a note of fear in the editorial comments. The possible danger of Bolshevism to organized government throughout the world was stressed in the more conservative papers. The *New York Times* declared that Rus-

sia had cast herself beyond the pale of civilization; the *New York Tribune* stated emphatically that Russia must now be treated as an enemy. But it was apparently more generally believed that whatever dangers the revolution had created, they would be passing. In its customary summary of newspaper opinion on November 17, the *Literary Digest* said that "no great alarm when the Bolsheviki seized Petrograd was felt by American editorial observers, who predicted an early collapse of the rebellion."

While Secretary Lansing stated that the United States would not recognize the Soviets and took steps to prevent any further shipment of supplies to Russia until a more stable government was formed, Ambassador Francis appealed to the Russian people over the heads of the new ministers. "There is no power whose authority is recognized throughout Russia," he declared in a public statement; "your industries are neglected and many of your people are crying for food. . . . A powerful enemy is at your gates. A desperate foe is sowing the seeds of dissension in your midst. . . . I appeal to you to be watchful of your true interests, and I make this appeal on behalf of my Government and my people, with whom you have ever borne friendly relations, and who cherish a sincere, deep interest in your welfare."

As upon the occasion of the March revolution, the immediately vital issue presented by the triumph of the Bolsheviki was whether Russia would remain in the war. The collapse of the eastern front under the Kerensky government had already clearly shown that little could be expected from her, but it was now feared that a separate peace would not only release German armies for fighting on the western front but would make Russia's vast resources available for the German war machine. The refusal to recognize the Soviet government in November 1917 was due not so much to hostility to the Bolsheviki themselves, although it was already an important factor in the general picture, as it was to the general belief that such a step would end all possibility of some other government, which might be willing to prosecute the war, coming into power.

The attitude of the Bolsheviki did nothing to disabuse the United States and the Allies of their fears that Russia would withdraw from the war. Their drive for peace got under way at once. While President Wilson thundered that "any body of free men that compounds with the present German Government is compounding for its own destruction," Lenin and Trotsky officially proposed immediate negotiations to conclude a democratic peace without annexation or indemnities, and with full self-determination for all nations. While they were ready to conclude a separate treaty if necessary, they hoped it could be a general peace. But the Allies pointedly ignored their proposals. Peace negotiations at the close of 1917 meant defeat for the Allied cause.

President Wilson first indicated the mounting concern over this problem in his annual message to Congress in December. The disclosure by Trotsky of the secret treaties whereby the Allies had agreed to divide up the spoils of war, disposing of the German colonies and making other territorial adjustments that ran directly counter to their professed aims, gave rise to the charge that imperialist ambition alone accounted for the prolongation of hostilities. The President felt compelled to recognize the validity of the Bolsheviki's peace formula, if not the justice of their attacks upon the Allies. He declared that no annexations, no contributions, no punitive indemnities expressed "the instinctive judgment as to right of plain men everywhere." But this crude formula, he emphatically stated, was being used "by the masters of German intrigue to lead the people of Russia astray . . . in order that a premature peace might be brought about before autocracy has been taught its final and convincing lesson, and the people of the world put in control of their own destinies."

His words had little effect in Russia. The Soviet leaders in Petrograd were determined upon peace and believed that the peoples throughout the world, including those of Germany, would rally to their support. "The American President Wilson, adopting the tone of a Quaker preacher," a government-

inspired editorial in *Izvestia* declared, "reads to the people a sermon on the higher practical morality. The people know that Americans came into the war, not in the interests of right and justice, but because of the cynical interests of the New York Stock Exchange."

Instructions had been given by Lansing to American diplomatic agents to have no communications whatsoever with the agents of the Soviet government. Ambassador Francis' belief that Lenin and Trotsky were reckless adventurers, in German pay and acting under orders from the German General Staff, carried great weight with the State Department. Other Americans in Petrograd, however, began to wonder whether our policy was not the most effective means of ensuring the Bolsheviki's complete capitulation to Germany. Edgar Sisson, who had arrived on the scene as agent of the Creel Committee, confidentially cabled Washington that unless constructive action was taken Russia would soon have to be counted wholly out of the war, and that the American ambassador appeared "without policy except anger at Bolsheviks. . . ." There were reports from both Colonel Raymond Robins, now head of the American Red Cross, and Jerome Davis, supervisor of Y.M.C.A. activities, that the strength and stability of the Soviet government could no longer be denied. The American military attaché actually saw Trotsky and assured him, unofficially, that the United States had no intention of interfering in Russia's internal affairs and that "the time of protests and threats to the Soviet Government has passed, if that time ever existed." By the end of December even Francis himself tentatively suggested entering into relations with the Bolshevik regime, possibly recognizing as well an independent Ukraine and Siberia, in an attempt to keep Russia at least neutral. It would be "exceedingly distasteful," he cabled home, but he felt that it might be advisable.

Secretary Lansing refused to consider any such change of policy. As early as December 10 he had warned President Wilson that Bolshevik domination meant Russia's withdrawal from the war, expressing the further opinion that the only hope for the Allies was the rise of a military dictatorship. His candidate was General Kaledin of the Don Cossacks. While hesitating to support him openly—"because of the attitude which it seems advisable to take with the Petrograd authorities"—he cabled our embassy in London proposing an indirect loan to Kaledin's forces through the British or French governments. "I need not impress upon you," he concluded these instructions, "the necessity of acting expeditiously and impressing those with whom you talk of the importance of avoiding it being known that the United States is considering showing sympathy for the Kaledin movement, much less of providing financial assistance." With such ideas, foreshadowing the interventionist policy of a later day, the Secretary of State naturally had no sympathy for any move that might strengthen the Bolsheviki.

A sharp rebuke was administered to Sisson for his interference with diplomatic affairs, our military attaché was recalled, and Ambassador Francis was distinctly instructed to follow the policy that he had himself originally advised. There would be no further consideration, even indirectly or distantly, of recognizing the Soviet government. Lansing declared that it was "a despotic oligarchy as menacing to liberty as any absolute monarch on earth." To reply to its suggestions in regard to peace, "would be contrary to the dignity of the United States."

The refusal of the United States, in common with the Allied powers, to recognize their government or accept their peace proposals did not deter the Bolsheviki from entering into direct contact with Germany. Envoys of the two governments met early in December and concluded an armistice. But Trotsky's goal remained a general peace—not merely a Russian-German peace. He repeatedly called upon the Allies to participate in the negotiations being held at Brest-Litovsk, twice postponing them to allow the Allies the opportunity to send delegates. When they continued to disregard all such appeals, he tried to arouse the people of the world to take action into

their own hands. "If the Allied Governments in the blind stubbornness which characterizes decadent and perishing classes," he declared in a ringing manifesto on December 29, "once more refuse to participate in the negotiations, then the working class will be confronted with the iron necessity of tearing the power out of the hands of those who cannot or will not give peace to the nations. . . ."

While the Allies stood fast in their refusal to enter into any peace parleys, the attacks of the Bolsheviki on the sincerity of their war aims could not be disregarded. Liberal elements in the United States and throughout western Europe, disturbed by the revelations of the secret treaties, were questioning the idealistic basis of the war as a crusade for democratic rights. Both Prime Minister Lloyd George of Great Britain and President Wilson felt compelled to answer these doubters, and to meet the challenge of what the latter declared to be a voice "more thrilling and more compelling than any of the moving voices with which the troubled air of the world is filled . . . the voice of the Russian people." Insofar as the United States was concerned, a clarifying statement on war aims was also strongly urged from Petrograd by Edgar Sisson as a direct means of countering the Bolshevik peace propaganda among Russian workers and soldiers. It should be brief, Sisson advised, "in short, almost placard paragraphs, short sentences," and in such form that he could distribute it throughout the country and also send it across the German lines into enemy territory.

An answer to these appeals was the Fourteen Points, presented to the world on January 8, 1918, in the President's special message to Congress. It reflected neither animosity toward the Soviet government nor criticism of its leaders. At the time Wilson believed the negotiations at Brest-Litovsk had been permanently suspended. He was ready to accept the principles underlying Lenin and Trotsky's peace proposals, declaring it to be his heartfelt desire that some way could be found to assist the people of Russia in attaining their hope of liberty and ordered peace. "Their conception of what is right, of what is humane and honorable for them to accept," the President said, "has been stated with a frankness, a largeness of view, a generosity of spirit, and a universal human sympathy which must challenge the admiration of every friend of mankind. . . ."

The Fourteen Points themselves were an attempt to demonstrate that the United States was prepared to go even further than the Bolsheviki in projecting a liberal program for the future peace. Article Six referred directly to Russia. It demanded as one of the basic terms of peace the complete evacuation of all Russian territory and settlement of the problem of Russia on a basis that would both assure her an unembarrassed opportunity for the determination of her own national policy, and a sincere welcome into the society of free nations under institutions of her own choosing. "The treatment accorded to Russia by her sister nations in the months to come," Wilson solemnly asserted, "will be the acid test of their goodwill, of their comprehension of her needs as distinguished from their own interests, and of their intelligent and unselfish sympathy."

The fear that Russia might make a separate peace, or even join forces with Germany, was becoming a nightmare. Wilson was more and more persuaded that no stone should be left unturned in trying to win her further support for the Allied cause. This is not to impugn the idealism underlying the Fourteen Points. The President was expressing a world-wide desire for a peace that would in reality make the world safe for democracy and end all wars. His address nevertheless had the immediate and highly practical objective of countering Bolshevik propaganda. For he again insisted that the democratic peace that was the common objective of the Russian and American people could not be concluded until the world was assured that Germany's spokesmen were really speaking for the German people, and not for a military party whose creed was imperial domination. In other words, the proposed negotiations at Brest-Litovsk could achieve no real purpose because the complete overthrow of German tyranny was an absolute requisite to any satisfactory settlement of world problems.

The speech was at once widely distributed throughout Russia. Hundreds of thousands of pamphlets were printed; posters
and placards pasted up in cities, towns and hamlets; newspapers
everywhere prevailed upon to publish it. In all, more than three
and one half million copies, one million in German, were sent
out from Petrograd and Moscow through the agency of the
Creel Committee. For a brief time it appeared that the Fourteen Points might actually have some effect on Russian policy.
Although the suspended negotiations at Brest-Litovsk were
renewed, the Soviet delegates refused to accept the harsh terms
Germany proposed. She demanded Russia's surrender of the
Baltic provinces, Poland and the Ukraine, where nominally
independent governments were to be set up under German
control. Disappointed and discouraged over the failure of the
peoples of the world to back up his peace program, Trotsky
bitterly attacked German imperialism. "We did not overthrow
the Czar," he declared, "in order to fall on our knees before the
Kaiser and beg for peace."

The breakdown of the negotiations did not, however, stiffen
Russian resistance on the field of battle. The Bolsheviki tried
to act upon the impossible principle of "no war; no peace,"
while the German armies continued to advance relentlessly,
penetrating deeper and deeper into Russian territory. "Russia
has fallen," the *New York Times* wrote despairingly, "and for
generations to come will take the place of the Balkan States as
a chessboard of international chicanery." It was hardly an
accurate prophecy. Few of those made about Russia in these
days—or during the next quarter-century!—would be. But in
the circumstances of February 1918 there appeared every reason
to believe in Russia's complete disintegration—political, economic, financial and social. The army was wholly demoralized;
the people discouraged and confused. And over all lay the
ominous shadow of Germany's military might.

As the Kaiser's forces advanced toward Petrograd itself,
there was for a time confusion in the ranks of the Bolsheviki
as to the policy they should pursue. Lenin's single-minded goal

was to save the revolution. He had favored peace on almost any terms. Now he hesitated in view of the brutally aggressive nature of the German demands. If there was any chance of obtaining effective aid from the Allies in defending Russia against the immediate enemy, he was ready to make a deal with them. Over against the opposition of those Bolshevik leaders who would have refused to traffic with any of the imperialist governments and favored a revolutionary war against all comers, the possibilities of such assistance were consequently explored. Was there any chance of it? Colonel Robins, acting as an unofficial envoy between the American embassy and the Soviet government, tried to assure Trotsky that substantial aid would be forthcoming if the Russian army took up the fight. But his assurances could not take any concrete form.

"Colonel Robins," Trotsky said one time, as later reported by the Red Cross official, "your embassy sends you here with a big bag marked 'American help.' You arrive every day, and you bring the bag into my room, and you set it down by your chair, and you keep reaching into it as you talk, and it is a powerful bag. But nothing comes out."

It was an ironic situation. But however strongly the Allies and the United States desired to have Russia remain in the war, the events of the past few weeks had convinced them both that there was little possibility of this so long as the Bolsheviki remained in power. The American public, indeed, was becoming more and more distrustful of the Soviet government every day, and more embittered against the policies it was pursuing. A constituent assembly had met only to be immediately dissolved when the Bolsheviki found themselves in a minority among its elected representatives. The program of property expropriation had been further carried forward with the repudiation of all foreign debts. Increasingly alarming rumors were reaching the outside world of internal disturbance and revolt, and of the bloody methods being employed to suppress all political opposition to Soviet rule. And early in February, Ambassador Francis reported that he had conclusive docu-

mentary evidence confirming his belief that Lenin and Trotsky were in Germany's pay. These documents would in time be generally discredited. The American ambassador's basic assumptions were shown by events to be unwarranted. But the opinion was nevertheless almost universal in these decisive days that the Bolsheviki were merely the tools of imperial Germany.

Under such circumstances there was little disposition to aid the Soviet government even if the means had been available. It was felt that to do so, or even to recognize it, would be playing into Germany's hands. Wilson and Lansing were fully agreed that support for Russia would actually mean support for the Central Powers. And the wish constantly remained father to the thought: the days of the Bolsheviki were numbered. Support for a government on the verge of collapse would have highly unfortunate consequences, it was believed, and embarrass relations with any rival faction sincerely disposed to continue the war.

With the complete demoralization of their own armies and no effective foreign aid forthcoming, the Bolsheviki reluctantly decided, after a close vote in the Central Committee, upon capitulation. Germany presented new terms even more drastic than those the Soviet delegation had originally rejected, but on March 3, 1918, Russia nevertheless surrendered completely and signed the Treaty of Brest-Litovsk. She lost territory accounting for over a quarter of her total population, vast natural resources and a great part of her manufactures. "We declare openly before the workmen, peasants, and soldiers of Russia and Germany, and before the laboring and exploited masses of the whole," read the formal statement of the peace delegates, "that we are forced to accept the peace dictated by those who, at the moment, are more powerful, and that we are going to sign immediately the treaty presented to us as an ultimatum, but that at the same time we refuse to enter into any discussion of its terms."

Public opinion in America was shocked and horrified. "The

signing of a formal peace on Germany's terms," the *New York World* declared, "marks the final act of betrayal on the part of the Bolsheviki. . . . Trotsky and Lenin have done their best by the Kaiser whether actuated by money, or lust for power, or the insanity of class hatred." Hardly anyone, however, questioned the almost universal belief that the Bolshevik leaders were agents of Germany. This was the easiest explanation for so catastrophic a development for the Allied cause. Colonel William B. Thompson, basing his opinion on his own experiences in Petrograd, tried to point out that Lenin and Trotsky were not traitors but internationalists, seeking through any sacrifice to make possible the ultimate triumph of their utopian dreams of world peace. To desert Russia whatever the circumstances, he warned, might be disastrous. "Presently Russia must and will stabilize herself," Colonel Thompson wrote. "Shall she have the aid of the United States in working out her problems, or shall she be left to the ministrations of Germany?" Fear and distrust, for all the high promise of the sixth of Wilson's Fourteen Points, was all too clearly cutting off American sympathy.

The Bolsheviki made one more last desperate appeal to the Allies. Although convinced that it was of little use and that to hesitate much longer in concluding peace would be the death knell of the Soviet state, Lenin agreed to withhold ratification of the Brest-Litovsk treaty if any means could be found to resist further German aggression. Trotsky again made through Colonel Robins official inquiries as to what aid Russia might expect from the American government should she refuse even now to accede to the German demands and renew the war. But he was careful to make it clear, in a note forwarded to our embassy on March 5, that the Bolsheviki were quite as willing to surrender to the Germans as they were to accept any restrictive conditions from the Allies. His questions were conditioned, Trotsky declared, on the assumption "that the internal and foreign policies of the Soviet Government will continue to be directed in accord with the principles of international socialism."

President Wilson had already, in effect, answered the in-

quiries of the Russian government. In a message to the All-Russian Congress of Soviets on March 11, dispatched before Trotsky's delayed communication had been received in Washington, he redefined American policy. It was based upon sympathy and friendship for the Russian people, the President declared, and the United States would avail itself of every opportunity to secure for Russia complete sovereignty and independence in her own affairs. But he also stated that the United States was unhappily not in a position at the time to render the direct and effective aid to Russia that it might otherwise wish to extend.

Military and other considerations may have gone far toward justifying this position, but there was the further clear implication behind the President's words that the United States would have nothing to do with the Soviet regime. As already noted, the wavering policy of this country—and that of the other Allied governments—had steadied to the point of accepting a Russian-German peace as an inevitable consequence of the Bolsheviki's control of the Russian government. Nothing further could be done to check the German advance in Russia, it was felt, until the Bolsheviki were overthrown and some government set up in which the capitalist world could have real confidence.

The reaction of the Soviet Congress to this restatement of our policy was sharp and hostile. It struck back at once in adopting a resolution described by Acting Foreign Commissar Zinoviev as a slap in the face for President Wilson. The Congress took occasion to express its warmest sympathy for all peoples suffering from the horrors of an imperialist war, and declared its firm belief that the happy time was not far distant "when the laboring masses of all countries will throw off the yoke of capitalism and will establish a socialist state of society, which alone is capable of securing just and lasting peace, as well as the culture and well-being of all laboring people."

The growing bitterness of ideological conflict between Bolshevism and democracy was now heavily underscored. Nevertheless final action on the Brest-Litovsk treaty was once more postponed in the hope that some further reply to Trotsky's communication might still be forthcoming. For the Bolsheviki, despite the tone of Wilson's message, did not believe that America could afford to stand aloof in this international crisis. "The United States cannot permit Germany to become the autocratic master of dismembered Russia and especially of her markets," *Izvestia* declared. "The United States cannot in its own interest acquiesce in Germany's plan of turning Russia into a German colony. And it, unlike Germany, is not interested in establishing its political power in Russia. On the contrary, in view of its rivalry with Germany and Japan, the United States is directly interested to have Russia politically and economically strong and independent."

This had been our attitude in all our earlier relations with Russia; it would again in time become our policy. But *Izvestia* reckoned without American hostility toward the Bolsheviki and failed to realize how little confidence we had in their good faith. Just as Lenin believed that continued war would mean the collapse of the Soviet state, so was Wilson convinced that the triumph of Bolshevism spelled Russian surrender to Germany. Each was prepared to sacrifice everything else for his major goal. For Lenin war or peace was only an incident in the final triumph of the revolution, while for Wilson the revolution had its only real significance as it affected the defeat of Germany.

In any event no further message came from the United States upon the question of possible aid, and the Soviet Congress finally prepared to take definite action on the German treaty. Ratification had already been approved by the Central Executive Committee and Lenin was determined to force similar action through the Congress. Nevertheless Colonel Robins has told the story of how he was sitting on the steps near the platform during this critical meeting, when Lenin called him over and asked him what he had heard from his government. Colonel Robins answered, "Nothing." Having also received the same reply in regard to possible news from the British government,

the Soviet leader then said: "I shall now speak for the peace. It will be ratified. . . ." This was on March 16, and that evening the final vote was taken. It was 784 in favor of ratification, 261 opposed. Russia was definitely and irrevocably out of the war.

Public opinion in the United States generally approved the resolution of the Wilson administration to have no traffic with the Bolsheviki. There was an occasional protest, such as that of Colonel Thompson, who felt our failure to accept the realities of the situation, however abhorrent Bolshevism might be to our capitalistic theories, had thrown Russia into Germany's arms. The press as a whole, however, did not see any alternative to the policy that had been adopted. The Bolsheviki had betrayed the Allied cause and threatened with their subversive propaganda the whole structure of the capitalist world. The reply of the Soviet Congress to President Wilson's expression of sympathy for the Russian people was generally interpreted, in the vehement characterization of Theodore Roosevelt, as a "mean and studied impertinence . . . a gratuitous and insulting expression for a class war in America."

In its official policy after Brest-Litovsk the United States continued to act upon the principle that the Soviet government did not have even *de facto* standing. The peace it had concluded with Germany consequently had no legal validity. Ambassador Francis remained in Russia, futilely trying to stem the Red tide sweeping over the country. He was constantly appealing to the Russian people to repudiate their leaders and disavow the peace treaty. In private correspondence he declared that should there be any movement along such lines, in whatever part of the country, he would try "to locate in that section and encourage the rebellion." Why did the Soviet government tolerate his presence under such circumstances? It at once clung to the hope that the United States would reverse its policy, and feared that the dismissal of the American ambassador might cause us to throw our support behind some one of the uprisings against Bolshevik authority.

There was a further ambiguity in the American position. In

a statement on March 12, 1918—that is, just prior to ratification of the Russian-German treaty—Acting Secretary of State Polk declared that the United States did not feel justified in regarding Russia as either an enemy or neutral power. Since she had in fact no government, and none of the acts of her so-called government could therefore be recognized, relations between Russia and America had in no way been altered by the events of the past few months. "The Government feels that it is of the utmost importance," Polk stated, "as affecting the whole public opinion of the world and giving proof of the utter good faith of all Governments associated against Germany, that we should continue to treat the Russians as in all respects our friends and allies against the common enemy."

What did such a policy involve? How could it be reconciled with actual conditions within Russia? Refusing to recognize or be friends with the Soviet government, we were irresistibly drawn into the role of foe. President Wilson had reiterated again and again that the United States had no intention of allowing itself to become involved in Russia's internal affairs. We would have no part in any war of factions. The willingness of the powers to let the Russian people work out their own destiny, he had declared, would be "the acid test" of their good will. But the fact that we were engaged in war with Germany, and that Russia under her Bolshevik rulers appeared to be swinging into the German camp, made such forbearance a seemingly impossible role. The pressure of events finally drove the United States to support an Allied program of intervention that was characterized by its open enmity to the Soviet government.

IX

INTERVENTION

THE issue of possible intervention in Russia, first raised as early as December 1917, became with succeeding months one of the most important and complicated of the many problems facing both the United States and Allied governments. As the war rose to a frightening crescendo on the western front, the dark shadow of events in eastern Europe appeared to cloud even the prospects of military victory over Germany. The democratic peoples were at once fearful of German domination over a prostrate Russia, and of the rise of a Bolshevik tyranny defying the capitalist powers. The counsels of Washington, London and Paris upon how the problem should be met were divided and confused. "I have been sweating blood over the question what is right and feasible to do in Russia," President Wilson wrote Colonel House on July 8, 1918. "It goes to pieces like quicksilver under my touch. . . ."

The pattern of events is incredibly complicated. There were two distinct phases of the interventionist movement as it finally developed. The one involved occupation of Archangel and Murmansk in North Russia, while the other and more important venture centered upon the Pacific port of Vladivostok. In each instance the nominal reason for intervention was the need to protect the large stocks of war supplies which the United States and the Allies had built up at these points, but there was the further underlying idea that recreation of an eastern front had become an imperative necessity if Germany were to be finally defeated. Other factors also entered into the situation. Despite all protestations to the effect that the landing of troops did not contemplate interference in the internal affairs of Russia, support was given to the anti-Bolshevik elements operating in both these areas. The horizon of military activities constantly expanded. Even when the collapse of Germany resulted in an armistice in western Europe, support for the counterrevolutionary movement against the Soviet government was not withdrawn. The United States found itself involved in a tangled and confused situation from which it hardly knew how to extricate itself.

When intervention was first suggested by Great Britain and France to protect the supplies at Vladivostok, the United States expressed emphatic disapproval of the proposal. For a time its position was apparently upheld by Japan. Her ambassador in Washington, at least, agreed with Secretary Lansing that the landing of troops in Siberia would arouse the hostility of the Bolsheviki and might well tip the scales in favor of Russia's complete surrender to Germany. As indications grew, however, that the Soviet government was entirely helpless in the face of the continued advance of the Kaiser's armies, Japan abandoned such a forbearing policy. In January 1918 her government not only declared itself in favor of immediate intervention, but vigorously asserted that such operations should be carried out only by Japanese troops. Although the United States and Japan were allies fighting against Germany, their underlying rivalry in the Far East was revealed by the Tokyo statement that the participation of American forces would "create a very unfavorable impression in Japan." England and France had originally contemplated some sort of joint action, but they now appeared ready to accept the Japanese view. While the Russians and Germans were negotiating at Brest-Litovsk, rumors and reports were consequently widespread that Japan was about to occupy Vladivostok and take over control of the Trans-Siberia Railroad.

The United States continued to oppose intervention. In reply to persistent requests from the Allied capitals that we endorse such action, Secretary Lansing reiterated our strongly held opinion that it would be both ill-advised and inopportune. Should such a move ever become necessary, we somewhat reluctantly admitted that Japan might be the logical nation

to undertake it. But the very fact that Japan wanted to act alone aroused our suspicions as to whether her desire to intervene arose wholly out of devotion to the Allied cause. Our principal contention in early 1918, however, was that intervention would be hotly resented by the Russian people. It would play into the hands of the enemies of Russia, a note dispatched on March 5, 1918, to the American ambassadors in Allied capitals declared, and particularly of the enemies of the Russian Revolution, "for which the government of the United States entertains the greatest sympathy, in spite of all the unhappiness and misfortune which has for the time sprung out of it."

Our strong stand held Japan in check. Her reluctant answer to the views expressed by Secretary Lansing stated that under the circumstances she would make no move until a general agreement had been reached between the United States and the Allies. The issue was merely postponed, however. It was in no way settled. During the next few months both London and Paris tried by every means possible to induce Wilson to withdraw American opposition to the Japanese program. The President found himself fighting a rearguard action in which he was battling not only pressure from the Allied capitals, but many of his own advisers. At the end of March, Secretary Lansing became convinced that Japan would intervene in Siberia sooner or later whatever we did, and that we might better accede to her proposals than fruitlessly oppose them. "Under the circumstances," he asked in a note to Wilson, "are not Japan's sensibilities more important than the sensibilities of the Russian people?"

Soon Ambassador Francis was urging intervention on the broader grounds that the time had come to aid the Russian people, in their own interest and that of the Allies, to overthrow a government that had betrayed the democratic cause. He believed it would be welcomed. "Russia is passing through a dream or orgy from which it may awaken any day," he cabled Washington, "but the longer the awakening is delayed the stronger foothold will Germany acquire. . . . I doubt the policy of the Allies longer temporizing with a government advocating the principles of Bolshevism and guilty of the outrages the Soviet Government has practiced."

While the problem of what to do in Siberia hung fire, events had given greater immediacy to the parallel issue of intervention in North Russia. For all its own complications, the situation here did not involve any factor exactly comparable to that presented by possible Japanese ambitions in Siberia. Allied policy had as its immediate objective protecting supplies at Murmansk, but it also aimed to maintain a foothold in Russia which might prevent further German advance. The Murman Coast was an area immediately threatened after the conclusion of peace at Brest-Litovsk. At this time—that is, in March 1918 —the Soviet government was not averse to accepting Allied aid where the German armies were so close to its capital. The Bolsheviki, hard pressed on all sides, not knowing which way to turn, were ready to follow a policy of playing off the Allies against the Central Powers in order to gain time for strengthening their own regime. They consequently approved the landing of troops at Murmansk to resist any German aggression in that direction, and Allied forces were welcomed by the local soviet.

Nevertheless friction soon developed over this move. As the Allies increased the number of their troops and extended their control over more territory, the Soviet government entered a vigorous protest. Foreign Commissar Chicherin declared in June that intervention had developed into an invasion of Russian territory unprovoked by any aggressive measures on the part of Russia. When the local soviet, under the influence, if not the actual control, of the Allied forces, broke off its relations with Moscow and entered into a special treaty with the Allied representatives at Murmansk, the growing estrangement between the Bolsheviki and the Allies was complete.

The United States had taken a limited part in these operations. An American cruiser had been sent to Murmansk upon the request of the Allies, and a small force of marines was

landed to join the Allied forces already ashore. President Wilson had authorized these steps subject to certain provisions. They were to be approved by the Russian people and under no circumstances involve either an attempt to restore the old regime or any interference with political liberty. These conditions had been theoretically satisfied through the local arrangements with the Murmansk Soviet, but its break with Moscow placed a different complexion on affairs. As the Allies undertook to support the local anti-Bolshevik administration and planned the enlargement of their field of operations to include Archangel, requests for American reinforcements became linked with the problem of intervention in Siberia. The United States was faced with a major decision upon its whole Russian policy.

A further development, strengthening the interventionist arguments of Great Britain and France, as well as those of Japan, had now taken place within Russia. A force of some 45,000 Czecho-Slovaks was attempting to cross Siberia and make its long, laborious way back to the western front. These troops had deserted from the Austrian army soon after the outbreak of war and had been permitted in 1917 to join the Russian forces to fight for the independence of the Czecho-Slovak Republic. Upon conclusion of the Treaty of Brest-Litovsk, they were left hopelessly stranded in the Ukraine. The Soviet government had consequently agreed to allow them to retreat through European Russia and across Siberia to Vladivostok, where they would supposedly be transported by the Allies half way around the world and again take up the fight for their independence in France.

A first contingent of the Czecho-Slovak force actually reached the Siberian port and the dramatic aspects of the whole undertaking awoke the admiration and amazement of the entire world. But friction soon developed between the main body of these troops and the people through whose territory they were passing. Local soviets, fearful of their joining the anti-Bolshevik elements in Siberia, tried to block the Czechs' further

passage eastward. At one point a serious clash occurred involving former German and Austrian prisoners of war released o
orders from Moscow. The situation became packed with dyna-
mite. To avoid further trouble the Soviet government tried t
disarm the Czecho-Slovaks, contrary to its original agreement
and the latter forcibly resisted. They were soon in open conflic
with the Red Guards and in June 1918 scattered warfare wa
being waged along the entire line of the Siberian Railway. The
Czecho-Slovaks who had already reached Vladivostok then decided to turn back and come to the aid of their comrades.

Siberia was already in the utmost confusion. Bands of White
partisans controlled a large part of the territory and under such
leaders as the Cossack Ataman Semenov, they were everywhere
waging guerrilla warfare against the Reds, laying waste the
countryside and massacring all those suspected of Bolshevik
sympathies. The entry of the Czecho-Slovaks into this bitter
civil war opened an even bloodier chapter of internecine strife.
With the Czechs joining forces with the anti-Bolsheviks, Soviet
authority east of the Urals virtually collapsed.

Interest in the Czecho-Slovak struggle for independence had
always been widespread in the United States, and a popular
demand at once arose for helping these patriotic troops, even
though they were proving quite capable of looking out for
themselves, to make good their escape from Russia. This involved keeping open both the port of Vladivostok and the
Siberia Railway if they were to be ensured free passage overseas. President Wilson, sharing the popular sympathy for the
Czechs, believed that the United States had an obligation to
stand by them in their struggle to win independence. The situation also provided a possible basis, in his opinion, for acceding
to the Allied demand for intervention in Siberia since it provided a framework for action which could be both strictly
limited in scope and morally defensible as noninterference in
Russian affairs.

The Allies had been quick to make the most of these developments, but they regarded them from a quite different angle

from that of President Wilson. The opportunity that now presented itself to them was not the limited intervention he envisaged, but the possible establishment of an effective eastern front against Germany. Their own operations in North Russia, the availability of the Czecho-Slovaks as the nucleus of a new army, the rise of anti-Bolshevik forces in Siberia, and large-scale intervention at Vladivostok became linked in the minds of the High Command as parts of an ambitious program to overthrow the Soviet state and launch a new attack upon Germany. At least the Urals might be held as a barrier to any further extension of Bolshevik power, and behind these mountains a White Russia, supported by the Allies, would compel Germany to keep her armies in the eastern theater of war and thereby strengthen the Allied position in the West.

This ambitious scheme was born of what was believed to be dire necessity. In the early summer of 1918 the struggle in Europe had entered a critical phase. Germany was transferring divisions from the eastern to the western front. The Allies felt they had no hope of defeating her that year, and they were further convinced that if time were given the enemy to draw upon the vast resources of prostrate Russia, the prospects of even ultimate victory would be indefinitely postponed. The Supreme War Council therefore urged that supporting forces be sent to the troops already in North Russia and that intervention should be at once undertaken in Siberia. Lord Reading, the British ambassador at Washington, pressed the issue home in conferences with Colonel House in mid-June in which he declared that it no longer involved merely a policy toward Russia, but the Allied cause itself. Even if her armies were defeated on the western front, he reported on the basis of military advices from London, Germany might be able to continue fighting indefinitely with Russia's food supplies and raw materials at her disposal. The Allies might be confronted with a German-Russian bid for world domination that would be irresistible unless a new front was formed in the East, with

Japan rallying the Czecho-Slovaks and anti-Bolsheviks in Siberia behind a fresh Allied army.

Fears of a German victory and mounting hatred of the Bolsheviki provided wide popular support in this country for such
a program. There was a demand for action in Congress. Senator King introduced a resolution calling for an immediate
military expedition to Russia; Senator Poindexter urged the
creation of an army of two million Japanese, with supporting
contingents from the Allies, to overthrow the Bolshevik regime
and carry the war to Germany. "If a force of Allied troops were
sent into Siberia," the *New York Times* declared, "it would
provide a supporting nucleus around which the people of
Russia could rally. . . . Is Germany to kill democracy by the
sword and the Allies by watchful waiting?" The *Washington
Post* declared the crisis admitted of no delay, and in an article
in the *Philadelphia Public Ledger*, former President Taft stated
emphatically that it was the time to act.

Wilson nevertheless continued to stand out against these
forces bearing down upon him from both at home and abroad.
He still could not reconcile a policy of intervention which
would constitute active opposition to the Soviet government
with his own declared pledges against interference in Russia's
internal affairs. Although he had no sympathy with the Bolsheviki, there was his own fervid statement that the attitude
of the powers toward Russia would be the proof of their good
will. For a time a possible solution to his dilemma appeared
in the proposal that a Russian Relief Commission be organized
to provide such substantial economic aid to the Russian people
that they would be effectively fortified against complete surrender to Germany. It was first suggested on June 13. Colonel
House was reported enthusiastic over the plan; Secretary Lansing strongly backed it, and Herbert Hoover was prepared to
take over the chairmanship if the President agreed to release
him from his duties as Food Administrator. "The creation of
this commission," Lansing wrote the President, "would, for the
time being, dispose of the proposal for armed intervention."

So moderate a program, however, in no way answered the demands of the Allies for creation of a new eastern front. The pressure upon Wilson grew stronger every day and the question was repeatedly canvassed in conferences at Washington. The military advisers of the President were highly sceptical of the whole project on strategic grounds. General March, Chief of Staff, General Pershing and General Tasker H. Bliss, our representative on the Inter-Allied War Council, all opposed the idea when it was first broached. But with its approval by Marshal Foch, they one by one advised the President to accept it. Secretary of War Baker held out almost alone. "If I had my own way about Russia," he wrote on June 19, "and had the power to have my own way, I would like to take everybody out of Russia except the Russians, including diplomatic representatives, military representatives, political agents, propagandists and casual visitors, and let the Russians settle down and settle their own affairs." Somewhat later he dismissed the whole plan as "nonsense . . . one of those sideshows born of desperation."

While Wilson still wavered, "sweating blood over the question" as he wrote Colonel House, a final appeal was cabled from the Supreme War Council on July 2. It flatly stated that Allied intervention was necessary to win the war, strongly urging American approval before it was too late.

"There is no doubt that if the Germans fail to gain a decision in the West in the next few weeks," this revealing document declared, "they will turn east and endeavour with all their power to paralyze any possibility of the national regeneration of Russia during the war. They know as well as we know that there is but the smallest chance of an Allied victory in 1919 unless Germany is compelled to transfer a considerable amount of her strength back again from West to East. It will therefore be a primary object of her policy to prevent the re-creation of an Eastern Allied front. . . . If the Allies are to win the war in 1919 it should be a primary object of their policy to foster and assist the national movement in Russia in order to reform an Eastern front or at least sustain such a vigorous spirit of inde-

THE ROAD TO TEHERAN

pendence in the occupied territories behind the German lines
as will compel Germany to maintain large bodies of troops in
the East. . . . If the policy of intervention however is to be
really successful, an adequate military force must be employed.
The Allied representatives in Russia are agreed that while economic assistance is important, military intervention is absolutely essential. . . ."

Whether it was this urgent plea that finally broke the President's resistance, or at what precise date he made up his mind
that further opposition to intervention seriously endangered
Allied unity, are questions to which the answer is not entirely
clear. But apparently a final decision was reached at a Washington conference on July 6, 1918. The United States could not
accept the full implications of the Supreme War Council's
program, but it would support a policy of limited intervention.
The conferees agreed that the creation of a new eastern front,
or any advance from Siberia west of the city of Irkutsk, were
alike impossible. Our participation would be restricted, despite
the pleas of the Allies, to the dispatch of small forces both to
North Russia and Vladivostok, and even such action would be
undertaken only with firm guarantees that there should be no
impairment of either the political or territorial sovereignty of
the Russian people.

It is clear from these developments that the United States
accepted intervention only with the greatest reluctance, that it
refused support to Allied plans for what would have amounted
to major operations against the Soviet government in order to
recreate an eastern front, and that in finally surrendering to
the insistent demands of the Supreme War Council, the President sought to uphold the principle of noninterference in
Russia's internal affairs as effectively as he could. Our general
policy was made clear in an *aide-memoire* drawn up by the
President for the Allied ambassadors on July 17, and in a
public announcement issued along the same lines by the State
Department on August 3.

The premise of these twin statements was that the United

States government, convinced that military intervention in Russia would add to the confusion in that country rather than cure it, and that it would not be of any advantage in winning the war against Germany, refused to participate in any such program or to sanction it in principle. It was, however, prepared to authorize military action in Siberia for the express purpose of helping the Czecho-Slovaks and of protecting the military stores at Vladivostok, and it yielded to the judgment of the Supreme Command in establishing a small force at Murmansk to guard Allied supplies and aid the Russian forces in that area resisting Germany. In carrying out these operations, the Allies were asked to unite in assuring the Russian people that their action in North Russia and Siberia did not contemplate interference of any kind in their internal affairs, and that their single object was to offer only such aid "as shall be acceptable to the Russian people in their endeavour to regain control of their own affairs, their own territory, and their own destiny."

The ambiguities and contradictions of this policy need hardly be emphasized. It can be understood only when it is borne in mind that American opinion was not only hostile to the Soviet government and prepared to ignore its very existence, but completely convinced that the Bolsheviki were about to be overthrown by the Russian people. On that basis alone could intervention, even as limited as President Wilson sought to make it, be in any way justified in the light of the President's former statements. On the other hand, it remains true that while Wilson surrendered on the immediate issue, his opposition to the Allies' broader proposals served to restrain them from what might have developed into even more serious involvement in Russia's internal affairs than the Archangel and Vladivostok ventures finally meant.

In any event a decision had been reached. The President was not happy about it. "I am greatly reassured by your generous approval of my action with regard to Russia," he wrote Victor F. Lawson on August 7. "It is a matter of the most complex and difficult sort, and I have at no time felt confidence in my own judgment about it." But there could now be no turning back. Preparations were made to dispatch an American force to North Russia consisting of an infantry regiment and a battalion of engineers, together with certain hospital and ambulance units, to join the Allied troops already in occupation. As for Siberia, an agreement was reached with Japan, compelled to accept joint intervention, whereby the expeditionary units of the two countries should be kept at a minimum, with small token forces from the other Allies, and ordered strictly to refrain from any interference in Russia's internal affairs. The American contingent totaled 7,000 troops; the Japanese was expected to number some 12,000. In the late summer of 1918 our forces disembarked at Archangel and Vladivostok to engage in operations whose purpose and extent were so obscure as to create both at home and in the field the utmost confusion.

Intervention naturally brought forth strong protests from the Bolsheviki and the embittered charge that the Allies were taking advantage of Russia's internal difficulties to follow a policy of selfish aggression. The Soviet government was especially aroused over developments in Siberia. For while the United States forces under General William S. Graves tried to maintain a strict neutrality in the factional strife in that part of the world, and confined their operations to keeping open the Siberian Railway in order to ensure free transit for the Czecho-Slovaks, the Japanese adopted a far more aggressive attitude. Disregarding their agreement to limit their troops, they built up their forces to some 70,000 men and began the occupation of strategic points in eastern Siberia which bore little relation to the professed objectives of intervention. They openly supported such anti-Bolshevik chieftains as Ataman Semenov and the even more notorious Cossack adventurer Kalmykov, both of whom General Graves denounced as bandits and murderers. "The imperialists of Japan," *Izvestia* wrote in alarm, "want to check the Russian Revolution and cut off Russia from the Pacific. They want to grab the rich territory of Siberia and enslave Siberian workmen and peasants."

To a certain extent the Soviet government distinguished between the role of the Allies in these operations and the position President Wilson was trying to uphold. "Although the Government of the United States has been obliged to consent to intervention," Foreign Commissar Chicherin declared, "this consent is merely formal." But general resentment against all the powers, including the United States, rapidly mounted as foreign troops in both North Russia and Siberia pressed inland, everywhere supporting anti-Bolsheviki uprisings against the Soviet government. These moves were denounced as bare-faced robbery. President Wilson himself was eventually attacked in the Moscow press as the prophet of imperialism, and his Fourteen Points were caustically described as a "deliquescent program of political rascality."

The Bolsheviki had every reason for their resentment. Allied intervention coincided with and was in part responsible for a renewed burst of counterrevolutionary activity, and the Soviet regime found itself in the late summer of 1918 passing through the most critical phase of its early development. The western territories of Russia were already lost to Germany; the countries of the Caucasus had either declared their independence of the Red regime or were in open revolt under the leadership of General Denikin; the Czecho-Slovaks were the spearhead of an anti-Bolshevik drive based upon Siberia which reached the banks of the Volga, and under the protection of Allied guns a Sovereign Administration of the Northern Region had been established with headquarters at Archangel. The area controlled by the Soviet government was no larger than the fifteenth century principality of Muscovy. With the Germans holding strong positions in the West from which they might further advance, and the Allies scheming to bring together all anti-Bolshevik forces to overthrow the Soviet regime and create a new eastern front, the outlook for Russia could hardly have been more confused or more precarious. "We were between the hammer and the anvil," Trotsky wrote of these perilous days.

Forced thus to meet foreign and civil war at the same time,

the Bolsheviki resorted to desperate measures. Trotsky proceeded vigorously to build up a new Red Army to meet all foes on the military front, and, following an attempt to assassinate Lenin at the end of August, Moscow proclaimed an official program of mass terror to stamp out the internal revolt. The savage and bloody suppression of all counterrevolutionary activity to which this led recalled to the Western World nothing so much as the excesses of the French Revolution. Wholesale arrests and mass executions were the Bolsheviki's answer to every suspected uprising against their authority. The Red Terror was designed to crush without mercy all those conspiring with foreign aid to overthrow the Soviet government.

The reaction abroad to these terroristic measures was an even more intense wave of anti-Bolshevik feeling. "My conclusion is that the only way to end this disgrace to civilization," cried Ambassador Francis, now at Archangel, "is for the Allies immediately to take Petrograd and Moscow." This suggestion proved hardly practical, but for a time the advance of the Whites awakened extravagant hopes. Public opinion in the United States universally rejoiced as the gathering momentum of counterrevolution threatened to overwhelm the Reds. What the *New York Times* called "the Allied economic, reenforcing and rallying expedition to Russia to aid her people to throw off the yoke of Germany" appeared about to win a great success, with the Bolshevik government snuffed out and its adherents forced to flee within the German lines before the Whites' triumphant advance.

In the meantime the war in the West was sweeping on to its startling and unexpected climax. The brilliant counteroffensive of the Allies after Hindenburg's final unsuccessful drive on Paris, pushed back the reeling German armies and changed dramatically the whole European picture. In November, after the collapse of Bulgaria, Turkey and Austria, a defeated Germany was ready for peace. Revolution overthrew the Kaiser, a provisional government accepted the armistice terms offered by the victorious Allies, and the war was over.

All this had no immediate effect upon the tangled situation in Russia. The Allies had become so deeply involved in their support of the anti-Bolsheviks that there could be no automatic cessation of hostilities even though the need for an eastern front no longer existed. But as the Red Army rallied to throw back the advancing Whites and relieve the immediate pressure upon the Soviet government, Allied support for the anti-Bolsheviks was not forthcoming in sufficient strength to turn the tide of battle. For a time it appeared possible that operations in both North Russia and Siberia were to be intensified and that the Allies, having vanquished Germany, would undertake to overthrow the hated Bolsheviki in an even bloodier and more ruthless war. Events soon showed, however, that none of the peoples of the Allied countries had any stomach for further fighting. There could be no rallying of a war-weary world for another crusade, however dark the picture of Bolshevism painted by conservative statesmen.

The United States refused from the first to be drawn into any such new struggle. Even before the Armistice, it denied all requests for strengthening its forces at Archangel or Vladivostok, and it clearly showed its opposition to further cooperation in a policy which was not "the course of our free choice but that of stern necessity." Yet while it wished after November 11 to abandon intervention altogether, circumstances made this highly difficult.

In North Russia, American troops were compelled to remain at Archangel throughout the winter of 1918-1919, in part because of the great difficulty—if not impossibility—of evacuating them from that frozen port, and in part because of an obligation to protect from the avenging arm of the Red Terror the forces which the Allies had encouraged to rise against the Soviet government. And conditions during the winter grew steadily worse for our troops. The mounting hostility of the Russian people who they had been led to believe would greet them as deliverers, friction among the various Allied contingents, the obscurity of the purposes for which they were fighting, and above all the bitter cold and harsh conditions of life steadily undermined morale. A mutinous flare-up in one company of infantry symbolized the growing discontent of the troops, and at home there was a mounting demand for their recall. With the spring steps were consequently taken to evacuate all Americans, regardless of every other consideration. By June 1919 the last men had been withdrawn. The Archangel expedition had cost two hundred American lives and an outlay of $3,000,000. What it had achieved was not so apparent.

Things were even more complicated in Siberia. Within a month of the original decision in favor of intervention, Secretary Lansing had gravely warned President Wilson of the disturbing signs and portents of Japanese aggression. "Frankly," he wrote on August 18, 1918, "I think the situation is getting beyond our control." The President agreed. When later that same month the Allies proposed sending a High Commissioner to Siberia, he instructed the Secretary of State to oppose any such move and to make clear that the United States did not contemplate political action of any kind. "The other governments," he wrote, "are going much further than we are, and much faster—are, indeed, acting upon a plan which is altogether foreign from ours and inconsistent with it."

Our position became increasingly difficult as the Japanese went blithely ahead with their own program regardless of American protests, promoting partisan strife between the Reds and Whites and intensifying the chaos and confusion which generally prevailed throughout Siberia. The American forces guarded the railway and tried to preserve such order as they could, but their refusal to do anything more than this not only disappointed the White partisans, but also led to increasing friction with our Japanese allies. The United States had won no friends for its policy in Siberia, however well meant, and its troops found themselves doing little "but talk, nurse the railroads, distribute pamphlets and show pictures to prove to the Russians what a great nation we were—at home."

Nevertheless the armistice on the western front no more

cleared the way to immediate withdrawal in Siberia than it had in the case of the American forces at Archangel. There were our responsibilities in keeping open the railway and in fulfilling our pledges to rescue the disorganized and scattered Czecho-Slovaks. And more important, there was Japan. As time went on the major objective of our Siberian policy became more and more to try to restrain the Japanese from digging in so deeply on the mainland that they could not be dislodged.

While the United States worried over how it might extricate itself from the imbroglio of intervention, with civil war continuing to rage between the hard-fighting Reds and the foreign-supported Whites, the peace conference met at Paris. Just as the war with Germany had been the major concern of the Allies throughout 1918, so the conclusion of peace with Germany was their absorbing preoccupation in 1919. The problem of Russia was only less important than that of Germany, but it is nevertheless not surprising that in the midst of the immense complexities which the Allied statesmen faced in redrawing the map of western and central Europe, policy toward Russia should be subordinated to what appeared to be more immediately critical issues. The uncertainties and confusion amid which the powers groped for a solution of the Russian question in part reflected this failure to concentrate upon it. On one occasion for example, President Wilson left an important decision to Colonel House, frankly stating that he had a one-track mind and was at the time wholly absorbed in the affairs of Germany.

With peace, in any event, the Soviet government had again attacked the Allied policy of intervention, Foreign Commissar Chicherin renewing his protests "against this wanton aggression, against this act of sheer violence and brutal force, against this attempt to curb the liberty, the political and social life of the people of another country." For all the harshness of these strictures, he nevertheless hoped for the reestablishment of friendly relations and recognition of the Soviet regime. On January 12, 1919, he tried to open negotiations, officially asking the United States to name a place and set a time for a general conference.

There was little disposition to accept these proposals. Although it was no longer possible to base our policy toward Russia on the supposition that the Bolsheviki were only the tools of Germany, the Soviet regime was more than ever an outcast among the nations. In common with the Allies, the United States felt that to recognize these declared enemies of the capitalist world would be to condone and encourage their revolutionary policies, while it was still hoped that the Whites would encompass the Bolsheviki's early downfall. In the conferences on this problem among the Allied statesmen gathered in Paris, Premier Clemenceau of France proposed drawing a strict *cordon sanitaire* about Russia and enforcing the blockade declared in 1918 so drastically that it would ensure the immediate downfall of the Soviets. Both President Wilson and Prime Minister Lloyd George were reluctant to carry their anti-Bolshevik policies that far. It would be playing against the free spirit of the world, they declared, if they did not give Russia a chance "to find herself along the lines of utter freedom."

The British statesman first suggested that the Supreme Council summon to the peace conference representatives of all the *de facto* governments in Russia with the purpose of working out a solution to the whole problem. The French, however, flatly refused to treat with the Bolsheviki in any way, shape or form. They would "make no contract with crime." President Wilson thereupon advanced the alternative proposal that if such a meeting could not be held in connection with the general peace negotiations, a separate conference might be held among the Russian factions in some other place than Paris. This plan was finally accepted and Prinkipo Island, in the Sea of Marmara, was selected for the proposed meeting.

No direct invitation was issued to the Bolsheviki. The proposal was announced to the world by wireless. But despite this indirect approach, reflecting the fear in Paris that contact with Moscow might somehow lead to the spread of the Bolshevik

contagion, the Soviet government at once accepted. Not so the rival factions in Russia. Representatives of the counterrevolutionary governments of Archangel, South Russia and Siberia said they would have nothing whatsoever to do with the Prinkipo conference. Declaring that they would not even sit at the same table with persons whom they regarded as robbers and murderers, the White Russians said that reconciliation with the Bolsheviki was impossible under any circumstances.

Faced with this rebuff the Supreme Council made no further effort to provide for representation of Russia at the peace conference, directly or indirectly. She was to be completely isolated. This solved nothing, however, and President Wilson at least felt that matters could not be left in this thoroughly unsatisfactory state. He proposed an immediate end to the policy of intervention and the withdrawal of all Allied troops from Russian territory. Neither the British nor the French government was ready for such a step. A special emissary from the British cabinet, Winston Churchill, hurried over from London not only to oppose Wilson's plan but to urge an increase in the Allied forces operating in Russia and more aggressive support for the anti-Bolsheviks. The sharp conflict in the views of the two statesmen came to a head at a stormy meeting on the eve of the President's return to the United States in mid-February, but it did not lead to any clear-cut victory for either Wilson or Churchill. The Allies neither abandoned intervention nor gave it the support that might conceivably have made it effective.

A short time afterwards an unofficial step was taken by the American delegation at Paris—or at least by Secretary Lansing and Colonel House—to get in touch with the Soviet leaders and explore the bases of a general settlement. William C. Bullitt—who was to become our first ambassador to the Soviet Union some fourteen years later—was sent on a secret mission to Moscow where he held a series of talks with Lenin, Chicherin and Litvinov. He brought back with him the outline of a program that the Soviet government declared it would accept if the Supreme War Council agreed to put it into effect by April 15.

This plan embodied five major proposals: an immediate truce among all Russian factions until the people themselves had an opportunity to determine what form of government they desired; the raising of the Allied blockade about Russia; a general amnesty for political prisoners; the withdrawal of all Allied troops from Russia; and the recognition by existing *de facto* governments, including the Soviet government, of their respective shares of Russia's foreign debt. Bullitt returned to Paris convinced that the Bolshevik plan was put forward in good faith and that it provided the basis for a reasonable understanding. His report further stated that the Soviet government was the only constructive force operating in Russia, that it was both politically and morally strong, and that Lenin, in whom he expressed great confidence, was ready to meet the Western powers halfway and was particularly anxious to conciliate the United States. "No government save a Socialist Government," was his final conclusion, "can be set up in Russia today except by foreign bayonets and any government so set up will fall the minute such support is withdrawn."

These proposals were not even considered in Paris. The Bullitt report was shelved and the period which the Bolsheviki had set for acceptance of their plan was allowed to lapse without further action other than an unsuccessful gesture toward economic relief proposed by the Norwegian explorer, Dr. Fridtjof Nansen.

An important reason for the attitude of the Supreme Council on this issue was the new successes being won by Russian Whites. Their victories over the Red Army strengthened the conviction of the Allied representatives in Paris that they would not have to deal with the Bolsheviki but could safely await the Whites' final triumph. In November 1918, Admiral Kolchak had assumed dictatorial control over the anti-Bolshevik government which had been set up in Siberia, with headquarters at Omsk, and by April of the next year the troops under his command were advancing victoriously toward the Volga. There would be even more serious threats to the Soviet regime

upon such other occasions as the advances of Generals Denikin and Yudenich, but the local support accorded Kolchak at this time appeared to hold out great promise of victory, and his position as Supreme Ruler was generally recognized by the other White leaders. To forward such a promising movement, the Allies consequently agreed to provide Admiral Kolchak with additional aid. Upon receiving his pledge that he would safeguard the freedom of the Russian people and recognize the foreign debt, President Wilson associated himself with the Premiers of Great Britain, France, Italy and Japan in this new program. While the United States never formally recognized the Kolchak government, it provided it throughout the remainder of 1919 with both economic and financial support.

The general approval of the American people for this policy was won by the growing threat of Bolshevism as a revolutionary menace to the whole capitalist world. It was spilling over the Russian borders in 1919, with Soviets established in Bavaria and Hungary, and the impact of these developments was reflected on this side of the Atlantic as well as throughout Europe. "The American people are at war with Bolshevism," the *Washington Post* shouted, "and will not compromise with the enemy for any reason whatever." This was not meant in a literal sense. The American people could not be aroused any more than those of Europe to a renewal of war on the grand scale still being urged by strongly anti-Bolshevik leaders in France and England. But support for Admiral Kolchak as the white hope of capitalism was universally upheld. Counterrevolution in Russia was believed to be the most effective means of preventing the further spread of Red propaganda.

The views and strategy of the Allied Powers were of course wholly wrong. Admiral Kolchak could not unite the Russian people to overthrow the Soviet government. They found the White Terror no less cruel and tyrannical than the Red Terror, and as his forces drove on toward the Volga, unrest throughout the territory he had conquered undermined his support. When the reorganized and revitalized Red Army began driving him back in the autumn of 1919, his followers melted away and the advancing Bolsheviki were everywhere welcomed as deliverers. His capital at Omsk fell on November 15; his army began to disintegrate. The disillusioned Czecho-Slovaks, once the spearhead of the anti-Bolshevik advance, turned against him. All Siberia seethed with Red revolt. By the end of the year even his most faithful adherents had to admit that counterrevolution had failed, and in February 1920 Kolchak himself fell into the hands of his enemies and was executed by a Red firing squad.

The complete collapse of the Omsk regime marked the beginning of the end of Allied intervention in Siberia and also of the civil war between Reds and Whites. There was to be a flare-up of the old struggle when, during the Russo-Polish War some few months later, France supported a renewal of the anti-Bolshevik campaign in the South which was launched from the Crimea under Baron Wrangel. But the Soviet government had now demonstrated its stability. It was extending its control over more and more of the area left to it at the end of the war in western Europe. The independence of the territories torn away by the treaty of Brest-Litovsk—Finland, Latvia, Estonia, Lithuania and Poland—had been generally recognized, but the Bolsheviki had strengthened their grip over northern and southern Russia and the greater part of Siberia. The Soviet regime remained an outcast. Unable to agree upon a common policy the Allies tried to ignore it. No European government officially recognized it. But it had nevertheless become a power with which the rest of the world had to reckon.

With the fall of Kolchak the United States finally proceeded to withdraw such troops as still remained in Russian territory. Those in the north had long since been recalled, and preparations were now made to bring back the forces in Siberia. After evacuating the last of the war-weary and homesick Czecho-Slovaks, all American units were ordered home. By April 1, 1920, the last of them had finally embarked.

Intervention had proved to be as complete a debacle in Siberia as in North Russia. The people had not risen to welcome the Allied troops, and nothing whatsoever had been accomplished. Upon the pretext of rescuing the Czechs and aiding the people of Russia to establish their own self-government, the Allies had warred against the Soviet government, directly or indirectly, and played their part in plunging Siberia into a period of partisan strife, banditry and chaotic confusion which only temporarily postponed the establishment of Bolshevik authority. The entire venture had profited the Allies not at all —unless we assume that it prevented the Soviet government from more directly supporting Bolshevik uprisings in Central Europe. It had unquestionably contributed to the incredible hardship and suffering endured during these years by the Russian people whose interests we were supposedly safeguarding. The fruits of intervention, moreover, were still being reaped more than two decades later. It had fastened upon Soviet Russia fears of capitalist encirclement that could not be shaken off, and these fears served quite as much as did the Western democracies' mistrust of Communism to impede the cooperation that was to become so necessary in the common struggle of the United Nations against the aggressive designs of a newly militarized Germany.

In participating in these Allied operations directed against the Bolsheviki and in extending aid to the reactionary Kolchak regime, the United States had submitted, against what had at first been President Wilson's better judgment, to the insistent pressure brought to bear upon it at the most critical period of the war. Our objectives, our actual role in political and military developments, and the results of intervention remained confused and often contradictory. It may be repeated, however, that while giving in to the Allies upon the principal issue involved, our influence during these years did work as a somewhat moderating influence upon the more ambitious ideas they for a time held as to the extent to which intervention might be pushed. Yet even this consideration cannot outweigh the fact that we followed a policy toward Russia in 1918 and 1919 that could hardly be reconciled with the democratic principles we professed, or with our declared intention to allow the Russian people to settle their own internal problems.

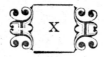

THE GREAT RED SCARE

As IMPORTANT for the future course of Russian-American relations as intervention in 1918-1920, were the repercussions in
the United States to what was happening within Russia. Hostility toward the Bolsheviki—or "Communists," in accordance
with the party name officially adopted in March, 1918—provided a basis for the popular support of our policy during these
years. Intervention then itself intensified this hostility. Official
and unofficial propaganda, which had been instilling hatred
of Germany among the American people as a weapon of war,
turned to damning the Bolsheviki as even greater enemies of
the social order to justify our support for counterrevolution.
It was not that this propaganda determined our attitude toward Soviet Russia. It only deepened the channels of distrust
and enmity which the Bolsheviki themselves had already carved
out by their violent, revolutionary program.

A first example of such propaganda, before the close of the
war, was the accusation that Lenin and Trotsky had betrayed
the Allied cause through their cowardly surrender to Germany.
Upon his return from Petrograd, Edgar Sisson had issued
through the Committee on Public Information in the autumn
of 1918 a series of documents which purported to give conclusive evidence of a gigantic German-Bolshevik conspiracy.
The revolution was depicted as having been wholly planned
by the German General Staff and financed by German funds.
"The present Bolsheviki Government is not a Russian Government at all," the Creel Committee stated on the basis of
these disclosures, "but a German Government acting solely in
the interests of Germany and betraying the Russian people as
it betrays Russia's natural allies, for the benefit of the Imperial
Government alone."

Despite the dubious character of these documents, which time has further discredited, they were generally accepted by the American public as providing official proof of a moral certainty. Since they were vouched for by our own government, such a reaction was only natural. "Filthy pocket-pickers and despicable degenerates of lucre," was the *Baltimore American's* happy characterization of Lenin and Trotsky, while the Soviet government was described as "an outlaw of civilization and a stench in the nostrils of humanity." Other newspapers were not quite so vituperative, but the Sisson disclosures were generally credited with having added "a new touch of foulness to treason." They played an important part in creating an atmosphere in which anything at all might be believed of the Bolsheviki, and no charges of corruption, tyranny and cruelty were too outrageous to be widely accepted.

Emphasis on the revolutionary aims of Communism, particularly after the establishment of the Third International in March 1919, soon added a further and more authentic cause for American hostility to the Soviet regime. The admitted and loudly proclaimed aim of the Bolsheviki to support a socialist state in Russia by spreading the gospel of Red revolt throughout the world, awoke both anger and fear. The conclusion of the war consequently led to no abatement of anti-Russian feeling. The ruthlessness which the Bolsheviki employed in strengthening their hold on power, and the cruel excesses of the Red Terror, stirred the world even more than the sins of Germany. The few voices in America seeking to justify or condone the course of events in Russia as an almost inevitable consequence of embittered civil war, were drowned out in a chorus of condemnation that often became shrilly hysterical. As Communism seemed about to spread over into eastern Europe, with Lenin and Trotsky still more urgently calling upon the proletariat throughout the world to shatter the chains of capitalist control, many Americans trembled with the fear that this virulent contagion would cross the Atlantic.

Governmental agencies made the most of these fears and

kept up a barrage of anti-Bolshevik propaganda throughout 1919 which was at least partially inspired by the need to justify the policy of intervention in both Archangel and Siberia. The continued presence of American troops in these areas after conclusion of the war inevitably awoke opposition to the administration's Russian policy. It did not necessarily reflect any sympathy for the Bolsheviki, or by any means bespeak any popular desire for recognizing their government. It was rather an expression of growing isolationist sentiment that called for the immediate withdrawal of all American troops still abroad and for a program of strict nonintervention in European affairs. Resolutions were introduced into the Senate demanding an explanation of why American boys were still fighting in Russia and insisting that they be at once brought home. Senator Borah broadened the inquiry in September 1919 by attacking the general policy of President Wilson as an unconstitutional exercise of executive authority. ". . . While we are not at war with Russia, while Congress has not declared war," Borah stated, "we are carrying on war with the Russian people. . . . Whatever is being done in that country in the way of armed intervention is without constitutional authority. . . . There is neither legal nor moral justification for sacrificing these lives. It is a violation of the plain principles of free government."

The administration's answer to all such criticism was an attempt to minimize the scope of American operations in Russia and to justify intervention in Siberia by the need to keep rail transportation open as a means for providing economic assistance to the Russian people. But at the same time this policy was upheld, together with our continued collaboration in the Allied blockade of Russia through our embargo policy, on the grounds that Bolshevism was such a dangerous menace to the capitalist world that everything possible should be done to aid those who were actually fighting it. "It is the declared purpose of the Bolsheviks in Russia," Assistant Secretary of State Colby wrote Senator Wadsworth in November, "to carry revolution throughout the world. They have availed themselves of every opportunity to initiate in the United States propaganda aimed to bring about the forcible overthrow of our present form of government. . . . It has seemed altogether inadmissible that food and other necessities of American origin should be allowed to become the means of sustaining such a program of political oppression."

Ambassador Francis, now finally back in the United States, soon added his voice to the pronouncements of the State Department. He had changed none of his original ideas. The United States, he declared, could not leave 180,000,000 people helpless and hopeless under the tyrannical rule of "a ruthless, conscienceless, and bloodthirsty oligarchy, directed by a man with the brain of a sage, and the heart of a monster." It would not only be a stultifying crime for the United States to enter into trade relations with the Soviet government, but it was our duty to society to do everything we could to "eradicate this foul monster—Bolshevism—branch, root and trunk."

President Wilson himself had swung far away from his original attitude of trying to maintain a strict neutrality in Russia's internal affairs. He vigorously attacked the existing regime as "a little group of men just as selfish, just as ruthless, just as pitiless, as the agents of the Tsar himself." On his memorable swing around the circle to support American membership in the League of Nations in the autumn of 1919, he touched only casually upon conditions in Russia but every reference was a scathing criticism of the Soviets. The Russian people, he declared in familiar vein, were friendly and lovable. His heart went out to them. But the intolerable tyranny of their government cut off every possible way in which we might aid them. He lent himself, as did other members of the government, to spreading the most extravagant and often wholly false rumors of the Bolsheviki's atrocities. "We are told by the newspapers," the President stated in one of his speeches, "that they are about to brand the men under arms for them, so that they will forever be marked as their servants and slaves."

If official spokesmen were thus intensifying fear and hatred

of Bolshevism, propaganda from nonofficial sources went to even greater lengths in envenomed attack. It originated in large part from various groups in this country and abroad representative of the old Czarist regime, or supporting one or another of the counterrevolutionary White Russian factions. Former Ambassador Bakhmetev, whom the State Department still recognized as the official envoy from Russia, and a Russian Information Bureau directed by A. J. Sack, conducted a well-financed campaign of anti-Bolshevik propaganda with the most lurid and sensational atrocity reports.

Direct appeals were also issued to the American public by these groups urging military assistance for General Denikin and Admiral Kolchak, whom they painted in glowing colors as the saviors of Russia and of democracy. They were successful in winning the support of many Americans to their cause. The publication *Struggling Russia* printed expressions of sympathy for the reactionary Kolchak regime from some twenty-seven prominent men including Ambassador Francis, Elihu Root, Nicholas Murray Butler, Samuel Gompers and six members of the Senate. The Omsk government was depicted as bearing aloft the banner of civilization against the onslaughts of as cruel, bloodthirsty, ravenous a set of men as the world had ever known.

The views of Russian *émigrés* and other adherents of the Whites were spread upon the records of a congressional investigation into Communist propaganda early in 1919. Witnesses in any way sympathetic toward the Communist revolution or even moderate in their views found it almost impossible to make themselves heard. Conditions in Russia were bad enough. There was no question of the disorganization, and in some areas virtual anarchy, prevailing in that unhappy country, nor of the oppressive and often brutal measures that the Reds had adopted to crush out counterrevolution. But the congressional investigators accepted every rumor at face value, almost regardless of its source, and responsibility for all the excesses of the civil war was invariably laid at the door of the Bolsheviki. The atrocities perpetrated by the armies of Denikin and Kolchak, although they were actually alienating the sympathy of great masses of the Russian people, were completely ignored. The public was deluged with lurid stories of the Red Terror; it heard almost nothing of the White Terror.

The press followed the lead of Washington and printed virtually every anti-Bolshevik rumor that came its way without pretense of verification. A startling example of this sensation-mongering was the widespread story of the "nationalization of women." The Bolsheviki had introduced certain changes in the existing Russian laws governing divorce and family relations. They apparently delighted in deriding what they called outmoded bourgeois ideals affecting social manners and morals. But there was no other basis for the story of the nationalization of women. It may have actually had its origin in the imaginary decree of a local soviet, which had been published as a joke in a Moscow paper, purporting to set up a Bureau of Free Love. Nevertheless the story received the widest circulation. Even after the State Department, attempting to draw the line somewhere, officially denied its authenticity, it kept bobbing up again and again. Senator McCumber read it into the *Congressional Record*, declaring the supposed nationalization of women to be so filthy and brutal that he was surprised that this country did not demand "the extermination of such beasts." Large numbers of Americans accepted the report as entirely true—what they might expect from such depraved barbarians as the Bolsheviki had proved themselves to be.

Sensational headlines told of other evil deeds credited to the Reds—their wanton destruction of property, their wholesale massacre of the bourgeois, their attacks upon religion. There was substance for some of these charges. Again it is necessary to emphasize that the Red Terror could hardly be defended upon moral grounds. But everything that did take place was magnified out of all proportion, and with little appreciation of the fact that the chaotic conditions prevailing in Russia were due to the activities of the Whites as well as to those of the

Reds. Editorial writers described the Bolsheviki as "assassins and madmen," "beasts drunk from a saturnalia of crime," and "ravening beasts of prey, a large part of them actual criminals, all of them mad with the raging passions of the class struggle." Their vile acts were said to make the crimes of Ivan the Terrible appear pale and insignificant.

The note of hysteria which so often marked these attacks upon Bolshevism may be at least partially attributed to a post-war reaction in which new victims had to be discovered for the violent campaign of hate formerly directed against the diabolic Huns. But it was also a consequence of growing fears, nurtured by the emotional fervors of war, of the spread of Red revolution to the United States. The conservative reaction ushered in with peace, the easy tendency to blame industrial unrest on foreign propaganda rather than to seek out its basic causes, the intolerance and bigotry that marked the rise of a fervent nationalism, and the jittery state of public nerves all played their part in the phenomenon known as the Great Red Scare of 1919.

There was a basis for these fears of the spread of Bolshevism just as there was for atrocity reports. However exaggerated they were, they were not made out of whole cloth. The objective of the Communists in this period—internationalists by their very definition of the class war—was world revolution. With the capitalist countries supporting the revolt against their regime in Russia, the Bolsheviki were convinced that their survival depended on their success in persuading the workers of other nations to rise as had the Russian workers. "The Communist Revolution," wrote Bukharin, "can triumph only as a world revolution." The Third International issued a ringing manifesto calling upon proletarians of the world to unite: "Down with the Imperialistic Conspiracy of Capital! Long live the International Republic of the Workers' Soviets!" The Soviet government itself was prepared to support this program. Although the Third International was theoretically a separate and distinct organization, it drew its strength from the same sources. Lenin and Trotsky held the strings of power in three interrelated and closely cooperating—if not actually identical—bodies: the Soviet government, the Communist Party and the Third International.

The common interest of these three organizations in stirring up Communist revolt in the United States was generally believed to be proved by the activities of Ludwig C. A. K. Martens, an emissary of Soviet Russia officially charged by Foreign Commissar Chicherin with the task of reopening trade relations between the United States and Russia. His presence in this country was completely ignored by the State Department, and the continuance of our embargo upon all exports to the Soviets in any event rendered any commercial negotiations quite futile. But Martens established offices in New York and in trying to spread abroad more favorable impressions of conditions in Russia, whatever his other activities, he soon found himself charged with being an agent of Communist propaganda.

He was investigated by a New York state legislative committee, the Senate Judiciary Committee, and finally by the Department of Labor. Despite his pleas that he was entitled to diplomatic immunity even though the government he represented was not officially recognized, and that he had neither engaged in objectionable propaganda nor in any way sought to interfere in the internal affairs of the United States, the ultimate verdict was against him. He was an agent of the Soviet government. The Soviet government was identified with the Communist Party and the Third International. Therefore Martens became subject to deportation, according to a decision handed down in December 1920 by the Secretary of Labor, as an alien member of an organization advocating the overthrow of the United States government by violence. Martens promptly left the country on orders from Foreign Commissar Chicherin and thus escaped actual deportation proceedings, but the incident deeply impressed the American public with the danger of Communist activity in the United States, and intensified the sharp discord already existing between Russia and America.

An even more ominous development in the minds of those

fearful of the spread of Bolshevism was the organization in September 1919 of an American Communist party. Indeed there were for a time two such organizations, growing out of a split within the old Socialist Party, but the so-called Communist Labor Party, led by John Reed, became the official affiliate of the Third International, advocating the dictatorship of the proletariat, the nationalization of business and finance, and close alliance with the Russian Bolsheviki. For a time driven underground, it emerged as the Workers' Party in 1921, putting up presidential candidates in successive national elections in the 1920's, and in the 1930's it officially became the American Communist Party. Estimates of the strength of this movement widely differed. While the National Security League declared the number of American Communists totaled some 600,000, their vote in 1924 was only 36,000 and party membership probably never rose above a small fraction of one per cent of the total adult population.

Despite their insignificance in actual numbers, the Communists were nevertheless charged with boring dangerously within the labor movement and with promoting the widespread and violent strikes which made 1919 a peak year in the history of American industrial strife. There were strikes in the steel industry, the building trades, and in coal mining; among railroad shopmen, longshoremen, stockyard workers, transportation employees. Seattle went through a violent general strike and Boston the crisis of a police strike. While in many instances these walkouts were a natural consequence of labor's postwar demand for higher wages to meet the rising costs of living, there was little question that the ferment induced by the triumph of the proletariat in Russia and the spread of Communist propaganda was working among American industrial employees. Some of the strike leaders were avowed Communists. Both the violence of their methods and in several instances their demands reflected the influence of events in Russia.

Whatever the responsibility of Communism for these industrial disturbances or the actual role of Moscow in fomenting them, the more conservative elements in American life saw everywhere the hand of the Third International. Popular revulsion against the course of revolution in Russia and fears of what might happen in this country should the Reds gain more control over labor, became interacting forces which steadily deepened our hostility toward the Bolsheviki. They were believed to be the ultimate source of the new dangers threatening American democracy, and consequently any possibility of re-establishing the old friendship between the Russian and American governments was pushed farther and farther into the background. Our resentment toward the Bolsheviki because of their withdrawal from the war and their repudiation of international obligations, and the additional friction which resulted from our intervention and support for the anti-Bolshevik forces in Russia, thus became greatly intensified by the growing conviction that they were directly interfering in our domestic affairs.

In March 1919 Secretary of Labor Wilson definitely stated that the Bolsheviki were behind the strikes that had broken out in Seattle, Butte, Paterson and Lawrence, plotting to set up a revolutionary government of soviets in the United States. Solicitor General Lamar echoed this warning. Socialists, anarchists and members of the I.W.W., he declared, were joining forces with a single end in view—"the overthrow of the government of the United States by means of a bloody revolution and the establishment of a Bolshevik Republic."

Some few newspapers refused to succumb to these alarms. "There is no more danger," the *Brooklyn Citizen* stated, "of anything in the shape of Bolshevism on this side of the Atlantic than there is that a majority of the American people will go insane." But when strike violence was supplemented by attempted bomb outrages, accusations that foreign influences were at work began to gain general credence. The discovery in the New York Post Office in April of a number of infernal machines, concealed in innocent-appearing department store

packages and addressed to government officials and prominent industrialists, including Justice Holmes of the Supreme Court, Postmaster General Burleson, Secretary Wilson, J. P. Morgan and John D. Rockefeller, awoke immediate alarm. And a month later actual explosions took place in eight different cities, wrecking among other homes those of Federal Judge Nott and Attorney General Palmer. While responsibility for these outrages was never fixed, the public generally accepted the emphatic conclusion of Judge Nott that they represented "a concerted and criminal alien plot of the Bolsheviki. . . ."

Taking up the alarm, the *New York World* ran a series of articles in June 1919 exposing the imminent danger of Red revolution. The Bolsheviki were said to have 2,400 paid agitators in the United States, to be financing some 265 periodicals reaching a total of ten million persons, and to have won the support of anywhere from five to nine million industrial workers. Their goal was to organize "the entire country on a Bolshevik basis." An equally fantastic exposure of revolutionary activity, appearing under the name of Rheta Childe Dorr, revealed that the foreign agitators were using the trade unions, the Socialist Party, public forums, the "liberal" churches and even the public schools as the vehicles for their sinister propaganda. Arthur Wallace Dunn also took up the challenge of this "gigantic conspiracy to overthrow the government of the United States." When "reduced to cold fact," he stated, the soviet system which the Communists were seeking to establish meant simply "anarchistic control as shown by the control of Russia."

The reaction to these outbreaks of violence and to the fearful explanations of what lay behind them was a nation-wide campaign to stamp out the menace of Bolshevism. Attorney General Palmer hit back at industrial strikers with blanket injunctions, excluded radical publications from the mails, and rounded up all foreign agitators for deportation. On December 22, 1919, the transport *Buford*, popularly known as the "Soviet Ark," sailed from New York for Russia with some 249 Reds "to be taken back to where they came from." Other radical witch hunts, climaxed by mass raids upon Communist headquarters throughout the country on New Year's Day, 1920, brought into the government's dragnet over six thousand men and women suspected of Bolshevist sympathies. Most of those arrested had to be released for lack of any evidence of subversive activities, but all aliens who had radical affiliations were held for deportation.

Mounting popular hysteria soon led to attempts not only to stamp out Communist activity but to suppress all liberal movements. The expulsion of five socialist members of the New York assembly in April 1920 was one startling example of this wave of intolerance. "These two men who sit there with a smile and a smirk on their faces," cried one irate assemblyman upon perceiving two of the socialist victims of persecution, "are just as much representatives of the Russian Soviet government as if they were Lenin and Trotsky themselves. They are little Lenins, little Trotskys in our midst."

The public was in no mood to view these developments rationally. It appeared to be caught in the grip of a paralyzing fear. Events in Russia and such violence as did occur in our own industrial strife threw the country completely off balance. "My motto for the Reds," cried Guy Empey, turning the campaign of hate he had formerly directed against the Germans upon the Bolsheviki, "is S.O.S.—ship or shoot. I believe we should place them all on a ship of stone, with sails of lead, and that their first stopping-place should be hell."

In time a more realistic attitude was to reassert itself. The nation became more willing to accept the truth of Radek's perhaps reluctant assertion: "Revolutions are not carried in suitcases. It is the local conditions that can alone develop revolution." In 1919 and the following years, however, the fear that Communism would wreak the havoc in this country that it had in Russia was a nightmare to the timid.

How much the official attitude toward the Soviet government was affected by these developments was revealed in a statement

made by Secretary of State Colby, who had now replaced Secretary Lansing, on August 10, 1920. Russia had become involved in hostilities with Poland when Polish troops invaded
her territory earlier that year and for a time this new danger,
combined with the advance of the Russian Whites under Baron
Wrangel, appeared to threaten the Bolshevik regime. But the
course of the war was soon reversed. The Reds advanced victoriously toward Warsaw and Poland found herself in desperate
straits. Under these new circumstances Allied policy appeared
to be working more than ever at cross purposes. France was
ready to recognize the Wrangel government and to support
Poland, Great Britain was unwilling to accept such a program,
and Italy actually entered into informal negotiations with the
Soviet government.

The Italian ambassador in Washington thereupon inquired
of the United States as to its attitude. Our policy in the Rus-
sian-Polish war was one of strict neutrality; we would not either
recognize or aid Baron Wrangel. The days of intervention were
over. But Secretary Colby went further than the immediate
situation by answering the Italian government's inquiry with
a lengthy note that laid down the basic principles that were
to govern our policy toward Russia for over a decade.

The preamble of this document expressed the continuing
sympathy of the United States for the Russian people and for
their efforts to reconstruct their national life upon the broad
basis of popular self-government. It reaffirmed our interest in
Russia's preservation of her territorial integrity. It declared
that the American people still had complete faith in the Russian people's ultimately discovering a solution to the grave
problems confronting them. But the existing regime, Secretary
Colby emphatically stated, in no sense represented the Russian
people, had come into power through force and cunning, and
was maintaining itself in office only through savage oppression. After charging the Soviet government with disregarding
its international obligations, he then indicted it on the serious
threefold count of promoting revolutionary movements in

other countries, using diplomatic agencies as the channels for subversive intrigue and propaganda abroad, and supporting and subsidizing the Third International.

"In the view of this Government," Secretary Colby declared, "there cannot be any common ground upon which it can stand with a power whose conceptions of international relations are so entirely alien to its own, so utterly repugnant to its moral sense. There can be no mutual confidence or trust, no respect even, if pledges are to be given and agreements made with cynical repudiation of their obligations already in the minds of one of the parties. We cannot recognize, hold official relations with, or give friendly reception to the agents of a Government which is determined and bound to conspire against our institutions; whose diplomats will be the agitators of dangerous revolt; whose spokesmen say that they sign agreements with no intention of keeping them."

This note went far beyond demonstrable fact in its accusations against the Soviet government. It clearly reflected the attitude induced by American horror at the reported atrocities of the Red Terror in Russia and domestic fears of the Red Menace in the United States. Moscow promptly denied the charges as false and malicious. In a note to the Italian ambassador in Washington, Foreign Commissar Chicherin further declared that Secretary Colby was profoundly mistaken in his apparent view that normal relations between Russia and the United States were possible only if capitalism prevailed in the former country. "The Russian Soviet Government is convinced," he concluded, "that not only the working masses but likewise the far-sighted businessmen of the United States of America will repudiate the policy which is expressed in Mr. Colby's note and is harmful to American interests, and that in the near future normal relations will be established between Russia and the United States."

Under such circumstances, this highly dramatic period in the history of Russian-American relations—four eventful years witnessing our concerted action against Germany, Communist

revolution, intervention and the Great Red Scare—drew to a close. There appeared to be no ground upon which the two nations could come together. For the first time in the long history of their relations, the conflict in ideologies completely overshadowed the traditional parallelism in foreign policies. Why? The principles of Communism appeared far more antagonistic to those of American democracy than those of a reactionary Czarism had ever been. And they had a dynamic force. Imperial Russia had not sought to convert America to monarchy, but Communist Russia preached the doctrine of world revolution.

The Soviet regime, soon to conclude peace with Poland and stamp out the last vestiges of counterrevolution by overwhelmingly defeating Baron Wrangel, was firmly established. It had created a socialist state. The United States refused to recognize it and did not conceal its deep hostility to everything for which it stood. In time, Chicherin's predictions were borne out. Common interests in trade and foreign policies once again pushed ideological friction into the background. Nevertheless thirteen years passed before capitalist America and socialist Russia entered into diplomatic relations and took up the difficult task of trying to resurrect an ancient friendship.

XI

CAPITALISM VERSUS COMMUNISM

SECRETARY COLBY'S note marked a definite crystallization of American policy toward Soviet Russia. Its basis was declared to be a continuing sympathy and friendship for the Russian people and an unimpaired faith in their future. But the two principal corollaries derived from this premise could hardly be reconciled. For while we emphatically stated that in acceptance of the right of every nation to determine its own government there would be no further intervention in Russia's internal affairs, we just as unequivocally refused to recognize or have any dealings whatsoever with the government that had been established. The contradiction in these two aspects of our policy was ignored because the American people were generally convinced that the Soviet regime in no way represented the Russian people. On the contrary, the control over the country asserted by the Bolsheviki was believed to be a denial of the basic rights of free government to a people whose struggle for liberty had enlisted our warmest sympathies. Intervention had proved to be a fiasco, but it was nonetheless fervently hoped in this country that the Soviet government would be overthrown.

Our policy of nonrecognition ran counter to general historic precedent. The United States was traditionally prepared to enter into diplomatic relations with any government, whatever its origin or the bases of its power, once it had demonstrated its stability. It is true that President Wilson had departed from this policy in our relations with certain of the Latin American countries, notably Mexico, but otherwise we had never before sat in moral judgment upon the governmental system of other nations. A realistic appraisal of the situation clearly demonstrates that the United States was not primarily concerned

· 168 ·

over whether the Soviet government represented the Russian people, but over the nature of that government as it affected our national interests. We feared a Communist regime as a challenge to our own economic and political system, and those fears were emphasized by the impact upon this country of propaganda emanating from Moscow. We refused to recognize the Soviet government because we did not wish in any way to strengthen its influence, and because we hoped that such a policy would encourage revolt against Bolshevism and eventually bring Russia within the fold of democratic capitalism.

The Wilson administration thus passed on to its Republican successors a heritage of friction, ill will and hostility between the Russian and American governments that far overshadowed such sympathy between the peoples of the two nations as might have survived the troubled period of active intervention. And the Republicans were not prepared to modify our official stand or to adopt any measures looking toward an attempted reconciliation of opposing views. They too withheld recognition. One by one the other powers overcame an enmity to Communism no less vehement than our own and entered into official trade and diplomatic relations. Great Britain, France and Italy took such action in 1924; Japan the next year. But at the close of the 1920's the United States was as unwilling to accept the implications of the triumph of Communism as it had been at their start.

Soon after the inauguration of President Harding in 1921 the Soviet government took advantage of the change in administration to make a direct bid for the reopening of trade relations. A message was indirectly relayed through Maxim Litvinov, then serving as Soviet envoy in Estonia, expressing Moscow's hope that the new American government would not obdurately persist in following the old path of hostility toward the Soviets. President Kalinin of the All-Russian Central Executive Committee appealed to President Harding to take into consideration the mutual advantage of a re-establishment of business relations, and the general interests of the Russian and American peoples "which imperatively demand that the wall existing between them should be removed."

Secretary of State Hughes lost little time in effectively rebuffing this advance. There would be no change in our policy. Trade relations could not be disassociated from political relations. The whole issue, Hughes further pointed out, was in a sense academic because under existing circumstances any economic recovery in Russia was impossible. Borrowing his idea from an earlier statement by Secretary of Commerce Hoover, he said that it was idle to expect any resumption of trade until the economic bases of production, conditioned upon private property, the sanctity of contracts and free labor, were securely established. "If fundamental changes are contemplated, involving due regard for the protection of persons and property and the establishment of conditions essential to the maintenance of commerce," Hughes then continued, "this Government will be glad to have convincing evidence of the consummation of such changes, and until this evidence is supplied this Government is unable to perceive that there is any proper basis for considering trade relations."

It was all too easy to read between the lines of this sharp rejection of Russia's overtures. There should be no dealing with her so long as the Soviet government adhered to the principles of Communism. We would not interfere in Russia's internal affairs directly, but we would exert all possible indirect pressure to break down the hold of Bolshevism. The bait of American economic supplies and American markets was dangled before Russia as the prize for modifying her domestic policies to conform to those of capitalism.

Another aspect of relations with Russia also confronted the new administration in 1921, involving political rather than economic issues. Whatever our attitude toward the Bolsheviki, the United States had consistently tried to safeguard the principle of Russia's territorial integrity. President Wilson had withheld recognition of the independence of Lithuania, Latvia and Estonia, onetime Baltic provinces of Czarist Russia, and we

did not enter into diplomatic relations with them until July
1922. But far more important was the status of Siberia. Japan
had not followed the example of the United States in withdrawing her troops after the failure of intervention. She remained in control of Vladivostok, a great part of the Siberian
coastline, and even the northern half of Sakhalin. Against this
continued infringement of Russia's territorial rights, the
United States vigorously and repeatedly protested. Japanese
troops stayed on, however, and the conviction grew in this
country that Japan was seeking to win permanent possession
of eastern Siberia or to set up a nominally independent government subject to Japanese control.

Here was the very eventuality that President Wilson had
feared when he reluctantly consented to intervention. The disturbing prospect facing the United States, as at the time of the
Russo-Japanese war, was that the Pacific balance of power
would be upset. It was still to our national interest that Russia
should remain strong and powerful in the Far East, whatever
her form of government, as an offset to the increasingly threatening rise of Japanese imperialism. In the Pacific area even
embittered ideological conflict between the United States and
Russia could not wholly eclipse their common interest in
blocking the establishment of Japan upon the Asiatic mainland. Just as we had tried to restrain the ambitious ideas of
Tokyo when intervention in Siberia was first proposed, so we
now exerted even stronger pressure for the recall of all Japanese
troops from Russian territories even though the Soviet government remained anathema to us.

The issue was one of those underlying the Washington Conference which President Harding summoned in the autumn of
1921 to settle outstanding political questions in the Far East
and to bring to a halt the impending naval race in the Pacific.
Soviet Russia, despite her protests, was not invited to take part
in these negotiations. While refusing to take a step that would
have represented recognition, Secretary Hughes nevertheless
declared that protection of Russian interests "must devolve as

a moral trusteeship upon the whole conference." On the part of the United States he thereupon insisted that Japan entirely withdraw from the Asiatic mainland and allow the people of Siberia to work out their own destiny.

The Washington Conference was a distinct diplomatic triumph for the United States in compelling a Japanese retreat in eastern Asia. Whatever the ultimate consequences of our surrender of the right to fortify our naval bases in the western Pacific, as written into the naval limitation treaty, the immediate consequence of this important international meeting was Japan's acceptance of the basic tenets of our Far Eastern policy. Her withdrawal from Siberia was a part of this general settlement. Other factors entered into the situation, but in large measure through our insistence upon evacuation, the last Japanese troops quitted the Maritime Provinces of Siberia within a year of the Washington Conference. Moreover in 1925 Japan recognized the Soviet government, which had fully established its control over Siberia after the Japanese withdrawal, and she surrendered her final foothold upon Russian territory in northern Sakhalin. Had it not been for our vigorous opposition to Japanese encroachments on the Asiatic mainland from 1918 through 1921, the Soviet government might well have been robbed of this territory along the Pacific shore or found itself at war with Japan for its recovery.

While our motive in upholding Russia's territorial integrity was to safeguard our own national interests in the Far East, a generous humanitarianism was responsible for a simultaneous move in behalf of the Russian people themselves. A run of poor harvests, greatly aggravated by the ravages of civil war and the consequent collapse of agricultural production in many parts of the country, caused a devastating famine in Russia between 1921 and 1923. The famous Russian author, Maxim Gorky, appealed to "all honest Europeans and Americans" for aid and through Herbert Hoover, in his capacity of Director-General of the American Relief Administration, there was an immediate popular response to this cry for help. Upon receiving satis-

factory assurances that our activities would in no way be restricted. Hoover marshaled all available resources for a far-reaching relief program. American generosity had in the past come to the assistance of the people of Czarist Russia; it now came to the aid of those of Communist Russia.

Although there was some opposition on the part of members whose enmity for Communism made them balk at even humanitarian relief, Congress appropriated some $20,000,000 for supplies and released a considerable quantity of surplus foodstuffs held by the War Department. An additional $26,000,000 was raised through private contributions and the Red Cross. In all, there were exported to Russia some 700,000 metric tons of food which was then distributed among the Russian people by a staff of two hundred Americans and eighty thousand Russians under the direction of Colonel William N. Haskell. No difficulties were experienced in carrying through this program and the Soviet government gratefully cooperated with the American Relief Administration. "Through this service," Colonel Haskell later reported, "America has not only saved millions of lives, but has given impulse to the spiritual and economic recovery of a great nation, and on our own behalf we have created in the assurance of goodwill from the Slav races a great inheritance for our children."

Neither protection of Russian interests at the Washington Conference nor famine relief, however, brought about any change in the political relations between the American and Russian governments. The frightened and hysterical tone which had characterized both official and unofficial attacks upon Bolshevism gradually gave way to more tempered expressions. There was less emotion and perhaps somewhat more reason in our attitude toward the Soviet government. But the underlying hostility was still there. While the trade embargo had finally been lifted in July 1920 and short-time credits were available for Russian purchasers, no further concessions whatsoever were made in regard either to a commercial accord or diplomatic recognition. The United States did not take part in the conferences held at Genoa and The Hague at which the Allied Governments tried to discover a basis for general European reorganization in cooperation with both Germany and Russia. We adhered strictly to the attitude that all such negotiations were entirely futile until a change of government in Russia made possible the re-establishment of her productive capacity.

When President Coolidge came into office in 1923 upon the death of Harding, there momentarily appeared a ray of hope that internal developments in Russia might make possible a renewal of commercial relations. Lenin had decreed adoption of the New Economic Policy, definitely modifying the doctrinaire principles of Marxian socialism. Referring to conditions in Russia in his first message to Congress, the new President noted "encouraging evidences of returning to the ancient ways of society." The favor of the United States was not for sale, he declared, but he was willing to make large concessions in the interests of closer collaboration between the two governments "for the purpose of rescuing the Russian people."

Three conditions were then suggested as essential requisites for any change in our policy: compensation for American citizens who had been deprived of their property through the confiscatory decrees of the Soviet government, recognition of the debts of the Kerensky government and abatement of the active spirit of enmity to American institutions. Whenever there was real evidence of these conditions having been met, Coolidge concluded, "our country ought to be the first to go to the economic and moral rescue of Russia."

Grasping at any straw which appeared to hold out the possibility of resuming normal trade, the Soviet government immediately declared its willingness to enter into negotiations with the United States upon the issues Coolidge had raised. But despite the relatively conciliatory tone of the presidential message to Congress, Secretary Hughes abruptly slammed the door shut again. "There would seem at this time no reason for

negotiations," he curtly replied to the overtures made by Foreign Commissar Chicherin. If the Soviet government wished to take the steps outlined by President Coolidge, he declared that it could do so without entering into any conference with the United States. And until such steps had been taken there would be no point in negotiations. "Most serious," Hughes concluded, "is the continued propaganda to overthrow the institutions of this country. This Government can enter into no negotiations until these efforts directed from Moscow are abandoned."

The bases for our nonrecognition policy were now more clearly admitted to be dislike of Communism rather than the inability of the Soviet government to speak for the Russian people. Propaganda was generally accepted as the sharpest point at issue. Under such circumstances no further gesture toward cooperation, even as tentative and conditional as that of President Coolidge, would be made again for a decade. Secretary Hughes remained convinced that we could not deal with the Soviets. His successor in office, Secretary Kellogg, was if possible even more conservative in his approach to the problem. He saw the bogey of Communist propaganda on every hand, at one point hysterically warning the Senate of rampant Bolshevism in Mexico. With the advent of the Hoover administration, what had become a fixed and settled policy was again reaffirmed by Secretary Stimson.

After the recognition of the Communist regime by the other powers, the United States nevertheless found it increasingly difficult to ignore the Soviet Union. We were taking part in various nonpolitical meetings sponsored by the League of Nations where Russia too was represented, and at the preliminary disarmament conference at Geneva, Ambassador Gibson crossed swords with Maxim Litvinov, now Commissar of Foreign Affairs, over the Soviet government's proposals for total disarmament. Russia also was accepted as a signatory of the Briand-Kellogg pact for the outlawry of war negotiated in 1928—a step which some observers felt was tantamount to recognition—even though Secretary Kellogg that very year bitterly attacked her government. The Communist propaganda of the Third International, he declared, despite Moscow's adherence to this international treaty, provided conclusive evidence "of the hostile purpose of the present rulers of Russia which makes vain any hope of establishing relations on a basis usual between friendly nations."

The ambiguities of this situation were even further emphasized in 1929. When controversy over the status of the Chinese Eastern Railway led to skirmishes between Russia and China along the Manchurian border, Secretary Stimson tried to call the Soviet government to account for what he termed its violation of the anti-war pact. Litvinov struck back sharply. "The Soviet Government," he declared, "cannot forbear expressing amazement that the Government of the United States, which by its own will has no official relations with the Soviet Government, deems it possible to apply to it with advice and counsel."

Public opinion throughout these years generally supported the policy followed by the State Department. The American people as a whole remained convinced that the very existence of the Communist regime in Russia threatened the stability of capitalistic institutions. It was almost universally accepted as a fact that the Third International, the Communist Party and the Soviet government were but three faces of the same governing body in Russia, and that the Soviet government could consequently be held directly responsible for the revolutionary propaganda that remained the stock-in-trade of Communists throughout the world. There was widespread agreement with Secretary Kellogg's thesis that it was impossible to have relations with "a governmental entity which is the agent of a group which hold it as their mission to bring about the overthrow of the existing political, economic and social order throughout the world."

The Soviet government's repudiation of foreign debts also created resentment not only in itself, but because of the broader significance given to this attitude. Secretary Hughes had re-

peatedly stated that Russian policy ran so completely counter to the accepted principles of international law that there was no warrant for trying to treat with the Soviet Union in any way. The public was largely convinced that a regime that so cavalierly ignored financial obligations would be equally free in regard to any other international commitments. What profit would there be in extending diplomatic recognition to the U.S.S.R. if it felt no obligation to observe the accepted usages of the law of nations?

The course of internal events in Russia further appeared to substantiate these doubts as to the wisdom of any dealings with the Soviets in the minds of most Americans. While the Red Terror had subsided with the end of civil war, there was repeated evidence of the brutal suppression of all elements hostile to the Communist dictatorship. The campaign for the liquidation of the kulaks in 1929-1931, with its forced requisitions of grain leading to what was widely described as "organized famine," outraged public opinion throughout the United States. Even more important in offending American feelings were continued Communist attacks upon religion. The known facts of confiscation of church property, bans upon religious instruction, and atheistic propaganda based upon the theory that religion was the opiate of the people, were sufficient in themselves, even without the exaggeration of anti-Bolshevik propaganda, to create in many quarters an unrelenting opposition to any official relations with such a godless regime. Church groups, and particularly the Catholics, singled out this aspect of Communism as a decisive reason for supporting a non-recognition policy.

A minority element within the United States, steadily growing as we shall see, questioned the entire basis of our Russian policy and advocated recognition as the only realistic course we could follow. Had a popular referendum been held at any time during the 1920's, however, it is highly probable that the State Department would have received an impressive vote of confidence. It was a conservative era, none more so since the nineteenth century, and despite our high confidence in capitalist theory and practice the climate of public opinion permitted no rapprochement with the dangerous radicalism of the Soviet Union.

Entirely apart from opinion upon our official relations with Russia, there was a striking universality about the keen interest, the consuming curiosity, in all things Russian during these years. Conservative and liberal alike followed the evolution of the Soviet state with the liveliest attention. Russia had greatly interested the American people in the days of the Czars; there appeared to be an equal fascination about her in these days of Communist dictatorship. As events unrolled in Russia—the New Economic Policy, Stalin's succession to Lenin, the developing cleavage with the Trotskyists, the first Five Year Plan and the extermination of the kulaks—the public was absorbed by the exciting drama. In country clubs, smoking cars and speakeasies; in college debating societies and church discussion groups; at meetings of local chambers of commerce and of labor unions; at conventions of the American Legion, tea parties of "parlor pinks," and bankers' luncheons, Soviet Russia was a perennial subject of spirited discussion. During the hectic days of the fabulous 'Twenties, it was an engrossing conversational rival to the scandals of the Harding administration, the jazz-age revolt of youth, prohibition and gangsterism, the home runs of Babe Ruth and the gyrations of the stock market.

The information upon which all this discussion was based was vague, contradictory and generally inaccurate. A number of Americans made voyages of discovery to the never-never land of Communism and came back to share their findings enthusiastically with an avid public. But what did they find? Whatever the Soviet government chose to show them, and it was almost always interpreted in the light of what the travelers had originally gone forth to seek. They returned, these American visitors to Russia in the 1920's, either to denounce or applaud on the basis of their individual preconceptions or prejudices. And those few who did not discover either a Utopia

or a Hell revealed such contradictions and paradoxes in the land of Bolshevism that their readers groped hopelessly for some solid foundation of fact upon which they could base a satisfactory opinion of what was really happening. For all the popular interest in Russia, the cloud of ignorance and mis-understanding which settled down between the people of the two nations could hardly have been more dense.

Books on the Soviets poured from the presses in an endless stream; the number of magazine articles was legion. "There has been more said and written about Russia," Will Rogers stated in his *Saturday Evening Post* "Letters of a Self-Made Diplomat to His President" in 1926, "than there has been about Honesty in Politics and Farmers' Relief." His advice to young authors on how to get published was simply to write on this all-absorbing topic. His own contribution to popular knowl-edge of the Communist experiment was not very enlightened. He discovered that "the real fellow running the show was a Bird named Stalin," sagely reported that he had not seen "a pair of silk stockings on a single lady on the street," and answered the profound question of whether everybody in Rus-sia was happy with a flat and unequivocal, "Well, they are not." The *Post's* millions of readers were confirmed in their opinion, we may well believe, that Communism had failed.

The general tenor of books and articles on Russia was at first strongly hostile; by the middle of the 1920's there was a fair mixture of writings pro and con, and at the beginning of the 1930's at least a start toward more informed, objective treat-ment. Walter Duranty and William Henry Chamberlin were writing unusually revealing dispatches for the *New York Times* and the *Christian Science Monitor* respectively, and such im-portant books as Maurice Hindus' *Humanity Uprooted*, C. B. Hoover's *The Economic Life of Soviet Russia*, and Louis Fischer's *The Soviets in World Affairs* had begun to appear. But the general list was endless. Sherwood Eddy wrote on *The Challenge of Russia* and H. R. Knickerbocker discovered *The Red Trade Menace*. Theodore Dreiser set out on a Moscow pilgrimage and returned with *Dreiser Looks at Russia*; J. N. Darling, the cartoonist, offered an expectant public *Ding Goes to Russia*; and even Ivy Lee, public relations counsel to big business, wrote *Present Day Russia*.

The magazine articles afforded graphic—and generally confusing—accounts of Soviet setbacks, reverses and collapses, matched by equally authoritative descriptions of gains, progress and triumphs. They ranged from "See Russia and Die, Laughing" to "Toward the Millennium." One could read "Red Poison" or "These Charming Russians"; "Why Things are Better" or "The Terror That Rules Russian Life"; "Russia Returns to Capitalism" or "The Economic Seesaw"; "Bolshevism as an International Menace" or "The Soviet Union and Peace." There were articles on "Russian Nudists" and "Puritan Bolsheviks"; on "The Bathtub Comes to Russia" and "Moscow Bread Lines"; on "The Five Year Plan of Atheism" and "Russian Communism as a Religion." Other writers delved into "Russian Efficiency," "Sex Standards in Moscow," "Russian Summer Resorts," "The Soviet Attitude Toward Romance" and "Who Has a Good Time in Russia?"

Throughout the 1920's, however, the popular attitude toward Soviet Russia reflected not so much the effect of this great mass of information, or misinformation, concerning the country itself as the interaction of economic and social developments in Russia and in the United States. The problems of postwar reconstruction and the general desire on the part of the American people to return to what President Harding so infelicitously termed "normalcy," had naturally created a sharp antagonism to the disruptive and threatening forces symbolized by Moscow. Even though the hysteria of the Great Red Scare had subsided, the fear of Communist propaganda persisted and it continued to be magnified as a frightening bogey for the suppression of all criticism of the capitalist order. The identification of radical activity or liberal reform with the subversive influences of Communist Russia became an accepted technique for the defense of "the American Way."

Vociferous proponents of "one hundred per cent Americanism" saw Moscow's Red hand in every criticism of laissez-faire, and they also looked upon every suggestion of closer relations with Russia as a patriotic betrayal. Such organizations as the American Defense Society, the National Security League, the National Civic Federation, the Daughters of the American Revolution and the American Legion were the noisy vanguard of anti-Bolshevism, but their attacks upon Communism, the Third International and the Soviet government were no more vehement than those of the American Federation of Labor. At its annual convention in 1928 the Soviet regime was excoriated "as the most unscrupulous, most anti-social, most menacing institution in the world today."

There was a curious paradox in the conservative attitude. There was no period in which faith in capitalism was greater than that of the 1920's. The rising prosperity of our fabulous years of plenty, which industrialists and politicians agreed was banishing the specter of poverty from the land, was accepted as incontrovertible proof of the fundamental soundness of our economic system. And in perfect consistency with these views, conservatives generally were fully convinced that the whole Communist experiment was a hollow sham. Either it would wholly fail and the Soviet regime finally collapse, or Russia's misguided leaders would find they could save it only by abandoning their more radical doctrines and returning to capitalism. In spite of such straightforward opinions on the relative value of these two economic systems, the conservatives' fears of Communism showed no signs of abatement with our continuing prosperity. Their faith in America somehow failed to modify their instinctive feeling that the United States could not afford to run the risk of encouraging Communism by recognizing the Soviet regime, or expose itself to the possible corruption of its own principles and institutions through any direct contact with Moscow.

The minority in favor of entering into relations with the Soviets did not necessarily dispute the basic tenets of the conservative majority. It merely refused to believe that the United States would succumb to any dangerous contagion by direct dealings with a Communist state. Except among extreme left-wing factions, unable to poll more than 49,000 votes for the Communist ticket in the election of 1928, there was virtually no popular support for the doctrines of Moscow. The basis for urging recognition of the U.S.S.R. was the practical common sense advantage of resuming trade and diplomatic relations with a government which we might not like, but whose stability could no longer be denied. Obviously international contacts with Soviet Russia could not be avoided when all the rest of the world had recognized its government. The State Department was following an ostrichlike policy, according to its critics, effectively preventing through its insular and short-sighted views any possible Russian-American rapprochement.

Senator Borah, determined opponent of intervention in 1919, led the political drive for recognition. As early as 1922 he introduced a resolution into the Senate calling for such a move and expressly criticizing the State Department for maintaining official relations with the envoy of the defunct Kerensky government. His forthright stand was largely responsible for forcing Ambassador Bakhmetev's final retirement, but the State Department nevertheless continued throughout the 1920's to let the financial attaché of the old Russian embassy remain as custodian of the funds of the Provisional Government. It consistently refused to consider any change in its policy, and the handful of senators who followed Borah's lead were unable to make any progress against a forbidding stone wall of official intransigence.

The most realistic move in favor of recognition came from American commercial and industrial interests looking on Russia as a market for exports. For all their generally conservative attitude, they were not so concerned over the nature of the Soviet government, either its economic or political principles, as they were anxious to trade with it. If recognition would open the avenues of commerce, they favored recognition, believing

hat we could take care of ourselves insofar as possible con-
amination with Communism was concerned. The State Department's continued refusal to allow the granting of long-term
redits to the Soviet Union and its ban upon accepting Russian
old, on the ground that the new regime had no legal title
o it, effectively blocked the restoration of normal commerce.
ndustrial firms exporting their products to Russia wanted the
omplete removal of all such restrictions. Trade, as one observer
hrased it, was proving thicker than Bolshevism.

The promotion of its commerce had always been a major
oncern of the Soviet government in seeking recognition. Rus-
ia had very real need in her program of economic rehabilita-
ion for American products, especially machine tools, agricul-
ural implements, automobiles, tractors and trucks. Every effort
vas consequently made to overcome the obstacles imposed by
ur policy. Representatives of the various state agencies which
ontrolled foreign trade, a government monopoly under the
oviet economic system, established offices in this country to
nake contacts with American business and to purchase essen-
ial supplies. The Amtorg Trading Corporation, incorporated
n New York, acted as a general agent for the Soviet export and
mport bureaus. It was inevitably attacked as a medium for
Communist propaganda disguised as a commercial organiza-
ion, but it continued about its real business notwithstanding,
ntering into important and valuable contracts with an in-
reasing number of American firms which proved more than
villing to do business with Stalin.

Preparations for the first Five Year Plan, introduced in 1928,
rovided a further impetus to the Soviet Union's efforts to
btain industrial equipment, and there was also a demand both
or American capital and American technical assistance in pro-
noting this far-reaching economic program upon which the
ountry was embarked. Returning from a visit to Russia about
his time, William S. Wasserman, of the investment firm of
)illon, Read and Company, reported that Foreign Commissar
itvinov had told him that the Soviet government was ready to

go more than halfway in meeting any American conditions for further economic assistance. Abstention from propaganda, adequate reparation for expropriated American property, settlement of the Kerensky debt were the specific concessions he proposed for the removal of restrictions upon trade and credits.

Soviet Russia was looking to America for help. Different as its own economic system might be, it recognized both what the United States had to offer in the way of material assistance, and also how much Russia had to learn from its capitalistic rival in industrial organization and manufacturing techniques. "Ford tractors, quantity production, American efficiency," Wasserman declared, "—these are the gods of every factory worker and peasant, and the secret idols of every Communist." Despite nonrecognition, there were increasing contacts between Russian and American business, and large numbers of engineers, technicians and industrial experts from this country went to Russia under contract with the Soviet government.

In such circumstances, pressure from firms selling their products in Russia brought about a gradual modification of credit restrictions. Upon inquiry from the American Locomotive Company, the State Department declared in 1927 that while it still disapproved of the sale of Russian securities in this country, it would not object to long-term credit advances to agencies of the Soviet regime. An even more marked forward step was the extension of its official blessing the next year to a long-term contract concluded between the International General Electric Company and the Soviet government, involving settlement of the company's claims for confiscation of its property and provision for Russian purchase of from $21,000,000 to $26,000,000 of electrical equipment. This was the largest order the Soviet government had placed in the American market, and the approval of the State Department aroused widespread conjecture as to whether it foreshadowed a complete change in policy. It had no such implications, as events proved, but opponents of recognition were nevertheless alarmed at any

suggestion of modifying our anti-Soviet stand for the sake of trade promotion.

Business interests themselves, however, were becoming more and more insistent that this was exactly what should be done. By the close of the 1920's, the day when Secretary Hughes could refer to Russia as "a gigantic economic vacuum" had long since passed. Our unofficial trade was growing. Russia had become an important export market despite the State Department. In the five-year period, 1921-1925, the annual total of Russian-American trade amounted to almost $37,000,000, or approximately three-fifths of the annual prewar total with Czarist Russia, and in the next five years it rose sharply to an annual average of approximately $95,000,000, or almost twice the prewar figure. Moreover, American exports now far exceeded American imports as against a close balance prior to 1914. While this Russian trade was still no more than about 3½ per cent of the aggregate of all our foreign commerce, the definite upward trend in exports made it appear highly significant.

This was all the more important after 1929, because the United States had entered upon the dreary period of economic depression. Any market capable of absorbing American exports had become doubly valuable. But while the Soviet government succeeded for a time under the impetus of the demand created by its Five Year Plan in maintaining its foreign purchases at a rate few other countries could equal, it continued to experience great difficulties in obtaining credits and foreign exchange. To meet these problems Russian exports were expanded upon such a low price basis that there were outraged cries—in part seeking to divert attention from domestic ills—that the Soviets were wickedly dumping wheat, coal, oil, manganese and wood pulp on the American market.

In response to this new development, sensationally played up as the Red Trade Menace, the Treasury placed an embargo on the import of certain of these commodities, said to have been produced by convict labor, while a demand arose in Congress for additional restrictions to safeguard American producers. Nevertheless American business interests generally looked upon the expanding Russian market for our exports as a more important consideration. In the face of attacks directed against "the shortsighted selfishness of a few business concerns which are engaged in encouraging the building up and strengthening of a system which aims to destroy our own," they continued to demand the resumption of normal trade relations.

The Russian-American Chamber of Commerce took the lead in this intensified campaign and it was supported by such business journals as *Business Week, Barron's, Nation's Business,* and *Sales Management.* A long list of companies could also be added to the American Locomotive Company and the General Electric Company as seeking to promote trade relations. W. A. Harriman and Company held important concessions for exploiting Russian manganese resources; both the Standard Oil Company and the Vacuum Oil Company had contracts with the Soviet government; the Ford Company entered into a special deal whereby it undertook to aid in the establishment of a Russian automobile industry while in return the Soviet Union agreed to purchase automobiles, trucks and tractors to a total value of $30,000,000 over a four-year period; and the Hugh L. Cooper Company provided important technical assistance for construction of the huge Dnieprostroy Dam. There were many others. As a direct consequence of such activities, a questionnaire sent in 1932 to fifty large American firms by Jerome Davis revealed an overwhelming sentiment in favor of American recognition of the Soviet Union.

The ground was thus being prepared, despite die-hard opposition in the State Department, for a major change in American policy. As the Hoover administration drew to its close in the midst of world-wide depression, a vigorous debate was being waged throughout the country as to whether the time had not come when with proper guarantees for the protection of American interests, and adequate assurance that the Soviet government would abstain from all propaganda activity, it would not be the part of wisdom to admit officially that there was a

oviet government. Our position had in many ways become idiculous. American delegations were sitting side by side with Russian delegations at an increasing number of international onferences; the two nations were signatories of the same international treaties; we were engaged in direct trade with Russia nd very much wanted to see that trade expand. While every ther important power had long since established relations ith the U.S.S.R., the United States alone stood out in stubborn refusal to reverse its original stand.

The ideological differences were still there. An exchange of mbassadors would not suddenly reconcile them. Among an ncreasingly large number of people, conservatives now as well s liberals, however, there no longer appeared to be the insurmountable barriers that had perhaps once existed to a renewal f the old friendship formerly binding both peoples and governments. Still, the step would not be taken while the Republicans remained in office. President Hoover made no move to modify the policy he had inherited from his predecessors. It was only when the continuing crisis of the depression brought bout not only a change in administrations but a further shift a public opinion that at long last the Soviet Union was formally recognized.

RECOGNITION

POSSIBLE recognition of the Soviet Union played no part in the election of 1932, but a victory won in the name of a New Deal in domestic policies clearly foreshadowed a shift in foreign policy on so highly controversial a question where the popular division of opinion had for so long been largely along conservative and liberal lines. Moscow had been too often disillusioned to expect very much merely from a change in administration. "The policy of hunger and of the preparation of a new war," *Pravda* declared in characteristic attack upon capitalism, "will continue to remain the policy of the American bourgeoisie." There were, however, definite indications that the incoming Democrats not only intended to break away from the traditional attitude toward the Soviets, but to lose little time in doing so.

Senator Swanson, chairman of the Senate Foreign Relations Committee, predicted in December 1932 that President Roosevelt would take up the Russian-American question promptly and move "in the right direction," and a poll of his committee revealed that some thirteen or fourteen of its members favored resuming diplomatic relations. An even more significant statement was made by Alfred E. Smith before a congressional committee on economic recovery. "I believe that we ought to recognize," he declared; "I do not know of any reason for not doing so." He brushed aside the danger of subversive propaganda with the comment that he did not believe the Russians were "making headway with this Communism." His attitude was at once assailed by another prominent Democrat, former Secretary of State Colby, whose views had not changed one whit since his attack in 1920 on the hostility of the Soviet regime toward the United States. "Despite denials and concealments

and disguises employed by as subtle propaganda as the world has ever seen," he declared, "this enmity continues to be the foundation of Soviet foreign policy." But for all such outcroppings of die-hard opposition to the U.S.S.R., newspaper comment on Smith's forthright statement was in general agreement, as it most certainly would not have been a few years earlier, with the *Norfolk Pilot's* comment that it was "a pleasure to see Al blow away the cobwebs."

A first official sign of a changing attitude in Washington was Roosevelt's inclusion of President Kalinin among the heads of governments to whom he addressed his first message on peace and disarmament in May 1933. Two months later a further step along quite different lines was taken when the Reconstruction Finance Corporation underwrote the sale of $3,000,000 worth of cotton to the Soviet government. And finally on October 10, 1933, the President definitely shattered the precedent of sixteen years by formally inviting the Soviet government to enter into formal negotiations.

"Since the beginning of my administration," Roosevelt wrote Kalinin in this important note, "I have contemplated the desirability of an effort to end the abnormal relations between the one hundred and twenty-five million people of the United States and the one hundred and sixty million people of Russia. . . . If you are of similar mind, I should be glad to receive any representatives you may designate to explore with me personally all questions outstanding between our countries." From Moscow came an immediate and cordial acceptance. "There is no doubt that difficulties present or arising, between the two countries," Kalinin answered, "can be solved only when direct relations exist between them; and that, on the other hand, they have no chance of solution in the absence of such relations. . . . I shall gladly accept your proposal to send to the United States a representative of the Soviet Government to discuss with you the questions of interest to our countries."

The primary reason for this dramatic reversal in a policy so consistently followed since the Bolshevik revolution of November 1917 was the growing desire, already noted, to promote our trade with Russia. The upward trend in exports which had graphically brought home the potentialities of the Soviet market for American manufactures had been abruptly reversed. Total shipments for 1932 fell precipitately to some $13,000,000, or about one-eighth their previous peak. While general world conditions were largely responsible for this decline, advocates of closer relations with Russia could nevertheless point out that our Russian exports were about one-third the total of those of Great Britain and approximately one-tenth of Germany's. The United States could not afford the luxury, it was said, of further curtailing our trade because of ideological differences with the Soviet Union. At the London Economic Conference early in 1933, Foreign Commissar Litvinov had stated that his government was prepared to place abroad orders for $1,000,000,000 worth of goods. Since all of our trade rivals had officially recognized the U.S.S.R., it was felt that unless we now followed their example, they would be in a position to freeze us out of such a promising outlet for American machinery, ferrous metals, textiles, leather and rubber products.

There were also other factors in the world situation of the early 1930's that pointed to the desirability of entering into relations with the Soviet Union. Whatever the immediate importance of trade, President Roosevelt was undoubtedly influenced by them. Events in the Far East had once again—as in 1905 and 1921—underscored the natural identity of American and Russian interests in the face of Japanese imperialism. The Manchuria incident of 1931 marked the collapse of the whole fabric of international accords reached at the Washington Conference a decade earlier. Japan was on the march. The expansion of her political power on the Asiatic mainland was an imminent and dangerous threat both to American Far Eastern policy, symbolized by the Open Door, and to the security of the immediately adjacent territories of the Soviet Union. "Some move in the direction of normal relationships with Russia at this time," Senator Johnson stated early in 1933, "would do far

more to remove perils from the Far East, and therefore from the world in general, than any other single act."

On this count Russian-American rapprochement was perhaps even more important from the Russian than from the American point of view. The Soviet Union had abrogated the treaties wherein Imperial Russia and Japan had sought to divide their spheres of influence in Manchuria. It had shown, and would continue to show, an apparent willingness to surrender claims that had been vigorously asserted under the Czars. Nevertheless complete Japanese control of the entire territory could not fail to awaken the alarm of Russia. There were many observers in the Far East who believed war between the two nations—a repetition of the conflict of 1904—was in the long run inevitable. The Soviet Union, in any event, welcomed Secretary Stimson's refusal to recognize Manchukuo in 1932. It was anxious to establish as close relations as possible with a nation that constituted a potential threat to Japan's eastern flank should a Russo-Japanese war ever develop.

Underlying these immediate reasons for renewing relations with Russia, were those developments within both the United States and the Soviet Union which appeared to make far less formidable the obstacles to rapprochement which had loomed so large upon the international horizon during the 1920's.

Economic circumstances seemed to be at one and the same time bringing Russia closer to capitalism and the United States nearer socialism. This is not to imply that either nation was forsaking the fundamental economic or political principles upon which its government was based. This was not the case. But the Soviet Union's experience in employing the assistance of the capitalistic world in its industrial expansion and its adoption of certain capitalistic techniques within the framework of its own economic system, now coincided with American experience in certain socialistic practices and experimentation under the New Deal.

Public opinion often overemphasized the importance of these apparent trends. With increasing regimentation and government controls in this country, and recognition of the profit motive and piece work in Russia, it was believed in some quarters that the two countries might eventually end up at about the same place. Whatever the validity of such ideas, they did serve to create a more friendly and sympathetic attitude on the part of the American public toward the Soviet experiment in Communism. Economic depression modified our strictures upon unorthodox policies that were apparently succeeding. Russia had for long been paying American capitalism the compliment of adopting many of its techniques in mass production; we began to demonstrate a sneaking admiration for some aspects of the Soviet system by exploring the possibilities of a planned economy. There was a marked abatement of old hostilities even though there was still much suspicion and distrust in the air.

Another factor which must be taken into account was the enthusiastic response to various manifestations of Soviet cultural life on the part of American intellectuals. The influence of this development can hardly be evaluated, but the more sympathetic attitude toward Russia that it promoted affected liberal circles to an increasing degree. Russian art and music, Russian theater and Russian moving pictures, were hailed both as enriching the cultural inheritance of all the world and as reflecting the vitality and strength of the Communist regime. There was a tremendous vogue for everything Russian, whether it stemmed from the earlier traditions of Imperial Russia or the modernist experimentation of Soviet Russia. The Moscow Art Theatre and the Russian Ballet, exhibitions of paintings arranged by the Committee on Cultural Relations with Russia, and the memorable moving pictures produced by Eisenstein and Pudowkin all contributed to this feeling that Russia had much to offer entirely apart from either economics or politics.

Writers in the leftist journals were continually emphasizing the vitality of Russian art. In an article in the *New Republic*, John Dos Passos paid eloquent tribute to Meyerhold and the experimentation of the little theater in Moscow. Breadth, variety and dynamic aliveness marked Soviet drama, he declared,

while the theater in the United States was petering out. In the same vein Gilbert Seldes wrote of Russian moving pictures and compared such films as "Potemkin," "Ten Days That Shook the World" and "Storm Over Asia" with the more tepid offerings of Hollywood. Admitting that they were propaganda, he dwelt upon the artistic integrity they nevertheless achieved, and a moral fervor which he thought illustrated the force behind the Bolshevik revolution.

The desire to trade with Soviet Russia and the growing feeling of common interests in the Far East were more important than this cultural sympathy. The audience reached by Russian art, music, plays and moving pictures was at best a small one. Nevertheless a Theatre Guild staging of *Roar China*, the Soviet art exhibition of 1929, the productions of the Moscow Art Theatre and the extensive showings of Russian films were a part of the background for Russian-American rapprochement in 1933.

A first ground for refusing recognition in the past had been the Soviet government's expropriation of American property as a part of its general program for establishing the national ownership of all means of production. In a number of cases, however, restoration had already been made. In entering into trade relations with the Soviet government, American firms had made individual settlements of all outstanding claims a part of their sales contracts. The demand for restitution of property had consequently lost much of its force. It was more generally accepted that remaining claims could well be made a subject for friendly negotiation, set against counterclaims of the Soviet government. Moscow had long since declared its willingness to discuss all such issues with a view toward adjustments equitable for all concerned.

The interrelated and even more delicate question of repudiation of the Russian foreign debt offered perhaps greater difficulties. But here, too, the Soviet government had shown a willingness to meet our demands halfway on condition that the United States would in turn recognize the claims of the Soviets for damages and losses resulting from American intervention in 1918. Controversial as this issue might be, moreover, it could not be considered an impossible obstacle to recognition. Debt repudiation was no longer a unique practice or a Communist monopoly. The whole system of intergovernmental debt payments had broken down under the impact of world depression. Six states, including France, had suspended all advances on their indebtedness in 1933; Great Britain and Italy were making only token payments. However conditions might differ in their cases, and however little we liked the action taken by our former Allies, there was no valid reason to single out Soviet Russia as the only debt defaulter with whom we would refuse to have economic or political relations.

Still more important was the propaganda issue. The declared aim of the Communists to overthrow capitalism and establish the dictatorship of the proletariat by revolutionary upheavals throughout the world had been consistently emphasized for sixteen years as the final and conclusive reason why the United States could have no dealings with Moscow. The Soviet government's denials of sponsoring such revolutionary propaganda were brushed aside because its officials were also the officials of the Third International, admittedly the directive of Communist activities in this country, as well as in all other capitalistic nations. No technicalities could alter the popular conviction, which has never been satisfactorily proved or disproved, that the Soviet government was actively intervening in our domestic affairs through direct aid and support for the small but highly articulate band of American Communists.

After 1928, however, a shift in emphasis upon the aims of Russian Communism held out the hope that Moscow's propagandist zeal was diminishing, and that we no longer had to fear its subversive influence. Not only the public statements of Stalin and other leaders of the Soviet Union, but the general policy they were pursuing clearly showed that their attention was centering more and more upon the task of building socialism at home. The principal task of Communism had become

the establishment of economic and social stability in Russia, wherever possible with the cooperation of capitalistic countries, rather than any further dissipation of its energies in fomenting a world revolution that failed to materialize.

The new direction given to Communist policy, marking a complete reversal of the earlier doctrine that Bolshevism could succeed only with world revolution, had not been brought about without grim and bitter internal conflict within Communist ranks. Some of the old Bolsheviks under the leadership of Trotsky fought adoption of the new party line advocated by Stalin as a betrayal of the revolution. But victory rested with the adherents of the new program. Trotsky himself was driven into exile, his followers expelled from the party, and soon all who clung to the old doctrines or who opposed Stalin's iron-handed dictatorship found themselves on trial for their lives as traitors to the state. While there was no reason to believe that Communism had permanently abandoned its long-term revolutionary aims, they appeared in 1933 to have been definitely subordinated to more immediate internal goals.

Newspaper and magazine comment demonstrated the marked extent to which these various developments had won over popular opinion to the projected change in our policy. The conservative-liberal line-up of the 1920's had not entirely broken down, but where hostility to the Soviets had been most pronounced there was at least a striking moderation of earlier views. Such magazines as *Harper's, Scribner's,* the *Forum* and *Collier's* showed a definite shift in opinion. Even the *Saturday Evening Post* now reluctantly admitted the advantages of closer trade relations with Russia. A poll conducted by the American Foundation among twelve hundred newspapers throughout the country, reported 63 per cent of those answering the questionnaire as favoring recognition. An additional 10 per cent were prepared to accept it under certain conditions, and only 27 per cent definitely opposed it. Three things were emphasized in these statements: the proved stability of the Soviet regime, the opinion that its political and economic philosophy was none of our concern and the imperative need to expand American trade.

Many newspapers also pointed out that the United States and Russia had a compelling interest in the preservation of world peace which should draw them together in the twentieth century as it had in the nineteenth. Their foreign policies generally followed parallel lines, one paper said, and they were already "marching side by side in the Orient." The *Christian Century* declared that for all the difference in their methods, they were at one in the basic objectives of a domestic program "to do away with want and injustice and to increase human opportunity." The comments of the press in general marked a far departure from the bitter antagonisms of a decade earlier. Time had modified the fears aroused by the first impact of the Bolshevik revolution and softened the harsh judgments of the Soviets' most implacable foes. It was not that the country had become reconciled to Communism or expected for a moment that recognition would resolve all ideological conflict. There was a note of caution in most of these expressions of opinion. Even the foremost advocates of recognition admitted serious reservations as to its possible consequences. The general reaction to Roosevelt's move to extend the Good Neighbor policy to Soviet Russia was perhaps most aptly summed up in the phrase of one editorial writer, "Let's see how it all works out."

Under these circumstances, generally creating a more favorable atmosphere than at any time since 1917, the United States and the Soviet Union held their first official negotiations in the autumn of 1933. The Russian representative appointed to meet with President Roosevelt was Foreign Commissar Litvinov. No better envoy could possibly have been selected than this plump, smiling, good-natured diplomat who so completely belied the popular conception of a Communist. Here was no long-haired, fiercely bearded Bolshevik, a dagger in one hand and a smoking bomb in the other. Litvinov bore no more resemblance, in either appearance or manner, to the cartoonist's stock drawing of a Russian Red than did the average American businessman.

Moreover there was no Communist leader who had shown a greater interest in restoring Russian-American friendship since the very first days of the revolution. Litvinov had wanted to come to the United States as an ambassador of good will in 1918, he appealed to President Wilson for American friendship during the Paris peace conference, and he had forwarded to President Coolidge the Soviet's unsuccessful bid for recognition in 1923. It was now his major objective, he told reporters upon landing in this country, to legalize the "reciprocal gravitation" of two nations which had "had no conflicts in the past and cannot anticipate them in the future."

Between November 8 and November 16 a series of private meetings was held at the State Department and at the White House at which Secretary Hull and Foreign Commissar Litvinov, and then President Roosevelt, thoroughly discussed all points at issue between Russia and the United States. Only the most brief and uncommunicative announcements of these conversations were made to the press, and there is still no public record of them. Just what may have been said in the course of the negotiations is not known. Upon their conclusion, however, the State Department released an official exchange of notes between Litvinov and the President which marked the formal establishment of diplomatic relations between the two governments, and set forth in general terms the common understanding that had been reached upon the issues that had for so long barred recognition.

Five matters were treated in this brief correspondence. Litvinov pledged his government to extend to American nationals in Russia the "free exercise of liberty of conscience and religious worship" as prescribed by existing laws and the conventions already concluded with other nations. He guaranteed their rights in regard to legal protection upon a basis no less favorable than that enjoyed in the U.S.S.R. by nationals of the most favored nation. Upon the related problems of the two nations' financial claims upon each other and outstanding debt obligations, he agreed that they should be considered together in later negotiations. All Soviet claims arising out of the military activities of American forces in Siberia were waived, moreover, and Litvinov joined with the President in issuing a statement that their exchange of views on debts and claims as a whole "permits us to hope for a speedy and satisfactory solution of these questions which both our Governments desire to have out of the way as soon as possible."

Finally, and most important, was the understanding reached upon the vexed issue of propaganda. The Soviet Commissar definitely stated on this point that it would be the fixed policy of his government "to respect scrupulously the indisputable right of the United States to order its own life . . . and to refrain from interfering in any manner in the internal affairs of the United States, its territories or possessions." It would itself refrain from all revolutionary propaganda and restrain all persons under its control from any such activity. Furthermore it would also be the fixed policy of his government, Litvinov declared, "not to permit the formation or residence on its territory" of any organization whose aim was the overthrow of the political or social order of the United States.

Concessions were made on both sides in the resumption of relations under these conditions. The United States abandoned its original position of demanding complete settlement of all claims and debts before recognition; the Soviet Union expressly assumed its debt obligations and surrendered its counterclaims in Siberia, although not in North Russia. We were prepared to extend full facilities for Russian trade, and the Soviet government pledged itself to refrain from all propaganda. Relations were restored, that is, on the practical basis that their respective forms of government were the two nations' own concern, and that they would henceforth seek to cooperate along such commercial or diplomatic lines as appeared to be to their mutual advantage.

The conclusion of the accord was hailed in both Washington and Moscow as a constructive step toward the revival of Russian-American friendship. Newspapers in this country greeted

it with almost universal approval. There was a temperate note in much of the editorial comment, and warnings that too much should not be expected in the way of any great increase in our trade. Nevertheless such conservative organs as the *New York Times* and the *Herald Tribune* expressed the firm hope that recognition would usher in a new era in the relations between the two countries. The *Baltimore Sun* declared that the move was only common sense; the *Cleveland Plain Dealer* characterized it as a triumph for realism, and the *Boston Herald* said that any other policy would be purely fanciful. Touching upon both the commercial and political advantages of recognition, the *Louisville Courier-Journal* declared that it would enable the United States "to stand with the strongest force for peace and disarmament in Europe."

Liberal organs naturally greeted with enthusiasm a development that they had long urged. In a world where the rise of Japanese imperialism and the triumph of Hitlerism in Germany already foreshadowed the approaching crisis of war, they were particularly encouraged over the new prospects for collective security that might result from Russian-American collaboration in foreign affairs. "It means more even than the return of common sense after the long reign of fantasy and fear," the *Nation* applauded. "It means the creation of a new force for peace in an international situation bristling with imminent conflicts."

For a time the promise of rapprochement held out in the Roosevelt-Litvinov exchange of notes appeared to be realized. The utmost cordiality marked the exchange of ambassadors that soon took place. The Soviet Union sent Alexander Troyanovsky as its first official representative to Washington; the United States designated William C. Bullitt for the post at Moscow. The latter appointment had in it an element of retribution in the light of Bullitt's unsuccessful efforts in 1919 to persuade the Allies to accept the peace proposals that he had brought back from his secret mission to Moscow during the Paris peace conference. He now reported the most friendly reception at the Russian capital, publicly expressing on a brief visit to this country, early in 1934, his conviction that the Soviet Union was firmly committed to a policy of international peace. He had every confidence, Bullitt further stated, in the integrity and sincerity of the Soviet leaders.

Negotiations for the settlement of questions still outstanding between the two governments, however, soon ran into unexpected snags, while other difficulties developed on both the trade and propaganda fronts. The Good Neighbor spirit proclaimed by Roosevelt and echoed in Moscow could not overcome so easily the suspicions and distrust of sixteen years. Russian-American friendship, for all the lively hopes entertained in both countries, was once again jeopardized by serious disagreements and mutual recriminations.

Discussions on the debt issue had been started at once by Ambassador Bullitt in Moscow. The American claims against the Soviet government amounted to some $188,000,000 (without interest) in the so-called Kerensky loans, representing our advances to the Provisional Government in 1917, and a total of $400,000,000 as compensation for American property confiscated by the Bolsheviki under their nationalization decrees. Against these demands the Soviet government presented claims to an unspecified amount for the damage done Russian property as a result of American intervention at Archangel. Both governments were willing to set these claims off against each other and to compromise upon a reasonable sum for the net amount still owing the United States. We were prepared to scale down the total to $150,000,000; Moscow offered to pay $100,000,000. No real difficulties consequently stood in the way of agreement on this phase of the negotiations. The United States, indeed, did not balk at accepting Russia's low figure.

A final settlement depended, however, on one other vital factor. The Soviet government conditioned any debt agreement upon our willingness to grant it further loans. The United States declared it was unable to do so. While it was willing to grant long-term credits through the Export-Import Bank, at

interest rates including provision for the gradual repayment of the original debt, an outright loan was blocked by the ban imposed by the Johnson Act upon any further loans to governments already in default. The Soviet government nevertheless insisted on this point, and Foreign Commissar Litvinov declared that a new loan had been promised in the understanding reached at Washington. The grounds for the Soviet Union's position were that it could not recognize its indebtedness to the United States upon any other terms without wholly invalidating settlements already reached with other countries in which corresponding claims had been completely waived.

The negotiations were shifted from Moscow to Washington in an attempt to overcome this impasse, but neither government would make any further concessions. Each felt the other was standing upon technicalities that concealed the promotion of selfish interests. After a final brief interview between Secretary Hull and Ambassador Troyanovsky on February 1, 1935, negotiations were abruptly terminated. The State Department bluntly announced that they had collapsed because of the Soviet government's refusal to accept the American proposals. It thereupon pointedly rebuked the U.S.S.R. for its alleged failure to live up to the terms of the Roosevelt-Litvinov understanding by abolishing our consulate-general at Moscow and reducing the embassy staff.

In the meantime, however, trade negotiations were making much more favorable progress, and in striking contrast to the failure on debts a commercial treaty was signed at Moscow in July 1935. In return for our extension to Russian products of all tariff concessions granted to similar imports from other countries under the terms of our reciprocal trade agreements, the Soviet Union undertook to make purchases in this country over the next twelve month period amounting to $30,000,000.

Satisfactory as this agreement was in some respects, the relatively small total for which Russia contracted nevertheless underscored the failure of our trade to expand as much as had been expected. Our exports had previously fallen, as we have seen, from over $100,000,000 to some $13,000,000. Guaranteed purchases of $30,000,000 consequently represented a marked gain, but one which still fell far short of our original hopes. The difficulties Russia continued to experience in obtaining satisfactory credits in this country as a result of the failure of debt negotiations were held to be partly responsible for this. There was a general feeling of disappointment in business circles that the fruits of recognition had not proved more worthwhile.

The summer of 1935 was nevertheless marked by the rise of more serious controversy between Russia and America than any misunderstandings growing out of debt or trade developments. At the seventh session of the Third Communist International—or "Comintern," as it was now more generally called —reports were officially made upon the progress of Communist propaganda in the United States. Our State Department at once vigorously protested through Ambassador Bullitt and called the Soviet government to account for what it termed a flagrant violation of the antipropaganda pledges made by Foreign Commissar Litvinov at Washington. The continuance of such activity by the Comintern, it was stated, would preclude the maintenance of normal friendly relations between the United States and the Soviet Union.

The sharp tone of this thinly veiled ultimatum aroused deep resentment in Moscow. The Soviet government, categorically stating that it could not "take upon itself, and has never taken upon itself, obligations of any kind with regard to the Communist International," refused to accept our protest. The ball was thus passed back to the United States in as challenging form as we had thrown it at Russia. Secretary Hull was constrained to handle the issue carefully if it was not to lead to an open break. Without further direct reply to Moscow, he consequently declared that the United States would await developments but that if the Soviet government countenanced further propaganda "the friendly and official relations between the two countries cannot but be seriously impaired."

The incident was highly disturbing—and all the more so for occurring within less than two years of recognition. It was widely questioned, however, whether Secretary Hull had been justified in adopting such a harsh attitude toward Russia. While there were possibly just grounds for our protest, the meeting of the Comintern actually demonstrated a striking moderation in its attitude toward revolutionary propaganda, and it clearly revealed not the strength but the weakness of the Communist movement in this country. Even conservative papers were not unduly excited over the issue Secretary Hull had raised, while liberal organs accused him of attacking the Soviet Union in order to offset charges that the New Deal was too receptive to socialist theories.

Friction between America and Russia was all the more regretted, moreover, because a growing tension in international affairs throughout the world was doubly emphasizing the importance of their solidarity. We had recognized the Soviet Union in the hope that it would make possible cooperation not only in trade but in foreign policies. "It is tragic," the *New Republic* wrote, "that the two most powerful nations and those whose interests are most nearly identical should quarrel without reason."

XIII

THE FAILURE OF A UNITED FRONT

THE five years from 1935 through 1939 were the most critical in modern history. The so-called "have-not" nations threatened the world with war in their ruthless determination to seize by force whatever territories they desired, and those powers whose goal was peace and international stability met the challenge of aggression with divided counsels and conflicting policies. Soviet Russia took the lead in demanding a United Front, calling upon the democracies to uphold collective security at whatever risk. But their conservative leaders appeared to fear Communism as a possibly even greater menace than Fascism. Chamberlain and Daladier followed the sorry road of appeasement, while Roosevelt, under isolationist pressure, subscribed to a program of illusory neutrality. The pacific-minded nations were unable to resolve their mutual suspicions and to join in common defense of their national security until global war gave final proof of the indivisibility of peace.

While the developing crisis in Europe involved most directly England and France on the one hand, and Germany on the other, its repercussions were world-wide and the roles played by Russia and America could not fail to have a critical significance. Together they might have succeeded in establishing an effective bloc to combat aggression, commanding Anglo-French support and confronting the Axis Powers with an array of economic and military might so formidable as to compel them to renounce their ambitions. But far from working together, the United States and the Soviet Union drifted further apart during these decisive years. Their common objective in the maintenance of peace, both in Europe and in Asia, was wholly lost to sight in the persistent conflict of opposing ideologies. A collaboration

that might have averted war never even entered the realm of possibility amid the confusions and fears of the 1930's.

The policy pursued by Russia, viewed with mistrust and suspicion at the time, followed what we can now see was a wholly logical pattern. It was based upon self-interest, and complete realism. Deeply involved in a far-reaching program of economic reconstruction, there was no nation to whom peace was a more vital necessity. The triumph of the Fascist forces symbolized by Mussolini and Hitler, together with the rise of Japanese militarism, gave a dread reality to the fears of foreign attack harbored by the Kremlin ever since 1918. Stalin had set aside the program of world revolution as a possible defense for Communism, and he was seeking aid wherever he could find it to build up the national security of the Soviet Union. His policy was one "of cultivating peace and friendly trading relations with all nations."

Russia signed nonaggression treaties with her neighbors, entered into a mutual assistance pact with France, and supported every move made by the League of Nations, which she had finally joined the year after American recognition, to promote disarmament and restrain military aggression. As the spokesman for Soviet policies at Geneva, Foreign Commissar Litvinov early and late urged effective measures to bring the armaments race upon which all Europe was engaged to a halt, making his own radical proposals for the total abolition of all arms and strongly backing up the more limited but still far-reaching program submitted by the United States. When the League conference finally broke up in failure in 1934, he unsuccessfully urged that it be kept alive as a continuing organization in order to provide the means for further American cooperation in international affairs.

Soviet Russia was also ready to enforce League sanctions against Italy when Mussolini wrote the first chapter of Fascist aggression in his wanton attack upon Ethiopia. She bitterly repudiated the farce of nonintervention during Spain's civil war and accepted the challenge of German and Italian support

for General Franco by directly helping the Loyalist government. She took part in the Brussels conference, summoned to
meet the crisis caused by Japan's onslaught upon China in
1937, vigorously urging effective action to re-establish a just
peace in the Far East. On every possible occasion Litvinov
strongly declared that the policy of his government "was, is,
and will be a policy for peace."

As Russia thus looked more and more to collective security
to ward off the mounting threat of war, the same potential
danger drove the United States deeper into isolation. The
enemy was not near at hand. The Atlantic Ocean would be our
equivalent of nonaggression pacts and the enforcement of
sanctions. Discouraged and disillusioned by the trend of events
in Europe, and believing that we could safely protect our own
interests whatever happened in the rest of the world, the American people were the first to reject the doctrine that peace was
indivisible.

The widespread feeling throughout the country that the
purposes for which the United States had gone to war in 1917
had been betrayed was a fundamental cause for our attitude.
The great crusade to make the world safe for democracy had
led only to the rise of Fascism and a renewal of Europe's age-
old quarrels. The bitter aftermath of war had been wrangling
over debts and unsavory charges of the role the munitions makers had played in forcing intervention. For a time after the
Far Eastern crisis in 1931 it had almost appeared that the
United States was ready to abandon isolation, but the public
soon withdrew its support from these tentative gestures toward
international collaboration. The failure of the League even to
attempt to restrain Japan in any decisive fashion, the breakdown
of disarmament, the ineffectiveness of the measures dealing with
Italian aggression and Anglo-French surrender to Germany in
the Rhineland convinced this country that collective security
was doomed. Congress undertook to insulate the United States
from what was now believed to be the certainty of another war
rather than to seek to avert it by joining a United Front against

aggression. A neutrality policy was adopted in 1935 whose objective was to avoid all possible foreign entanglements and prevent the repetition of those developments that had brought us into war in 1917.

The very fact that Soviet Russia was now in the forefront of the movement for collective security seemed to intensify this new trend toward isolation. The old fear of Communism exerted its pervasive influence on public opinion. Russia's proposals for disarmament at Geneva and her declared willingness to impose sanctions against aggressor nations were discredited as moves designed to promote world revolution rather than to bulwark world peace. Some ulterior purpose was seen behind every move Litvinov made toward international cooperation. His demand at the Brussels conference for effective measures not only to combat Japan's new aggression but to re-establish the bases for enduring peace in Eastern Asia was interpreted as an attempt to sow dissension among the Western democracies.

Was the Soviet government entirely sincere in its protestations in favor of peace? Was there any real warrant for our refusal to accept at their face value the pacific pledges repeatedly made by Moscow? Our suspicions were not entirely spun out of thin air. The armaments program of the Soviet Union, the secrecy which shrouded so much of the Kremlin's activity for all the apparent openness of the declarations of policy at Geneva, and above all the continued interference of the Comintern in the domestic affairs of foreign countries, provided at least some grounds for the widespread feeling that the U.S.S.R. continued to hope that circumstances might enable it to impose Communism upon the rest of the world. While the Comintern was soft-pedaling its revolutionary program, Communist parties throughout the world still followed Moscow's direction in supporting only such policies as were primarily in the interests of Soviet Russia. Nevertheless the evidence of our own envoys in Moscow, and that of many other observers, repeatedly emphasized the absorption of the Soviet Union in its program of national rehabilitation and its consequent vital concern over security from war. The strongest ground for accepting the sincerity of Russia's devotion to collective security was that it was so directly in her own interests. Stalin was essentially practical and realistic in his appraisal of the world situation.

Our new ambassador in Moscow, Joseph E. Davies, perhaps saw more clearly what was actually happening in Russia and evaluated the Kremlin's policies more soundly than any other American in official life. He reached his post in January 1937, with the immediate assignment of seeking renewal of the Russian-American trade agreement first concluded in 1935, and was further instructed to hold himself in readiness to take up at any time the difficult and still unsettled problem of debts. No trouble was experienced on the first of these issues. The Soviet government once again agreed to continue the old arrangement, promising to increase its purchases in the United States to $40,000,000 during 1937 in return for most-favored nation treatment on our imports of Russian goods. As subsequently revealed, Moscow was also anxious to reach an understanding on debts. Reversing the position it had originally insisted upon, the Soviet Foreign Office now stated that Russia did not need an American loan. In June 1938 Davies was presented with a written proposal, officially approved by Stalin, which he was requested to discuss directly with President Roosevelt. The prompt and generous response of the Soviet officials to all his overtures for the settlement of these problems convinced our ambassador of their good faith, and of the Soviet Union's strong desire to maintain the friendliest possible relations with the United States.

Davies' observations upon other phases of foreign and domestic policy confirmed the favorable impression he had received from his own negotiations on matters of exclusively American interest. In his reports to the State Department, many of them later published in his best-selling book *Mission to Moscow*, Ambassador Davies repeatedly emphasized his conviction that the leaders of Soviet Russia were honest, forthright

and sincere. He believed that their policy, as dictated by the growing menace of Hitlerism on the west and Japanese militarism on the east, was one of peace, and that with "very little activity on the part of the Comintern," there was no danger from Communism so far as the United States was concerned. Finally, Davies declared that Soviet Russia was more friendly to the United States than to any other nation, that our common interest in world peace was a strong bond, and that everything possible should be done to promote a Good Neighbor Policy for "friendly relations in the future may be of great general value."

The American public did not at the time have access to the objective, reasoned reports of Ambassador Davies. On the contrary, everything which it heard of Soviet Russia tended to deepen the hostility so long felt toward Communism. Set against the pacific speeches of Litvinov at Geneva and the Kremlin's adherence to principles of collective security were developments within Russia that shocked and horrified popular opinion in their brutal denial of democratic rights. Furthermore there was apparent evidence of the continued subversive activities of the Comintern. The seemingly insurmountable obstacle to American confidence in the declared aims of Soviet statesmanship, and to any real measure of Russian-American collaboration, remained a conflict in social and political principles completely submerging the underlying identity in the goals of foreign policy.

The violent and bloody purges of 1937 and 1938 first deadened the admiration we had begun to feel for Soviet Russia. The tremendous forward strides she had made in economic reconstruction and the promise of political reform believed to be implicit in the Constitution of 1936 were overshadowed by the terrible spectacle of mass trials and cold-blooded executions of all suspected enemies of the state. Whatever their supposed justification, they could not be reconciled with our own ideals of justice and individual liberty. The mysterious nature of these arbitrary arrests, trials and punishments only added to the horror with which the American public read of them. In later years they were interpreted as a ruthless but imperative suppression of treason. "There were no Fifth Columnists in Russia in 1941," Davies has written, "—they had shot them." Regardless of whether such an easy dismissal of the political implications of the purges is wholly justified, Americans could not in any event condone the trials at the time. Communist tyranny was interpreted as a sign of the inherent weakness as well as of the inherent evil of the Soviet state.

Occasional voices were raised to declare that however indefensible the methods employed by Stalin in stamping out all opposition and subversive activity, they should not blind American opinion to the dangers that drove him to adopt such a policy. Writing in the summer of 1937, Walter Duranty regretted that the Kremlin's enemies were able to use the bewildered reaction of the world to the Communist purges as a means of weakening the international prestige of the U.S.S.R. More generally, however, there was nothing but condemnation for the trials that carried over to every phase of Soviet policy and practice. William H. Chamberlin, formerly regarded as an objective if not friendly observer, wrote of the "brutalitarian state" and contributed to the *American Mercury* an article on "Stalin: Portrait of a Degenerate," in which he compared him to "Scarface" Al Capone and described Russia as a terror-ridden madhouse. Even the *Nation* and the *New Republic*, once such strong defenders of the Soviets, bitterly condemned the trials and executions. In "A Letter to Stalin," Bruce Bliven called upon the Russian leader to withdraw from the dictatorship and open the way to a legal opposition to the Communist Party as the only means for restoring American confidence in Russia.

At the same time Communist agitation in this country, now directed toward organizing a United Front against Fascism in accordance with the new party line, was no less resented because the emphasis upon world revolution had abated. It was still interference in our internal affairs. It still constituted an undercover threat to democratic capitalism. The Communists were

advocating policies believed to be dictated by Moscow in the interests of Soviet Russia without regard to either the domestic or foreign objectives of American policy. Moreover they appeared to be making headway in gaining new converts to their cause under the pretense of bringing all democratic elements into the United Front, appealing both to radicals discontented with the slow progress of reform in rooting out the evils of capitalism, and to liberal and pacifist groups which despaired of the pusillanimous attitude of conservative governments in the face of Fascist aggression. There was no question of the Communists' control over some few leftwing unions in the C.I.O. and of their dominant influence in other radical organizations. They were aggressively active in the League for Peace and Democracy and in the American Youth Congress.

While the actual number of American Communists may not have materially increased at this time, a resolute army of "fellow travelers" zealously followed the party line, and the movement as a whole made up in zeal and determination what it may have lacked in numerical strength. Conservative alarms were inevitably awakened. Conforming, however innocently, to the doctrines of Nazi propaganda seeking to build up Communism as more than ever a world menace, isolationists and reactionaries were once again on the warpath. Something like the witch hunts directed against the Reds in 1919 and 1920 were repeated in wholesale attacks upon all those suspected of any radical sympathies or undue friendship for the Soviet Union. The Dies Committee, authorized by Congress to investigate all subversive activity in the United States, almost completely disregarded Fascist propaganda in its zeal to ferret out every possible shred of evidence disclosing alleged Communist influence. Scores of moderate liberals were accused of being pro-Communist because they were associated with organizations supporting the United Front. As an indication of how conservative reaction took advantage of this situation, there were even attempts to block the progressive policies of the New Deal through the implication that they were inspired by Communism.

The popular indignation aroused by Communist agitation, whether real or imaginary, deepened hostility toward Moscow just as purported Bolshevist plots had poisoned our relations with the Soviet Union in the immediate postwar period. The United Front, a large part of the American public firmly believed, was but another weapon in the armory of Communist propaganda. Its purpose was not to promote collective security but to confuse and divide the democracies. Many Americans made no secret of their belief that Stalin's dictatorship was not only as ruthless and tyrannical as Hitler's, but even more hostile to democracy because it was the directing force behind the Comintern. In conservative circles at least, it was hoped that if war broke out in Europe, it might somehow be channeled into a crusade against Communism and accomplish the purposes which Allied intervention had failed to achieve in 1918.

As America allowed these various developments at home and abroad to feed her growing distrust of Soviet Russia and committed herself ever more firmly to isolation as a foreign policy, events in Europe were hurrying toward the final tragic failure of collective security. After quietly absorbing Austria, Hitler demanded the recovery of the Sudetenland from Czechoslovakia. In panic and confusion the democracies prepared to appease the aggressor and at Munich they surrendered supinely to the Nazi dictator. A four-power pact was concluded among Great Britain, France, Germany and Italy on September 29, 1938, with the dismemberment of Czechoslovakia accepted as the basis for an illusory peace. It paved the way for Hitler's complete conquest of Czechoslovakia the following spring, for Mussolini's occupation of Albania and for the attack upon Poland. Aggression was given a clear signal to go ahead. Nevertheless Prime Minister Chamberlain returned from his travels to tell cheering crowds in London of "peace in our time."

Neither the United States nor Russia took part in the ill-fated negotiations at Munich. But for quite different reasons.

We were wholly committed to our policy of neutrality. Roosevelt's appeals for peace on the eve of the crisis were little more than a perfunctory gesture, as our determination to avoid any entanglement in European affairs had been made abundantly clear. The door to possible Russian participation, however, was slammed shut by England and France. Although it had agreed with France to come to the aid of Czechoslovakia in the event of attack by Germany, and was ready to stand by its pledges, the Soviet Union was completely ignored. It was neither invited to take part in the Munich conference nor consulted upon decisions in which it was quite as much concerned as any of the participants. Moscow was ostracized.

"To avoid a problematic war today," Litvinov declared at Geneva in emphasizing his government's readiness to cooperate with France in immediate military measures for Czechoslovakia's defense, "and receive in return a certain and large scale war tomorrow—moreover at the price of assuaging the appetites of insatiable aggressors and of the destruction or mutilation of sovereign States—is not to act in the spirit of the Covenant of the League of Nations. To grant bonuses for sabre-rattling and recourse to arms for the solution of international problems . . . is not to act in the spirit of the Briand-Kellogg Pact."

The men of Munich paid no heed. Distrusting Soviet Russia perhaps even more than the United States did, they were apparently afraid to call upon her for the assistance she was ready to proffer in resisting Hitler's demands. Outraged at what he regarded as the betrayal of collective security, convinced of the validity of his suspicions that England and France were playing Hitler's game rather than attempting to restrain Germany, Stalin thereupon began to fall back upon a policy of wholly nationalistic self-defense. It apparently seemed to him to be Russia's only recourse in a world drifting into war without any concert of the peace-minded nations to stem the fatal tide.

There were many tragic elements in the international situation at the close of 1938. Perhaps none more tragic than the position of the United States and Soviet Russia. They were potentially the two most powerful nations in the world, and the two most strongly dedicated, from reasons of intensely practical self-interest, to the maintenance of peace. Had they somehow been able to agree upon a common policy, throwing their tremendous influence behind the battered cause of collective security even at this late date, Hitler would at least have faced a united world. But with Europe hovering on the edge of war, America and Russia each despaired of collective security, retreated into isolation, and for all their common danger remained themselves divided by distrust and suspicion.

The precarious nature of the peace so ingloriously formulated at Munich became more apparent with every passing week. "The acid test," President Roosevelt stated shortly after the conference, "is whether anyone is ready to disarm." No one was. The armaments race was being pursued throughout Europe more and more feverishly. There was every reason to believe that Hitler was but waiting the opportunity to renew his drive for a Greater Germany. Roosevelt once more sought to call Germany to account. "Words may be futile," he declared in his annual address to Congress in January 1939, "but war is not the only means of commanding a decent respect for the opinions of mankind. There are many methods short of war, but stronger and more effective than mere words, of bringing home to aggressor governments the sentiments of our people." But despite the implied threat, it *was* only words—and they were futile. Our neutrality laws remained a notice to all the world that we had no intention of reaching out across the Atlantic to take any effective action to relieve the mounting crisis.

From Ambassador Davies, now transferred to Brussels, there came some two weeks later in a letter to Harry Hopkins a proposal which he wished placed directly before the President. Chamberlain's peace "had proved a flop," he wrote. World leadership had passed to the totalitarian states, with Russia completely quarantined by the reactionary policies of England

THE FAILURE OF A UNITED FRONT

and France. Under such circumstances Davies pointed to the very grave danger that "the Chamberlain policy of throwing Italy, Poland and Hungary into the arms of Hitler may be completed by so disgusting the Soviets that it will drive Russia into an economic agreement and ideological truce with Hitler." Could such an ominous development be in any way prevented? "Specifically there is one thing that can be done now, in my opinion," the ambassador declared, "and that is to give some encouragement to Russia to remain stanch for collective security and peace."

A few years earlier, perhaps a few months earlier, something might have been possible—but now? The United States had hardly disguised its belief that the United Front was a cover for Communist revolution despite Davies' earlier reports. Our attitude had done nothing to free the Soviet Union of its fear that the Western democracies would encourage Hitler to launch a crusade against Communism as a means of saving their own skins. Stalin had not forgotten 1918. There was no way in which we could encourage Russia to stand stanchly for peace other than by breaking down the walls of our own isolation and political distrust. And the American people, through their Congress, had taken their stand. Europe's crisis was none of our direct concern. We were going to sit this one out.

The startling events occurring between March and September 1939, confused and obscure as they were at the time, now appear to have followed a definite and almost inevitable course. With Germany's denunciation of the Munich accord and occupation of Czechoslovakia, an England startled out of the complacency induced by the soft phrase "peace in our time" frantically wooed the Soviet government. She began to seek the aid and cooperation previously spurned. But there were still reservations. For all Chamberlain's emphatic insistence that ideological differences no longer counted, a highly conservative ministry's hostility toward Communism even now prevented the British government from taking the one step that might have revived Moscow's shattered confidence in the Anglo-

French entente. England wanted Russian help for an attack in the west, but she would make no guarantee of assistance if Hitler turned to the east. She refused to conclude a formal military alliance.

Stalin would have none of such halfway measures. He was safeguarding Russia's interests, not pulling Anglo-French chestnuts out of the fire. Speaking before a party congress in Moscow, he bitterly condemned both England and France for their cowardly surrender to Hitler at Munich. He charged the two nations with actually inciting Germany to attack Russia. Under such circumstances, he gravely warned, the Soviet Union had no alternative other than to seek to strengthen its ties with *all* nations. Two months later this hint of a changed policy was given further substance. Litvinov, the persistent advocate of collective security, was dismissed. It could clearly be read between the lines that collaboration with England and France having failed, it would now be wholly abandoned. In his first public speech Molotov, the new Commissar of Foreign Affairs, bluntly informed the world that it was Russia's intention to resume negotiations for a trade agreement with Germany. Actually she was prepared to go much farther. The decision had been made to seek a political truce as well as a commercial treaty with Hitler.

While preliminary conversations to this end were proceeding with the utmost secrecy, August witnessed another half-hearted effort by England and France, along the line of the negotiations earlier in the year, to reach some sort of understanding with Russia for the defense of Poland, marked as the next victim of aggression. The atmosphere was tense. The prospects of war daily grew more menacing. Here in America a public far more alive to the dangers in the situation than it had been a quarter of a century earlier when the first World War was developing during another lowering summer, watched the drama with a dread expectancy. Wishful thinking guided a good deal of the public comment on events. It was natural to cling to the hope of peace. On August 12, however, Under Sec-

retary of State Welles solemnly warned President Roosevelt that in his opinion a declaration of war was probable in a week or ten days.

Would Russia reach an eleventh-hour agreement with England and France and confront Germany with a combination that even Hitler might hesitate to challenge? Or would the obscure rumors of a Russian-German treaty result in an understanding enabling the Nazi dictator to defy England and France with his eastern front secure from attack? What was Soviet Russia's policy—that "riddle wrapped in a mystery inside an enigma," in Winston Churchill's pungent phrase?

The answer was given to the world on August 21, 1939. Russia and Germany had reconciled their differences and agreed to sign both a trade agreement and a nonaggression treaty. While the conversations with the British and French military missions that had been sent to Moscow were not at once broken off, the refusal of the democracies to sanction the movement of Russian troops through Poland and the Baltic countries as the only realistic method for stopping Hitler, killed whatever slight hopes of success they may ever have had. Poland saw in the Soviet Union's insistence upon precautionary measures against "indirect aggression" a threat of Russian invasion of her territory perhaps more dangerous than the menace of Hitler's Germany. Whatever the justification for these fears, England upheld her ally's position. Faced with such an impasse, the shift in Russian policy first noted after Munich had been carried to its logical conclusion.

If it was impossible to crush aggression by a United Front, Stalin felt the next best thing for Russia was to attempt to divert any immediate German attack from the Soviet Union. He had believed the democracies were inciting Germany to attack Russia. If he was now turning the tables on them, it was no more and no less than another Munich. There is little reason to believe, however, that the Russian dictator was ever convinced that the Soviet Union could stay indefinitely out of a general European war. He was buying time in order to build up Russia's defenses so that she could singlehandedly, if necessary, safeguard her own national interests.

The announcement of the Russo-German treaty burst upon a startled and bewildered world. The likelihood of such an agreement had long since been foreseen in informed diplomatic circles. Our State Department had been many times warned of it, not only by Ambassador Davies but by other American diplomats in Europe. Under Secretary Welles had accepted the pact as a definite possibility well before its conclusion and further believed that it presaged war. Four days before it was signed, he summoned the Inter-Departmental Neutrality Committee to conclude the arrangements to make this country "ready for the worst." The American public, however, was not prepared for the shock of such an unlooked-for shift in European alignments. To the average man it was a wholly mystifying development for which there at first seemed to be no adequate or satisfactory interpretation.

Newspaper comment was confused and contradictory. The *New York Times* thought the treaty might turn out to be nothing but "a grandstand flourish in the game of playing one side against the other." Both the *Boston Transcript* and the *Philadelphia Evening Ledger* agreed that it was probably little more than a Russian bid for better terms in the negotiations with England and France. The *Wall Street Journal's* primary interest was in the proof it afforded of how immaterial were the actual differences between Hitlerism and Stalinism, while the *Chicago Tribune* ran the heading "The Comrades Join the Kamerads." With second thought, editorial writers began to take it more seriously as a startling diplomatic victory for Germany and a staggering blow to the morale of the democracies. Finally the *Times* sought to find such comfort as it could in the new alignment. "At least there is a democratic front," it said on August 24. "The sham fronts are down and the anti-democratic systems are on one side and the democracies on the other. Inevitably we are more deeply engaged in the conflict." For all the growing realization that Germany was

now in a position to avoid the perilous risks of a two-front war, prevailing editorial opinion nevertheless appeared to lean to the side of a probable postponement of actual hostilities.

Time was running out, however. While the democracies struggled to adapt themselves to the new international line-up, Germany increased the pressure she had been exerting upon Poland. It grew every day more apparent that Hitler was determined to challenge France and England once again, with all preparations made for war. And this time they would not stand aside and let him wreak his will upon still another victim of aggression. Appeasement had run its course. When finally the attack upon Poland came, on September 1, the two allies of western Europe reluctantly accepted the gage of battle thrown down by the Nazi dictator, convinced that surrender now meant that the next attack would be directly against them.

The twenty-year armistice had come to an end. The world faced the war it had long foreseen and been so tragically helpless to prevent. The curtain was rung up on a conflict whose spreading waves would in another two years engulf even the two great nations which in September 1939 stood aside in transitory isolation.

XIV

IN A WORLD AT WAR

Upon the outbreak of war both the United States and Soviet Russia immediately declared their neutrality, but there was a sharp divergence in their attitude toward the struggle. American sympathies were almost wholly with England and France. While we hoped desperately to avoid being drawn into the conflict, public opinion favored the Allies so strongly that we would soon give concrete expression to this sentiment by modifying our neutrality law to make possible their purchase of munitions in the American market. The Soviet Union, on the other hand, appeared on the surface to be almost as fully committed to the support of Hitler. It was bound to Germany both by the anti-aggression treaty and a trade pact, making Russian supplies available for the Reich's armies, while the influence of the Comintern, acting through foreign Communist parties, was thrown against neutral aid to the democracies on the pretense that the struggle was nothing more than another chapter in imperialistic war.

Theoretically there should have been strong grounds for understanding between the United States and Russia. Each had followed, however different the circumstances, the same policy in retreating into isolation. Our neutrality laws had been widely criticized as encouraging German aggression; Moscow's conclusion of a treaty with Berlin had been attacked as affording Hitler even more direct aid. In both instances, national peace and safety were the dominating motives for the policy adopted and actually, as events were to prove in decisive fashion, the interests of Russia and America had never been more nearly identical. Neither could escape the challenge of Fascism, however frantically they tried to insulate themselves behind ocean barriers or the shield of buffer states. They were destined

to find themselves in time fighting as partners in a common cause, irresistibly drawn together, as they had been so many times in the past.

There was a complete blindness to all this in 1939. Neither nation could recognize the other as a potential ally. Their opposing philosophies and the distrust born of almost a quarter of a century of mutual misunderstanding, completely obscured the possibility of any united defense of the peace which was the basic goal of their foreign policies. For almost two years they went entirely different ways. Far removed from the actual scene of conflict, the United States found no need to take any political measures in self-defense other than to tighten its bonds with Latin America. Soviet Russia sensed a danger nearer to hand which she felt could be met only by occupying the territories of her small neighbors in order to build a stronger wall against possible attack. We felt free to offer economic support to the embattled European democracies; Russia felt the necessity of supplying Germany to gain time if nothing more.

The wholly realistic policy Stalin adopted under these circumstances served to widen still further the breach between the United States and the Soviet Union. Every move he made alienated American sympathies. The conclusion of a Far Eastern border truce with Japan, which would later be broadened to embrace a nonaggression treaty, was interpreted in America not from the point of view of Russia's national defense but as a further betrayal of the democratic cause. For it encouraged Japan to expand an imperialistic program already threatening American interests in the Far East and creating a very real danger on our western flank.

The far more shocking agreement with Germany for the division of Poland, closely followed by Russian occupation of the eastern half of that country, could not be viewed at this time in any other light than making Stalin and Hitler partners in aggression. *Collier's* declared that the two dictators were "old-style land grabbers and empire builders wearing new sets of labels and mouthing new slogans." The *New Republic* said

Stalin was "playing the imperialist game as shrewdly as any," and advised a thoroughly realistic view of Soviet policy if we were not to be surprised at future developments. The demands being simultaneously made upon the Baltic states—Latvia, Lithuania and Estonia—further substantiated these interpretations of Russian imperialism. When they were eventually absorbed into the Soviet Union, American public opinion denounced Russian policy as no less heinous than Germany's invasion of Czechoslovakia or Poland.

Even more disastrous to Russian-American understanding was the U.S.S.R.'s assault upon little Finland. When that nation, for which we had the greatest sympathy if for no other reason than her faithful observance of debt obligations, heroically resisted Russia's demands for territorial concessions, there was an immediate upsurge of pro-Finnish sentiment throughout the country. The Soviet invasion of November 1939 inspired a popular condemnation of Communist policy that brought relations between Washington and Moscow almost to the breaking point. At no time in their history—not even in the grim aftermath of the first World War—had Russia and America confronted each other with greater antagonism. The fears and suspicions of those who had regarded the Soviet Union as an even greater menace to the democratic world than Hitler's Germany appeared to be justified.

Speaking before the American Youth Congress in February 1940, President Roosevelt lashed out against Russia in terms which clearly identified her as a partner with Germany in overthrowing the structure of world peace. "The Soviet Union, as everybody who has the courage to face the facts knows," he stated, "is run by a dictatorship as absolute as any dictatorship in the world. It has allied itself with another dictatorship, and it has invaded a neighbor so infinitesimally small that it could do no conceivable harm to the Soviet Union. . . ." Recalling the hope once entertained of Russia's peaceful role in world affairs, the President declared that it was now "either shattered or put away in storage against some better day." There were

few of his countrymen, ignoring the strategic considerations underlying Russian policy in Poland and the Baltic countries, who then believed that "some better day" could ever condone what they regarded as Moscow's criminal duplicity.

Somewhat later Foreign Commissar Molotov answered in kind in an address before the Supreme Soviet in Moscow. "I will not dwell upon our relations with the United States," he said, "if only for the reason that there is nothing good that can be said about them. We have learned that there are certain people in the United States who are not pleased with the success of Soviet foreign policy in the Baltic countries. But, we must confess, we are little concerned over this fact, inasmuch as we are coping with our tasks without the assistance of these displeased gentlemen." Striking back at charges made by Under Secretary Welles that the Soviet Union had "deliberately annihilated" the sovereignty of the Baltic states, he accused the United States in turn of imperialistic designs in Latin America which were being promoted "behind a well-advertised 'concern' for the interest of the entire hemisphere."

The analogy was not entirely justified. American troops had invaded no neighbor states. But the strategy of national security ran along somewhat parallel lines. One may perhaps wonder what our policy toward the Caribbean countries might have been if, with Germany threatening us as closely as she threatened Russia, they had rejected our proposals for mutual security and hemispheric defense.

Throughout the Russo-Finnish war our policy was one of benevolent neutrality toward Finland and we took every possible step short of severing diplomatic relations with Moscow to extend her aid and comfort. Statutes which would have cut Finland off from the American market for supplies were not invoked; the money she sought to pay us on her debt account was set apart in a special fund for the benefit of the Finnish people, with further payments suspended, and in protest against Russian bombings a moral embargo was placed upon further shipment of either airplanes or aeronautical equipment to the Soviet Union.

The question of providing Finland with credits for the purchase of additional supplies in the United States soon arose in Congress. On this issue the administration moved carefully, favoring such action but only for agricultural and manufactured goods which definitely fell outside any category of military equipment. The measure finally enacted in March 1940 consequently approved a loan of only $20,000,000, and barred the purchase through these funds of any munitions. This caution resulted from the feeling that the European situation was much too tense for the United States to run the risk of an actual break with Russia, but it was criticized in many quarters. In refusing to give the Finns more direct assistance, Dorothy Thompson wrote in her syndicated column, the United States had "slapped Finland in the face." Popular sentiment generally was expressed in the wide and generous support given not only to the Finnish Relief Fund but to the more belligerent Fighting Funds for Finland.

A result of sympathy for the victim of aggression was renewed attack upon the aggressor. In January 1940 a Senate inquiry had called upon Secretary Hull to answer questions dealing with the failure of the Soviet Union to live up to the terms of the accord concluded in Washington in 1933. There had been "divergencies in the interpretation of the agreements in question," the Secretary of State declared, and the United States had never received satisfactory assurances upon the U.S.S.R.'s observance of its anti-propaganda pledge, "irrefutably" covering activities of the Communist International. It was a report whose hostility toward Soviet Russia was carefully veiled in diplomatic language but it clearly revealed the attitude of the administration. While the Senate took no further steps after conclusion of the inquiry, the House assumed a more belligerent stand. It failed by only three votes to adopt an amendment to the annual State Department supply bill

striking out the salary appropriation for our ambassador in Moscow.

The drive against Communism in this country was pushed with undiminished vehemence. Both party members and fellow travelers had found themselves thrown completely off balance by what was to them a sudden and unexpected reversal of the party line in the conclusion of the Russo-German pact. Their troubles had been increased with the outbreak of the Finnish war. Having vociferously condemned Nazi aggression and called for a United Front for the past five years, they now had to throw overboard all their previous international formulas, castigating the Anglo-French acceptance of Hitler's challenge in attacking Poland as promoting imperialist war. From the strongest advocates of collective security, they became the most outspoken adherents of isolation. The League for Peace and Democracy gave way to American Peace Mobilization. Such a change in tactics so clearly revealed the hand of Moscow that not only conservatives but liberals as well now rose in their wrath against the Comintern's invasion of our domestic affairs. Gallup polls revealed that the American public by a majority of some 70 per cent considered Communist propaganda a greater menace to the United States than Nazi propaganda.

The Communist Party program during 1940—of course an election year—was one of bitter opposition to Roosevelt because of his foreign policy. Since aid for the democracies could not be reconciled with the Soviet Union's role in the war, American Communists subordinated the interests of their own country to the supposed interests of Russia. Writing bitterly upon what he termed the Stalinist penetration of America, Eugene Lyons violently denounced this "Moscow-dictated fake-pacifist movement." With the Communists being held responsible for almost all strikes and other labor disturbances, especially those in national defense industries, the Dies Committee expanded its investigations and bore down still more heavily upon all those suspected of Communist leanings or radical tendencies.

All such evidence of mounting antagonism to the Soviet

Union and of hatred of Communism was topped by the vitriolic attack made upon Russia by former President Hoover in April 1940. Writing in *Collier's*, he flatly demanded the immediate recall of our ambassador in Moscow and declared that recognition of the Soviet Union had been "a gigantic political and moral mistake." He did not believe there had ever been any justification for departing from the policy followed by the Republicans. What had happened immediately after the exchange of the Roosevelt-Litvinov notes? Hoover stated that overnight we were flooded with conspiracy to overthrow our institutions, and that the Communist Party showed a 100 per cent increase in membership. The intellectual and spiritual life of the nation had been poisoned; class hatred had flourished as never before in our history. "We cannot even remotely recognize this murderous tyranny," the former President exclaimed, "without transgressing on every national ideal of our own."

Although popular sentiment did not necessarily go the whole way with Hoover in the vindictiveness of his attack, his views had wide support. It was impossible for the American people to judge the international situation objectively. Even after the conclusion of peace between the Soviet Union and Finland, in which the United States played an influential role, led to some abatement of the anti-Russian feeling, the conviction of Soviet perfidy remained. There were few Americans who gave to Russia's policy the possible interpretation of an attempt to bulwark her defenses, by whatever means, against an overwhelmingly powerful neighbor who might attack her despite all anti-aggression treaties. A fog of misunderstanding and prejudice, for which the Kremlin's secrecy and deviousness was in part responsible, completely obscured the national vision.

Our own realization of the direct menace of Germany was awakened only by the shattering events of the late spring of 1940. As Hitler launched his armies upon western Europe and France collapsed in tragic defeat, America was startled out of her complacent sense of security. Our attention was dramati-

cally centered upon the Battle of Britain. The possibility that
England would fall and a triumphant Hitler win control of
the Atlantic caused us to redouble our efforts to provide the
Allies with the tools of war and to embark upon a tremendous
program of national defense. And these new circumstances also
compelled us to re-examine our policy toward Soviet Russia.
Her international position now became of far too great importance for us to· think of her only in terms of her policy
toward Poland, the Baltic countries or Finland. What the
Kremlin now did might well determine the outcome of the
entire war.

What was the actual role of Russia in this sudden and terri-
fying expansion of European conflict? Was she drawing closer
to Germany and likely to enter into a military alliance? Did
Stalin hope to maintain his neutrality? Was there any likelihood that Hitler might after all turn upon Germany's traditional foe and carry out what had so generally been thought
to be his original objective of driving into the Ukraine? A
sobered America realized that here were possible lines of development directly affecting her own future. To at least some
far-sighted observers, the need to detach Russia from Germany
and restore some measure of good will between Washington
and Moscow became of paramount importance. We could no
longer afford the luxury of quarreling on ideological grounds.
We could not allow our dislike of Communism to stand in the
way of a rapprochement in foreign policy if there were any
possible way to bridge our differences.

In the spring of 1940 Russian-American relations were at
their nadir. A trade agreement was still in effect, but there were
cautious reservations on both sides. Our outspoken criticism
of Russia's incorporation of Latvia, Lithuania and Estonia
into the Soviet Union had been followed by the freezing of
those countries' credits, thereby tying up gold reserves taken
over by the U.S.S.R. which were on deposit in this country.
The moral embargo upon the shipment of airplanes to Russia
remained in effect. There was actually no American ambas-

sador in residence in Moscow, Laurence Steinhardt, who had succeeded Davies, having left the capital in May. These were all immediate barriers to the re-establishment of friendly relations, but they were after all only symptomatic of our general distrust of the Soviets. The real task facing those who would have brought the two powers together was to awaken a mutual realization that Hitler was potentially their common enemy, and to demonstrate that the logic of events pointed to the imperative need of their collaboration in stopping him.

Sumner Welles apparently played a major role in trying to reconcile America and Russia after the collapse of France. The annual trade agreement was successfully renewed, Ambassador Steinhardt returned to Moscow and the moral embargo upon airplane shipments was finally withdrawn in January 1941. But more important was a series of conversations, eighteen meetings in all, between the Under Secretary of State and Soviet Ambassador Oumansky in which the possible bases for a more cordial understanding were thoroughly and laboriously explored by the two statesmen. Their course was never an easy one. A primary interest of Russia was to increase her purchase of military supplies, but the United States was fearful they would make their way to Germany. We had adopted an export control system. Essential materials and munitions of war not needed for our own national defense program were largely earmarked for Great Britain, in accordance with the role we assumed during this period of becoming "the arsenal of democracy." Nevertheless Welles went as far as he could in meeting Oumansky's insistent demands. Permits were withheld for the export of machine tools, essential to our industrial program, but on assurances that they would not be transferred to Germany, increasing quantities of American wheat, cotton, copper and petroleum products made their way across the Pacific to Vladivostok.

Welles was no friend of Communism. His essential conservatism cut him off from any political sympathy for Moscow. But he became convinced after the failure of Germany to win

the Battle of Britain that Hitler's next move would be to attack Russia. The Soviets would thus be unable, in his opinion, to avoid joining the forces combating Fascism for all their attempts to remain neutral. The Under Secretary's information upon the likelihood of Germany's turning eastward, obtained from abroad early in 1941, was so precise that he actually set the date for it as some time in June. This confidential information he gave to the Soviet ambassador, gravely warning him of what his country might expect just five months before the actual event. But while Oumansky relayed the prediction to Moscow, the Kremlin gave no hint of its own policy. Foreign Commissar Molotov had visited Berlin in November 1940, an uneasy world wondering whether it might mean that Russia was prepared to join the Axis, but nothing had happened. Stalin was keeping his own counsel, and there was no reply to the warnings Welles had conveyed to his ambassador. Officially the Soviet dictator discredited any suggestion of a deterioration in Russian-German relations.

What slight hopes may have existed early in 1941 of breaking through the barriers to a more cordial understanding between the United States and Soviet Russia were now to be subject to another devastating shock. In April came announcement of the conclusion of the Russo-Japanese nonaggression treaty. It had been known that Foreign Minister Matsuoka was seeking such an agreement and Secretary Hull tried to minimize its importance. It was merely "descriptive of a situation which has in effect existed between the two countries for some time past." But the severe blow to our position in the Far East could not be denied. Russia had apparently cleared the way for Japan's imperialistic advance in southeastern Asia, launched immediately after the fall of France, by removing a possible threat on her northern flank, just as she had given the signal for Germany's attack upon Poland by freeing Hitler of the dread fear of a two-front war. Public opinion was thoroughly aroused over what it interpreted as still another act of unmitigated treachery. The hope that Russian diplomacy was slowly emerging from the fog of ambiguity that had hung over it for the past two years, the *New York Times* commented almost more in sorrow than in anger, was banished. Everything was again plunged into confusion. The only favorable aspect of the entire world situation was that the Soviet Union had at least not openly joined the Axis.

The Russo-Japanese pact, in any event, appeared to doom the slow and hesitant rapprochement between the Soviet Union and the United States. There could be no further economic aid, it was generally felt, for a nation so closely tied to both ends of the Axis. Further licenses for exports to Vladivostok were withheld. Russian funds in the United States were frozen. "I might as well go home," Ambassador Oumansky is reported to have told a State Department official early in June. "I can do nothing in Washington."

Public opinion would probably have agreed with him. Little realizing that the next tremendous climax in the overwhelming drama of the war was just over the horizon, the American people had virtually written Russia off as a nation they could never trust, as one with whom cooperation was impossible.

This was the general atmosphere when with an unexpectedness comparable to that which had marked the conclusion of the Russo-German pact two years earlier, Hitler launched his sudden attack upon the Soviet Union without even bothering to renounce his treaty with Stalin. German armies were on the march from the Arctic to the Black Sea, glaring headlines told an astounded American public on June 22, 1941, while the Nazi dictator confidently promised the swift annihilation of his new enemy. The war against Soviet Russia was to be a quick diversion, enabling him to secure the supplies which would then permit him to turn once again on embattled England.

While Prime Minister Churchill immediately announced that any "man or state who fights against Nazism will have our aid," it was a full twenty-four hours before any official announcement on this new development was made in Washington. The State Department then moved cautiously. After

conferring with President Roosevelt, Under Secretary Welles
issued a somewhat equivocal statement. There was no mincing
of words in his denunciation of Germany, but he also took
occasion vigorously to criticize the Soviet Union. He especially
singled out its suppression of freedom of worship, long one of
the sorest points of contention in our continuing controversy,
declaring that insofar as the American people were concerned
"this and other principles of communistic dictatorship are as
intolerable and as alien to their own beliefs as the principles
and doctrines of Nazi dictatorship." Having thus paid his respects to Communism, Welles then went on to state that the
major issue nevertheless remained whether Hitler could be
halted. "In the opinion of this Government, consequently,"
he concluded, "any defense against Hitlerism, any rallying of
the forces opposing Hitlerism, from whatever source these
forces may spring, will hasten the eventual downfall of the
present German leaders, and will therefore redound to the
benefit of our defense and security. . . . Hitler's armies are
today the chief dangers of the Americas."

It was a curious statement. For all the State Department's
foreknowledge of Hitler's plan, it failed to state definitely
what our actual policy toward Russia would be. Its ambiguity
appeared to reflect the confused state of public opinion, and it
may well have been purposely phrased to give the American
people time to reconcile themselves to the difficult readjust-
ments th y had to face.

The ation was dangerously divided, in the summer of 1941,
into the two general camps of interventionists and isolationists.
Even for the former group there was some question as to where
America stood in the face of Russia's entry into the war. "We
are not going to pretend," the *New York Times* stated, "that we
have anything in common with the brutal despotism of Stalin."
The Committee to Defend America by Aiding the Allies con-
tented itself with the statement that Germany was waging war
upon all mankind and "the peril to the United States is increasingly grave." But if the interventionists hesitated, the

isolationists had not a moment of doubt as to the significance of this new turn in events. It was the final, irrefutable proof that the United States should stay out of the war.

Former President Hoover declared that "collaboration between Britain and Russia . . . makes the whole argument of joining the war to bring the Four Freedoms a gargantuan jest." Senator Wheeler's comment, reflecting a point of view for so long common among isolationists, was terse and pointed: "Just let Joe Stalin and the other dictators fight it out." Predicting that the interventionists would now undertake a campaign to whitewash the Communist purges, Soviet confiscation of property and persecution of religion, the invasion of Finland and Russian seizure of half of prostrate Poland, Senator La Follette foresaw a day when these events would be made "to seem the acts of a 'democracy' preparing to fight Nazism." Senator Taft went even further in embittered opposition to both American intervention in the war and to the Stalin dictatorship. "A victory for Communism," he flatly stated, "would be far more dangerous to the United States than a victory for Fascism."

There was no hope of united support behind aid for Soviet Russia under these circumstances. The distrust of Communism added an explosive element to the friction that already divided the ranks of interventionists and isolationists. Nevertheless the administration was convinced, as Welles' statement had made clear despite its criticism of Russia, that Hitler's armies were the real menace to America. On June 24, President Roosevelt consequently stated that the United States was prepared to extend all possible assistance to the Soviet Union. The Treasury released funds frozen only the week before, and a general license was granted for exports to the U.S.S.R. Further measures would be taken, it was made clear, when it was more definitely known what Russia needed in the way of supplies.

The country accepted this decision. For all the vociferous outcries of the opponents of Roosevelt's foreign policy, and the continued hostility toward Communism, Germany was in fact

considered the real danger to the United States by majority opinion. A survey at the end of June indicated that Russia's entry into the war had caused no material change in the line-up of isolationists and interventionists, but the public apparently favored continued aid to the Allies and it was willing to include Soviet Russia among those nations to whom it would be extended. The difficulties of reconciling opposition to Communism with support for the Soviets obviously created a major problem. America and Russia, as Walter Lippmann rephrased the traditional paradox, were "separated by an ideological gulf and joined by the bridge of national interest." Germany's invasion, however, had at least brought home to both powers that there was such a bridge, and that it actually spanned the ideological gulf.

There was another complicating factor in the situation. Could Russia hold out against the German attack? If she could do so successfully, any aid extended to her would be aid to the entire democratic cause, but if she could not withstand the swift rush of Hitler's armies and made a quick peace, American supplies to the Soviets would be wholly wasted and might even fall into Germany's hands. At the opening of the new campaign, the opinion was generally held—by a popular majority of 70 per cent according to Gallup polls—that Russia's armies would succumb within a matter of weeks and Stalin make a peace that would throw open the vast resources of his entire country to Germany. Three-fourths of our own general staff, it has been reported, were convinced that Russia could no more withstand the Wehrmacht than had Poland, France and the Balkan countries. Possibly she could hold out a little longer, some military authorities conceded, but not long enough to justify any program of all-out American aid.

These pessimistic views were strenuously combated by a few persons better informed upon actual conditions within Russia. Here perhaps former Ambassador Davies rendered his most notable service. Immediately upon the announcement of Russian-German hostilities, he had stated in an interview with the

United Press that the Red Army would amaze and surprise the world. It was just common sense, he insisted, for the United States to give Russia all possible help because the Soviets "were fighting the greatest danger to our security in the world, the menace of Hitler's aggression and lust for world dominion." At a conference with Welles on July 7, he strongly urged our backing up the unequivocal stand taken by Prime Minister Churchill, and during the ensuing months, both in reports to the State Department and in public statements, he continued to emphasize his conviction that Russia would put up a strong resistance, refuse to make peace and despite early reverses fight out the war to its bitter end.

Only one possible consideration might move Stalin to make peace with Hitler, Davies declared in a speech made in October. That was the belief that further resistance was hopeless because the United States and Great Britain either could not or would not forward the supplies to enable him to keep on fighting. "If we would eliminate the possibility of another Russo-German treaty or a separate Russo-German peace," our former ambassador recorded in his diary record of this address, "then—in my opinion—we must do these things. We must stand by our guns and deliver the goods. We must stop expecting other nations to have the courage of our convictions. We must satisfy the Soviet Union that we practice what we preach as to the right of nations to self-determination. This means that during and after the war we do and will accord to them the right to decide what kind of government they want for themselves. By so doing we can retain and deserve their confidence. By so doing we can make clear our belief that the American and Russian people can live as friends in a world devoted to peace."

In the meantime President Roosevelt had demonstrated his determination to implement just such a policy. Toward the close of July, he dispatched Harry Hopkins as a special emissary to Moscow to sound out the situation and discover just what the United States could do. Upon reaching the Russian

capital, Hopkins at once entered into prolonged discussions with Stalin and was frankly, candidly told what were Russia's greatest needs. The Soviet dictator also disclosed a great deal more concerning the actual condition of Russian armies than had been divulged to any other foreigner, and he allowed Hopkins unusual freedom of investigation for himself. The President's envoy returned from his visit, to join Roosevelt and Churchill at their famous Atlantic Conference, convinced that assistance to the Soviets would not be wasted and that the United States should make every effort to meet Stalin's specific requests.

An exchange of notes between Under Secretary Welles and Ambassador Oumansky had already revealed agreement in principle on a program for American aid. President Roosevelt and Prime Minister Churchill now issued, on August 15, 1941, a joint message reaffirming their common policy, pledging themselves to expedite as speedily as possible shipment of the goods Stalin had outlined to Hopkins as immediately necessary, and proposing a conference among American, British and Russian representatives to consider the long-term aspects of the situation. The Russian dictator at once accepted this invitation. Preparations were thereupon made for an Anglo-American mission, headed by Lord Beaverbrook for England and W. Averell Harriman for the United States, to meet and confer with the Soviet leaders in Moscow during September.

This conference reached a full accord. The requests for aid made by the Soviet Union were granted, and an agreement signed as to the specific types and quantities of arms and munitions that the United States and Great Britain would undertake to deliver. In October, Roosevelt confirmed these arrangements in a note to Stalin pledging delivery of American supplies up to a total of $1,000,000,000, with provision for easy repayment over a ten-year period after the end of the war under the terms of our lend-lease legislation. Stalin accepted our offer with a warm expression of gratitude on November 4, 1941, and three days later the President certified the arrangement to the lend-lease administration on the stated ground that "the defense of the U.S.S.R. is vital to the defense of the United States."

Although America was still at peace, events were by this time drawing us perilously close to active hostilities in both Europe and the Far East. We had become involved in a "shooting war" with German submarines in the Atlantic; we had at long last broken off trade relations with Japan. As Germany pursued her attacks on both merchantmen and American war vessels off our eastern shores, and Japanese troops poured into Indo-China and threatened the Philippines, our position could hardly have been more critical. Still it was not actual war. The country as a whole somehow hoped that peace could be maintained, but it remained bitterly divided as to what our policy should be.

The question of aid to Russia, even though it was subordinated to the larger issues now at stake, contributed its quota of heated controversy. It was still strenuously opposed in many quarters, both on the ground that it was a dangerous fiction to believe that the Soviet Union's defense was in any way vital to this country, and because of an hostility toward Communism that could not be shaken whatever the stakes of international diplomacy. The suppression of religious freedom in Russia, although President Roosevelt tried to point out that persecution of the church had been on political rather than religious grounds and had now been stopped, became a topic of bitter debate. The influence of the Comintern, even though the party line had once again shifted with Russia's entry into the war, continued to be attacked as unwarranted interference in our domestic affairs. Stalin's pact with Japan was advanced as evidence that despite the Russo-German war, we still had no reason to trust the good faith of the Kremlin. An ingrained suspicion of everything for which the Soviet Union stood, and particularly of what appeared to be the tortuous shifts of Stalin's policy, could not be easily dispelled.

Nevertheless increasing evidence of the perils confronting

the United States, both in the Atlantic and in the Pacific, could not help but emphasize more and more the importance of "the bridge of national interest" that now so clearly joined Russia and America. The determined resistance that the Red armies offered to Hitler's advancing forces pushed further into the background our fears that the Soviets would collapse or Stalin make another deal with the Nazi dictator. Congress clearly indicated that for all the opposition of isolationists and Red-baiters, the country as a whole supported the administration's policy toward Russia when early in the fall it sharply rebuffed a move to withdraw the use of lend-lease funds in extending her aid.

Some three-quarters of a century earlier, during the crisis of our Civil War, Russia had given both sympathy and tacit support to the Union because it was to the immediate interest of her Czarist government to uphold this country as a counterpoise to the British Empire. We had intervened in the Russo-Japanese war in 1905 to prevent Japan from imposing too harsh a peace upon Russia because it was to our national interest to have a strong bulwark in the Far East against the rising power of Japanese militarism. For a time during the first World War Russia and America had joined forces in combating Germany's challenge to world peace. Even during its tragic aftermath our hostility to Bolshevism had not prevented us from standing out firmly against any dismemberment of Russia that would weaken her role in the Far Eastern balance of power. Now our mutual interests were more closely identified than ever before in our opposition to an aggressive Fascism that threatened the peace and freedom of the entire world.

One more startling event, however, was needed to drive home with compelling force the lesson we had refused to learn as the forces of aggression were gathering their terrible momentum during the 1930's. Japan provided it. The bombing of Pearl Harbor on December 7, 1941, shattered the illusion that the United States could not itself be attacked. Two days later Germany, and also Italy, underscored with their declarations of war what the Japanese had so dramatically demonstrated. Neutrality had safeguarded the United States no more than it had the Soviet Union. Peace was indivisible. America and Russia were both once again at war—fighting a common foe.

XV

THE STRUGGLE AGAINST HITLER

AFTER Pearl Harbor there was no more question of the United States avoiding direct participation in what had now become a global conflict. The heated controversy between intervention-ists and isolationists was immediately silenced; a united people entered upon the war with a full determination to see it through to final and complete victory over their enemies. The nations to whom we had been extending economic aid now became our military allies. A danger directly shared compelled a further reorientation of our official relations with the Soviet Union and of the popular attitude toward the Communist regime.

Even though we had been acting since November on the principle that the defense of Russia was vital to the defense of the United States, it was not easy to accept the full implications of this new relationship imposed by war. For all the growth of a more friendly attitude following the outbreak of Russo-German hostilities, the American people could not unreservedly cooperate with a government that they had so generally con-demned for a quarter of a century. A dawning realization that Stalin had been trying by every possible means to strengthen Russia's defenses against the ever-present likelihood that Hitler would turn eastward, served to explain much that had both mystified and outraged public opinion in the previous two years. Here at least was a logical reason, if not complete justifi-cation, for the Soviet Union's invasion of neighbor states and also for its conclusion of a nonaggression pact with Japan. Still, the suspicions originally aroused by the Russian dictator's devious and highly secretive strategy remained, superimposed upon a continued dislike of his arbitrary rule at home.

A first step toward combating such popular prejudice and bringing about greater unity and understanding among all the powers now arrayed against Hitler was the Declaration of the United Nations signed in Washington on January 1, 1942. Its most significant feature was the inclusion of Soviet Russia. It is true that she had already concluded a wartime pact with Great Britain, and through her ambassador in London accepted the principles of the Atlantic Charter drawn up during the previous August by President Roosevelt and Prime Minister Churchill. Nevertheless there were still ample grounds for disagreement upon war aims, while a further difficulty was the fact that Russia was not at war with Japan. It was consequently a dramatic triumph for Anglo-American diplomacy to have the U.S.S.R., in common with the twenty-five other United Nations, reaffirm without reservation the Atlantic Charter pledges against territorial aggrandizement, undertake to employ its full force against those enemy powers with which it was at war, and agree not to make a separate peace or armistice.

The Declaration of the United Nations was signed in behalf of Soviet Russia by Maxim Litvinov. The swinging pendulum of Russian-American relations had most appropriately brought him back to Washington in the new role of ambassador on the very day of Japan's attack on Pearl Harbor. His long prewar campaign to forge a United Front against Fascist aggression had failed. The United States and the Soviet Union had gone their separate ways. It was only poetic justice that Litvinov should now sign the pact in which the Russian and American governments joined the grand coalition against Hitler, "convinced that complete victory over their enemies is essential to defend life, liberty, independence and religious freedom, and to preserve human rights and justice in their own lands as well as in other lands."

American public opinion accepted the Declaration of the United Nations with universal approval. Whatever might be thought of Communism, there could be no hesitation about welcoming Soviet Russia into an accord placing her squarely alongside the democracies both as to the objectives of the war and military operations. Moreover the magnificent defense of

Moscow, and the brilliant counteroffensive launched in the winter of 1941-1942 by the Russian forces, had in themselves aroused a fresh admiration for the Soviet Union and strengthened the growing conviction that it was as fully committed to the defeat of Hitler as was the United States. Whereas all the world had expected Russia's defenses to crumble away before Hitler's savage onslaught, the Soviet armies were spectacularly dispelling the myth of German invincibility and giving the people of the United Nations a revived confidence in ultimate victory. They had revealed the inner strength, the tough, unbreakable core, of the new Russia to which ignorance, misunderstanding and prejudice had so largely blinded us. Entirely apart from our own paramount interest in the maintenance of an eastern front against Germany, the Russian people and their government commanded a heightened respect among all Americans.

The Soviet regime might be an arbitrary dictatorship, destructive of both private property and individual liberty, but it was functioning so effectively that its critics could no longer belabor it for weakness and inefficiency. More important, the Russian people had shown themselves singleheartedly united behind Communist leadership in heroic, self-sacrificing defense of their homeland. Whatever might be said of the methods Stalin had employed in building up this mighty state, of the terrible cost of establishing socialism, here was striking proof that many of the ideas about the Soviet Union popularly held in this country had been founded on a total misconception of what was actually happening in Russia and of the sentiments of the Russian people.

There were, however, many contradictory crosscurrents in popular thinking upon Russian-American relations in 1942. Perhaps four principal schools of thought emerged from the confusion. The first was made up of enthusiasts for Russia ranging all the way from faithful followers of the Communist Party line, who surprisingly found themselves back in the role of fervent supporters of a United Front, to many of the Soviet

Union's former most severe critics, now accepting Stalin as a lost sheep returned to the fold. Adherents of the second school prided themselves upon a more practical approach to the new situation. They remembered the Red purges and the Comintern. While prepared to collaborate with the U.S.S.R. as a war measure, these observers remained sceptical of its policies and were none too certain of the future. The third group was made up of obdurate conservatives and former isolationists who could still find nothing good in anything tarred with the brush of Communism, covertly opposed any real measure of aid for the Soviet armies, and clung to the old hope that the war might result in the destruction of both the Hitler and Stalin dictatorships. Finally there were those elements in American life who strongly advocated the greatest possible measure of collaboration with the Soviet Union on the ground that it was not only essential to the winning of the war but to the equally grave problem of winning the peace.

Some of those who had been most envenomed in their past denunciation of the Soviet government were found in the first category, tumbling over each other in praising everything Russian to the skies. Forgotten were yesterday's accusations of treachery and double-dealing; forgotten were the bitter charges of the betrayal of democracy; forgotten the old resentment against Communist propaganda. Soviet Russia became a nation miserably misunderstood, and Stalin a man greatly wronged. Illustrative of this attitude, often cropping up in strange and unexpected places, was an address delivered at the annual congress of the Daughters of the American Revolution in the spring of 1942. "Stalin is a university graduate and a man of great studies," Mrs. Tryphosa Duncan Bates-Batcheller declared amid what the magazine *Life* described as an obbligato of gasps from her audience. "He is a man, who, when he sees a great mistake, admits it and corrects it. Today in Russia, Communism is practically nonexistent."

There was a curious melange of truth, exaggeration and falsehood in many such statements seeking to compensate for

past criticism of a regime whose friendship we now wished to bolster up and maintain. The tendency in many instances was to be as unrealistic in praise as we had once been prejudiced in condemnation. There was a disposition to consider everything we had not liked about the Soviet system, an error of which the Communists now fully repented. Their introduction of such capitalistic techniques as differential wages, the speed-up system and interest-bearing bonds was interpreted as complete abandonment of the principles of Marxism. The ideological differences between the United States and the Soviet Union, that is, were to be resolved by stating that they no longer existed. Russia had somehow become, although these observers had not realized it until she went to war with Hitler, a state whose domestic policies quite as much as her foreign policies paralleled those of the United States.

Such a point of view was believed to be not only naïve but also dangerous by those who foresaw future difficulties as great as those of the past if the policy of friendship with Russia was oversold under the stimulus of a wartime alliance. Something more than wishful thinking was necessary, it was contended, if the basic and continuing differences in Russian and American philosophy were not to hamper our cooperation in either war or peace. The Soviet Union as an ally presented problems that could not be resolved by unwarranted assumptions of the conversion of the Communists to American ways of thinking.

William Henry Chamberlin tried to direct the popular attitude toward Russia along what he considered practical lines in an editorial appearing late in 1942 in the *Saturday Evening Post*. He pointed out that just as there had been too many indictments of the Soviet Union in the past, so now there were too many unthinking eulogies. The Russian experiment had proved that a socialist economy could be made a going concern, Chamberlin wrote, but it nevertheless remained just as true as ever that the price paid for it was heavier than any free people would willingly pay. The United States should welcome Russia as an ally in the war and seek her cooperation in peace, he maintained, without expecting her to adopt American social and economic ideas any more than we intended to adopt Soviet doctrines. Chamberlin then went on to warn of the difficulties of doing business with the Soviet Union because of its control of foreign trade and brought up the issue of the subversive propaganda of the Comintern—only to conclude, perhaps somewhat paradoxically, that "in the present crisis these are minor considerations."

This analysis of the situation marked a startling reversal of the *Saturday Evening Post's* earlier attitude of violent hostility to everything concerning the Soviet Union. It directly reflected the underlying change in public opinion since our entry into the war. At the same time there was still a latent note of very definite mistrust of our ally, as shown in the doubts expressed in regard to future trade and in the emphasis placed on the dangers of Communist propaganda, that gave a special significance to Chamberlin's final statement. While cooperation might be well and good when both the United States and Soviet Russia were menaced by Hitlerism, the editorial seemed to imply, it might not prove either so practical or necessarily so advantageous upon the conclusion of the war.

There were former foes of Soviet Russia, indeed, who continued quite openly to maintain the position that only the immediate demands of national safety justified any collaborations whatsoever with a Communist regime just as guilty as ever of brutal tyranny at home and revolutionary propaganda abroad. There might be no further public statements to the effect that Communism was actually a greater menace to the American way of life than Fascism, but conservative opposition to the U.S.S.R. was not very far beneath the surface. It would continue to make itself felt in frequent criticism of Stalin's policies and possible postwar ambitions.

Notwithstanding the overenthusiasm of so many newly won friends of Russia and the scarcely veiled hostility of those who thought only in terms of the immediate emergency, a steadily growing number of Americans adhered to the more realistic

school. They believed that cooperation between the two nations should be strengthened in every possible way and directed quite as much to the future peace as to the present war. Russian-American friendship should be the rule rather than the exception, it was asserted. The prewar period of mistrust and suspicion ran counter to what had again and again been proved to be the underlying community of interests in Russian and American foreign policies. The challenge of Hitler thus presented an opportunity, of which full advantage should be taken, to revive more permanently the friendship which had so generally characterized relations between the two countries before the advent of Communism.

A striking demonstration of renewed interest in Russia in all its phases was the great mass rally of the Congress of American-Soviet Friendship held in New York's Madison Square Garden on November 7, 1942, upon the occasion of the twenty-fifth anniversary of the Bolshevik revolution. The keynote of the entire gathering was unity in both war and peace. Congratulatory messages were received from President Roosevelt and General Eisenhower, while the galaxy of prominent speakers who addressed the 20,000 delegates represented almost every element in American life. Thomas W. Lamont, of the firm of J. P. Morgan and Company, pled for greater tolerance in our attitude toward Russia, declaring that Americans had no mandate to censor other people's politics or religion. President William Green of the American Federation of Labor called for aid to Russia that should be both real and vital. Senator Pepper stated that it behooved the United States to be worthy of such a good friend as Russia. Professor Ralph Barton Perry of Harvard warned against a policy of first trying to destroy the Soviets, then ignoring them, and finally treating them as poor relations.

The principal address was delivered by Vice President Wallace. It was in the first instance a renewed pledge on the part of the government that aid for the Soviet Union would be maintained as a primary goal of our foreign policy, an objective which the Vice President said he felt confident the American people wholly supported. But it went far beyond this immediate plan of giving the Soviets "priority number one." Both America and Russia had learned the tragic lesson of their retreat into isolation, Wallace declared, and they were now working toward a common middle ground of political and economic democracy which would assure united support for a world organization for peace. "I am here this afternoon," he stated, "to say that it is my belief that the American and Russian people can and will throw their influence on the side of building a new democracy which will be the hope of the world."

While the country as a whole was seeking to discover a satisfactory basis for adjusting its views on Soviet Russia, definite measures were being taken in the realm of international politics to provide for the future collaboration upon which such emphasis had been placed at the Congress of American-Soviet Friendship. The newspapers of June 12 had carried under imposing headlines the simultaneous announcement from London and Washington that Foreign Commissar Molotov, secretly visiting the two capitals, had signed in behalf of his government new and more binding agreements between the Soviet Union and the two great democracies of the West. Great Britain and Russia concluded a twenty-year alliance providing for common action to preserve peace and resist aggression in the postwar period. The United States and Russia reached a more informal but nevertheless comprehensive political understanding, and also signed a definite mutual aid agreement.

Two urgent problems had made the conclusion of these new accords essential if there were to be continued confidence between England and the United States on the one hand, Soviet Russia on the other. The first issue was the attitude of the Soviet government toward its so-called "strategic frontiers" on the west, and the second concerned the possible creation of a second front in Europe to relieve the immediate strain upon the hard-pressed Russian armies.

The primary interest of the U.S.S.R., as that of Great Britain

and of the United States, was national security. It was prepared to adhere to the Atlantic Charter, but it was not willing to surrender its right to the territories it had seized in Poland, the Baltic states, Finland, Bessarabia and Bukovina in 1939 and 1940. Molotov denied that their retention would violate the principles of the Atlantic Charter, and took the position that they were absolutely essential to Russia's national defense in the postwar world. Great Britain was prepared to acknowledge such claims in large part, upon the same realistic basis as that on which they were advanced by the Soviet Union, but the position of the United States was definitely against any territorial agreements even appearing to invalidate the principle of self-determination. Although there was no question of a secret treaty, Roosevelt did not wish to be confronted at the future peace conference with any such conflict between the commitments of our allies and the objectives of American policy as had tied Wilson's hands at Paris in 1919.

A compromise to this thorny issue was consequently worked out, largely through Roosevelt's instrumentality. The Soviet Union agreed to postpone action in regard to the future disposition of the territories on its western border until after the war in return for the guarantee of its national security represented by the Anglo-Russian alliance, with American assurances of moral support and postwar collaboration in safeguarding the peace and security of freedom-loving nations. Obviously the future of Poland and the Baltic countries was not in any way settled by this compromise. The problem was merely postponed. But it was hoped that it could be shelved at least for the duration of the war.

On the question of a second front, both Great Britain and the United States made it clear that they were in full agreement with Russia that one should be created just as soon as possible. It was expressly stated, in announcing the conclusions reached during the Roosevelt-Molotov conversations in Washington, that the two statesmen found themselves in unity upon the urgency of such a move—in Europe in 1942. No further explanations were made as to what this commitment might actually mean, but in connection with Russia's willingness to accept formal treaty engagements containing specific pledges against both territorial aggrandizement and interference in the internal affairs of other states, it gave comforting assurance of a general understanding among the three principal partners in the United Nations.

The mutual aid agreement between the United States and the Soviet Union, described as "an additional link in the chain of solidarity" among the United Nations, carried collaboration one step further. It superseded all earlier arrangements in regard to the supplies we were prepared to send Russia, setting up a lend-lease master plan similar to those in effect with Britain and China. No definite provision was made for the postwar settlement of lend-lease advances, but it was stipulated that repayment should not burden the commerce between the two nations.

Whatever may have been specifically in the minds of Churchill and Roosevelt in their emphasis upon the urgency of a second front, the course of military developments during the summer and fall of 1942 soon created widespread doubts as to the extent to which their two countries were prepared to comply with these apparently implicit pledges. As the Russian armies were once again rolled back by an even fiercer German offensive than that of the previous summer, the public took over the issue and began to clamor for action. Wholly ignorant of the over-all military strategy decided upon by their leaders, both the British and American people urged that something be done to draw off German strength from the eastern front before Russia went down to possibly irretrievable defeat. In September the situation was vividly dramatized by a statement made in Moscow by Wendell Willkie. His spectacular world tour brought him to the Russian capital at the height of the controversy, and after several meetings with Stalin—including an elaborate banquet at which he toasted the Russian dictator

as "a man who kept his eye on the ball"—he expressed his views in no uncertain terms.

"I am now convinced," Willkie told the correspondents in Moscow, "we can best help Russia by establishing a real second front in Europe with Great Britain at the earliest possible moment our military leaders will approve, and perhaps some of them need some public prodding. Next summer might be too late."

Our very unofficial emissary of good will was clearly enough expressing an attitude he had found among the Soviet officials. The Moscow newspapers, indeed, were becoming openly scornful of what they implied was the reluctance of the United States and Great Britain to run the risks that land operations in western Europe involved. They flatly charged that the democracies appeared more than willing to let Russia bear the real burden of war. Finally on October 4 Stalin himself came out with a blunt criticism of Anglo-American strategy in answering a series of written questions sent to him by the Moscow representative of the Associated Press. "As compared with the aid which the Soviet Union is giving the Allies by drawing upon itself the main forces of the German Fascist armies," the Russian dictator declared, "the aid of the Allies to the Soviet Union has so far been little effective. In order to amplify and improve this aid, only one thing is required: that the Allies fulfill their obligations promptly and on time."

Whatever the understandings—or possible misunderstandings —among the heads of government, relations among the United Nations appeared to be drifting perilously close to open dissension. The old distrust between the Soviet government and the Western democracies had not been as fully dissipated by the agreements reached in June, and subsequent conversations between Churchill and Stalin in Moscow, as had been hoped. That at least was clear. Public opinion in the nations concerned was highly disturbed. In the fall of 1942, as the tremendous battle over Stalingrad was drawing to its climax, the need to strengthen interallied trust and confidence appeared to be the most vital consideration in the conduct of the war.

November thereupon dramatically brought a first sign of the determination of Great Britain and the United States to fulfill their pledges to the Soviet Union and to take the offensive against the Axis Powers. American and British troops were landed in Morocco and Algeria, and in conjunction with the British Eighth Army, already driving Rommel across the burning sands of Libya, a great campaign was launched to oust Germany completely from all North Africa and clear the Mediterranean. Was this the long-awaited second front? For a time hopes ran high that these operations would lead to immediate invasion of southern Europe, force the transfer of heavy German forces from the eastern front and relieve the pressure upon the Russian armies. It would soon be demonstrated that these hopes were premature. The North African campaign would prove far more prolonged and difficult than an excited public here and abroad anticipated when the startling announcement that it was under way was first made. Nevertheless the landing of Anglo-American forces in this new theater of war appeared to relieve the tension that had developed between Moscow and the West.

Stalin promptly made handsome amends for his publicly expressed doubts upon the intention of the Allies to abide by their pledges. "The Soviet view of this campaign," he stated on November 13 in reply to another set of questions from the Associated Press, "is that it represents an outstanding fact of major importance demonstrating the growing might of the armed forces of the Allies and opening the prospect of disintegration of the Italo-German coalition in the nearest future. . . . It is yet too soon to say to what an extent this campaign has been effective in relieving immediate pressure on the Soviet Union. But it may be confidently said that the effect will not be a small one and that a certain relief in pressure on the Soviet Union will result already in the nearest future."

Almost simultaneously with the opening of the North African

campaign, moreover, the Russians themselves followed up their triumphant defense of Stalingrad by taking the offensive on a broad front against the forces which Hitler had been so confident would knock Russia completely out of the war. Again to the amazement of all the world, the Red armies drove ahead so irresistibly that as the winter progressed they succeeded step by step, in winning back all the territory conquered by the Nazis during the previous summer. The campaign in North Africa and the Soviet counterattacks in southern Russia marked the winter of 1942-1943 as a turning point in the European struggle, holding out the most favorable prospects of ultimate Allied victory since Russia and America had entered the war.

With England and the United States fervently congratulating Russia on her astounding successes, and the Soviet government returning the compliment with praise for their operations in North Africa, the new year opened upon a confident note for the United Nations. Both the military and the political situation appeared so favorable that the American public began to think far more seriously of the future peace than it had heretofore dared. Popular discussion of Russian-American relations took a new turn. With full collaboration in the war apparently assured, there came from many quarters an insistent demand that everything possible be done to assure the continuance of such concerted action when Hitler should be finally overthrown. Everywhere voices were raised to point out that close cooperation between the United States and Soviet Russia would be no less vital in time of peace than in time of war, and that events had demonstrated beyond shadow of doubt both the futility and the danger of the two great powers allowing any friction over internal policies again to blind them to the underlying similarity of their objectives in foreign policy.

Wendell Willkie was one of the most outspoken and influential of Russia's new-found friends. His advice to his countrymen, doubly effective because it represented the views of a champion of private enterprise and a Republican political leader, was to seek above everything else to understand the Russians.

"Work in ever closer cooperation with them while we are joined together in the common purpose of defeating a common enemy," he urged in an article in the *New York Times Magazine* early in January 1943. "Learn all we can about them and let them learn about us." To what end? Collaboration in peace as well as war. "Geographically, from a trade standpoint, from a similarity of approach to many problems," Willkie declared, "the Russians and Americans should get along together."

For all this enthusiasm over Russia, fears and suspicions of her future policies continued to lie close beneath the surface. Feelings which were the fruit of the long years of hostility between the two world wars could not be entirely eradicated from American thinking. Throughout the greater part of 1943, the popular attitude toward the Soviet Union swung erratically between the two extremes of deep admiration for Russian achievements on the field of battle, and grave misgivings as to how Russia might make use of these victories. Fears were expressed both of a separate peace and of the Soviets' single-handed defeat of Germany. The old ghost of possible world revolution walked again. The conviction that the United States had to accept in good faith the pledges of cooperation that Stalin had already made slowly gained ground through the year, but recurrent instances of dangerous friction could hardly be avoided.

"As the Red Armies plunge forward," the *New York Times* wrote on February 14, 1943, "they are raising many questions in many minds as to what order they have written on their banners, and the greater the Russian victories grow the more insistent they become. They are raised in private conversations, in the press, over the radio and in Congress. And these questions carry the danger that they will provide a fertile ground for the latest Nazi propaganda with which Hitler hopes to escape the consequences of defeat—the propaganda which raises the bogey of a Bolshevist domination of Europe in an effort to scare the world, divide the United Nations and therewith pave the way for a compromise peace."

To these questions the editorial found an answer in the binding engagements into which Russia had entered—her pledges to eschew all aggression, territorial aggrandizement and interference with the right of other peoples to determine their own form of government. But it revealed its own latent suspicion of the attitude of the Kremlin in declaring that perhaps even more explicit agreements were necessary "in order to give concrete meaning to the Atlantic Charter and to erect a common defense system for the future."

Another angle of the world situation inevitably promoting controversy was the Soviet Union's role in the Far East. Its critics emphasized the part they believed the United States had played in preventing a Japanese attack upon Russia through our operations in the Southwest Pacific, and they lost no opportunity to point out that in this part of the world we had received no cooperation whatsoever. The U.S.S.R. and Japan were still bound by a nonaggression treaty. There had been no indication that Stalin had any intention of taking part in that phase of the global war which perhaps most nearly affected American interests. Informed opinion realized that any diversion of Russian attention or Russian forces from the western front might prove disastrous insofar as the war in Europe was concerned until Germany was finally and completely defeated. Nevertheless former isolationists, declaring that Japan rather than Germany was the real menace to American national security, used the Soviet Union's failure to break off relations with Tokyo as another stick with which to belabor the alleged duplicity of its foreign policy.

A violent controversy also raged over the extent to which the United States was making good its pledges to increase the flow of supplies to Russia. Rumblings of discontent in Moscow became the basis for bitter debate in the United States between those who clung to their suspicions of the Soviet Union, and those who felt that we still had to prove our good faith before we could expect wholehearted Russian cooperation. On the one hand were charges that Stalin was pursuing his own nationalistic course, fighting his own war for all the efforts of the United Nations to develop an over-all strategy. On the other, attacks were leveled against the policy of the United Nations for failing to recognize the importance of Russia's tremendous war effort and for actually letting her down. The seeds of a third war might well be planted, it was stated, if America should doublecross Russia at this critical juncture in world affairs.

Perhaps to let in some light on this troubled situation, Admiral Standley, at this time American ambassador to Russia, stated in a press conference in Moscow that the Soviet government was concealing the extent of American lend-lease aid and purposely allowing the Russian people to get the impression that they had been deserted by their allies. Under Secretary of Welles at once announced that the ambassador had made his comment without prior consultation with Washington, but for all the fears that it might further disrupt American-Russian good will, the Soviet government took it in good part. It immediately made official acknowledgment of the effectiveness of our assistance, publicly broadcasting the actual figures of the supplies we had already delivered to the Russian armies.

What had been the extent of such aid? In the course of the debates on renewal of the lend-lease agreements, conducted against the background of this controversy and dispute, the official record was released to the public both here and abroad on March 11. Since her entry into the war the total value of all shipments to Russia was $1,825,600,000, including 2,600 planes, 3,200 tanks, 99,000 military vehicles and 130,000 submachine guns. Moreover, in the twelve months ending March 1, 1943, some 29 per cent of all lend-lease supplies had been set aside for the Soviet Union, and in such important categories as planes, tanks and military vehicles the percentage was higher than that for any other single country. These statistics were impressive. They went far toward stilling criticism, whether from Moscow or from doubters in this country, as to the wholeheartedness of American support for Russia. "The supplies received through lend-lease," Ambassador Litvinov declared,

"have been an enormous help, and as such deeply appreciated by the people of the Soviet Union, who are fully aware of its extent."

Whether the dying-down of controversy over American aid to Russia after renewal of the lend-lease legislation was the principal factor, or whether it more directly resulted from the realization that the Soviet Union was not going to win the war singlehandedly in the spring of 1943, the sharp criticism of the Soviet Union subsided after March. There was still evidence of latent mistrust, as when the Kremlin's suspension of diplomatic relations with the Polish government-in-exile revived the issue of strategic frontiers, but the United States showed itself increasingly anxious to maintain relations on the most cordial possible basis. Official policy was directed toward binding the Soviet Union firmly to the cause of the United Nations, and public leaders repeatedly emphasized the importance of establishing a basis for collaboration that would enable Russia and America to meet their problems in a spirit of mutual trust and confidence.

An issue of the magazine *Life* wholly devoted to the Soviet Union was a striking example of the intense popular interest in Russia, and its tone underscored the amazing reorientation in prevailing opinion about a regime which such a short time before had been so universally condemned for both its internal and external policies. For while *Life* treated somewhat gingerly the difficult issue of strategic frontiers, its portrayal of Russia and her leaders was remarkably sympathetic. "Clearly it is up to both the U.S.S.R. and the U.S.," this influential magazine stated editorially, "to seek a broader and more enlightened base for their future relationship. On Russia's part, we think she must try to overcome the suspicion which she seems to harbor against all democratic peoples. Russia should realize that she has strong friends in the United States; and she should give these friends help and encouragement by opening the channels of information and good will."

Wendell Willkie also urged the cause of Russian-American

friendship once again in his phenomenally popular *One World*. The hesitations of those in the democracies who feared and mistrusted Soviet Russia, dreading the inroads of an economic order that would be destructive of their own, were dismissed as a sign of weakness. The best answer to Communism, the Republican leader declared, was "a living, vibrant, fearless democracy—economic, social, and political." Our own ideals should be safe if we truly lived up to them. "No, we do not need to fear Russia," Willkie concluded. "We need to learn to work with her against our common enemy, Hitler. We need to learn to work with her in the world after the war. For Russia is a dynamic country, a vital new society, a force that cannot be bypassed in any future world."

Among administration spokesmen, Vice President Wallace pled most eloquently for a more general realization of how closely identified were the fundamental goals of the Russian and American people, and how dependent they were on one another if these goals were to be attained. "It is vital," he declared in one among many such statements, "that the United States and Russia be in accord as to the fundamentals of an enduring peace based on the aspirations of the common man."

The cause of unity was even more definitely promoted in Moscow. In striking contrast to the grudging and ungracious tone of so many of his former comments on the United Nations, the late spring of 1943 found Stalin paying eloquent tribute to the successes Anglo-American arms were now winning in North Africa, and strongly emphasizing the importance of friendship between Soviet Russia and her allies. On the occasion of the anniversary of the signing of the Russian-American mutual aid agreement, Moscow newspapers also extolled American help in the war and the promise of future American collaboration in terms such as they had never before used. "Soviet-American friendship," *Pravda*, organ of the Communist Party, declared, "is in accordance with the historical traditions of the two great nations, which feel a mutual sympathy and respect."

More important than such expressions of opinion was the dramatic announcement on May 22, 1943, of the dissolution of the Comintern. Throughout the entire history of Soviet-American relations, this agency for the promotion of revolutionary Communist propaganda had been the greatest barrier to any real understanding between Russia and America. Both the United States government and the American people were convinced that the Soviet government had violated its antipropaganda pledges in the Roosevelt-Litvinov agreement of 1933 by continuing to allow this organization, so clearly controlled by the Communist Party in Russia, to direct the activities of American Communists. While it had remained very much in the background since Russia's entry into the war, the American Communist Party having withdrawn from membership, the very existence of the Comintern was a constant threat of interference in our internal affairs.

Its dissolution, therefore, did more than any previous move on Moscow's part to convince many still doubtful Americans that Communist Russia had in reality swung far away from its original program of world revolution. It did not reconcile the underlying conflicts of capitalism and Communism. There was no guarantee that writing-off the Comintern necessarily represented a permanent change in the policy of the Kremlin. Nevertheless it fertilized the soil for a more hardy growth of the tender shoots of Russian-American friendship, and it led to a rising popular demand in this country for still more effective cooperation.

During the following months, the course of the war also emphasized the need for a further clarification of our relations. The armies of the Soviet Union, having successfully checked Hitler's attempts to launch a new drive eastward, counterattacked with such force that the Germans were soon in full retreat. Once again to the amazement of the entire world, Russia staged a spectacular offensive that drove the Nazis not only back to the Dnieper, but through even that strong defensive barrier. In the meantime, British and American armies had conquered Sicily, won in Italy their first foothold upon the European mainland, and were driving upon Rome. Fascist Italy had collapsed under the impact of these blows. Mussolini had fallen from power and the Badoglio government swung Italy into the Allied camp as a co-belligerent against the Axis powers. With greatly intensified bombing of Germany added to these advances in Italy and Russia, the imperative necessity of a closer understanding between the Soviet Union and the Western democracies was equally recognized in Moscow, London and Washington. The doubts and misgivings which still marked their relations, and occasionally broke out in open controversy, endangered the successful prosecution of the war and clouded the prospects of the peace that was beginning to become a more tangible possibility.

In order to convince Germany that she had no reason to hope for a falling-out among the allies, and to provide a common basis for both war and postwar policies, a tripartite conference was consequently held in October among the foreign ministers of Soviet Russia, Great Britain and the United States. Its scene was Moscow, and from the American point of view it represented far and away the most important effort since the start of the war to give enduring vitality to our rapprochement with Russia. There was some scepticism as to the possible results of the conference as Secretary Hull took off by plane for the Soviet capital, but it was heartily supported by public opinion throughout this country.

After two weeks of negotiation, new accords were announced which went far beyond the expectations of most observers. No definite agreements on specific postwar problems were proclaimed. The conference had not performed the miracle of settling every point at issue among the several powers. Nevertheless a joint declaration, in which the Chinese government also concurred, reaffirmed in the most binding terms the determination of the United States, Great Britain and Soviet Russia to continue hostilities against those Axis powers with which they were at war until they had laid down their arms on the

basis of unconditional surrender, and further pledged the continuance of united action for the postwar organization and maintenance of peace and security.

The four powers agreed to act together in all matters relating to the surrender and disarmament of the enemy, to take in concert such measures as were necessary to provide against violation of the terms of surrender, not to employ their military forces within the territories of other states except after joint consultation, and to cooperate in bringing about a practical agreement upon postwar disarmament. Still more important, their declaration of policy recognized the necessity of establishing "a general international organization, based on the principle of the sovereign equality of all peace-loving States, and open to membership by all such States, large and small."

The announcement of these accords on November 1 was hailed enthusiastically in the United States. Indeed, they received within a few days the most signal mark of public approval that any move in foreign policy could obtain. The Senate had been debating a possible resolution in favor of world organization. The provision for such an agency as outlined in the Moscow accords was at once incorporated in this resolution, almost word for word, and it was approved by the Senate with the overwhelming majority of 85 to 5. Only time could tell the effectiveness of these measures looking toward American participation in a new world order, but it was universally agreed that the Moscow conference, and the approval extended to its conclusions by the Senate, were among the most memorable developments in the whole course of American foreign relations.

A month later still further confirmation was given to this new evidence of cooperation between the Soviet Union and the Western democracies. Under highly dramatic circumstances President Roosevelt, Prime Minister Churchill and Premier Stalin met at Teheran, the capital of Iran. The conference results underlined their determination that the three nations, in the words of the declaration issued on December 1, 1943, should "work together in the war and in the peace that will follow." Perhaps even more important than any agreements reached, however, was the atmosphere of good will in which the meeting of the three statesmen was held. "We came here with hope and determination," Roosevelt and Stalin joined Churchill in announcing. "We leave here friends in fact, in spirit, and in purpose."

Apart from their implications as to united action for the defeat of Germany and a future world organization for peace, the conferences at Moscow and at Teheran held out striking promise for the continued collaboration in international affairs of the United States and the Soviet Union. The two nations had been drawn closer together than at any time since the Communist revolution, perhaps than in all their history.

Since the time over a century and a half ago when Francis Dana tried to persuade Catherine the Great to recognize the newly won independence of the United States, the points of difference between Russia and America have often seemed more important than those interests which the two great nations have had in common. The world crisis precipitated by Hitler, however, brought out as never before our mutual concern in the most vital of all issues facing the modern world—the preservation of peace. Moreover, for all the continued differences in our approach to national as distinguished from international objectives, here too the impact of a world-wide threat of Fascism has illuminated a basic similarity in ultimate goals. The peoples of both Russia and America are working toward a future in which they may be free to develop to the utmost their own resources and their own capacities. The one nation may be following a road marked "capitalism," the other a road marked "socialism," but the final destination in each case is a social order in which a decent livelihood, personal dignity and lasting peace can be assured for the common man.

The past history of Russian-American relations reveals that the two countries are almost inevitably drawn together in time

of crisis. They have had no grounds for conflict that have involved them in war against each other, and they should be able to continue to live together in harmony. But the challenge of today overshadows any such limited conception of their international responsibilities. It is a challenge to work together for world peace. The common danger drawing us together in the future should no longer be the possible threat to our national interests of a political or commercial rival, but any threat to peace in any part of the world from any quarter.

America and Russia have survived dissension and controversy and conflict in the past. Our traditional friendship has not been based upon sentiment and casual gestures of good will, but upon each nation's realistic appraisal of its own national interests. The record is a reasonably consistent one from the days of our early cooperation in defense of freedom of the seas to those of our united action against the menace of Fascism. There should be no reason, having for so long endured the perils of conflicting ideologies, why we should not respect one another's rights to self-government in a future world wherein we can together exert an influence that might well prove decisive in favor of a just and lasting peace. The road which has led to Teheran should in the future link Washington and Moscow even more closely.

BIBLIOGRAPHICAL NOTES

CHAPTER I

THE basic material for this account of Russian-American relations has been derived from the official documents of the State Department, especially valuable for the important period from 1917 through 1919; such records as are available in the writings of our envoys in Russia, which range from *The Mission to Russia* of John Quincy Adams to *Mission to Moscow* by Joseph E. Davies; and an extensive sampling of contemporary comment in newspapers and magazines throughout the entire period, especially *Niles' Register, Harper's Weekly,* the *Literary Digest* and the *New York Times.* Full use has also been made of earlier studies of various phases of Russian-American relations, particularly those based on Russian documents, and the author would gratefully acknowledge his debt to these books, monographs and articles.

There is no full-length treatment of the subject of this book. Two important surveys dealing with limited periods are J. C. Hildt, *Early Diplomatic Negotiations of the United States with Russia,* Johns Hopkins University Studies in History and Political Science, Vol. 24, 1906, and B. P. Thomas, *Russo-American Relations, 1815-1867,* Johns Hopkins University Studies in History and Political Science, Vol. 48, 1930. On the period between 1917 and 1927, Frederick L. Schuman, *American Policy Toward Russia Since 1917,* New York, 1928, is immensely helpful although additional documentary and other material has become available since it was written. Every writer on our relations with Russia is also particularly indebted to Frank A. Golder for articles based upon his examination of the Russian archives for the earlier period of our relations with the Czarist government. More specific reference to these monographs will be made under the appropriate chapters.

Among more general articles on the history of Russian-American relations are Oscar S. Straus, "The United States and Russia: Their Historical Relations," Reprint from the *North American Review,* 1905; Jerome Davis, "One Hundred and Fifty Years of American-Russian Relations, 1777-1927," *Annals of American Academy of Political and Social Science,* Vol. 132, 1927; DeWitt Clinton Poole, "Russia and the United States," *New Europe,* September 1941; and Roger Dow, "Prostor: A Geopolitical Study of Russia and the United States," *Russian Review,* 1941. There is also interesting treatment of this topic in Walter Lippmann's recent and highly stimulating *U.S. Foreign Policy,* New York, 1943.

CHAPTER II

MATERIAL on Francis Dana is most easily available in William P. Cresson, *Francis Dana*, New York, 1930, while the indispensable record of John Quincy Adams' stay in St. Petersburg is his *Mission to Russia*, in Vol. 2 of the *Memoirs*, Philadelphia, 1874. Quotations from Jefferson are taken from *The Writings of Thomas Jefferson*, Vol. 5, Washington, 1853. There is interesting material on our early trade with Russia in Samuel Eliot Morison, *The Maritime History of Massachusetts*, Boston, 1921, and James Duncan Phillips, "Salem Opens American Trade with Russia," *New England Quarterly*, Vol. 14, 1941. Special articles on the topics of this chapter are Frank A. Golder's "Catherine II and the American Revolution," in the *American Historical Review*, Vol. 21, 1915, and "The Russian Offer of Mediation in the War of 1812," in the *Political Science Quarterly*, Vol. 3, 1916. The entire period is treated in J. C. Hildt's *Early Diplomatic Negotiations of the United States with Russia*, as noted above.

CHAPTER III

THERE is important material for this chapter in Adams' *Memoirs*, Jefferson's *Writings* and also the *Writings* of James Monroe, Vol. 6, New York, 1903. The pertinent diplomatic correspondence on the events leading up to announcement of the Monroe Doctrine is found in "Correspondence of the Russian Ministers in Washington, 1818-25," in the *American Historical Review*, Vol. 18, 1913. Among useful specialized articles are William S. Robertson, "Russia and the Emancipation of Spanish America," *Hispanic American Historical Review*, Vol. 24, 1941, and the same author's "The Monroe Doctrine Abroad in 1823-24," *American Political Science Review*, Vol. 6, 1912. See also Dexter Perkins, *The Monroe Doctrine, 1823-26,* Cambridge, 1927; E. H. Tatum, Jr., *The United States and Europe, 1815-23,* Berkeley, 1936; and B. P. Thomas, *Russo-American Relations, 1815-67,* noted above. There is material on Russian settlements in North America, among many other books, in H. H. Bancroft's volumes on Alaska and California in his *History of the Pacific States*, San Francisco, 1886; Joseph Schafer, *The Pacific Slope and Alaska*, Boston, 1885; Robert G. Cleland, *A History of California: the American Period*, New York, 1922, and Henry W. Clark, *History of Alaska*, New York, 1930. The most fascinating reading on Russian activities, popularly written but based on Russian sources, are two books by Hector Chevigny: *Lord of Alaska: Baranov and the Russian Adventure*, New York, 1942, and *Lost Empire*, New York, 1937.

CHAPTER IV

THERE is some material on John Randolph's experiences in Russia in both Hugh A. Garland, *The Life of John Randolph*, New York, 1850, and William C. Bruce, *John Randolph of Roanoke*, New York, 1922; letters from St. Petersburg of James Buchanan are to be found in Vol. 2 of *The Works*

of James Buchanan, Philadelphia, 1908; and accounts of Cassius M. Clay's stay in Russia in J. R. Robertson's *A Kentuckian at the Court of the Tsars*, Berea College, 1935, and Albert Parry's "Cassius Clay's Glimpse into the Future," in the *Russian Review*, Spring, 1943. Frank A. Golder has written on "Russian-American Relations During the Crimean War," in the *American Historical Review*, Vol. 31, 1926, while of outstanding importance for the 1860's is his "The Russian Fleet and the Civil War," *American Historical Review*, Vol. 20, 1915, giving the first account of the real objectives behind the fleet's visit to American waters. In addition to the diplomatic correspondence found in *American State Papers* and B. P. Thomas' previously noted study, other useful sources are E. A. Adamov, "Russia and the United States at the Time of the Civil War," *Journal of Modern History*, Vol. 2, 1930; Harold E. Blinn, "Seward and the Polish Rebellion," *American Historical Review*, Vol. 45, 1940; and Albert Parry, "John B. Turchin: Russian General in the American Civil War," *Russian Review*, April 1942. The author has also drawn heavily in this chapter upon *Harper's Weekly* and contemporary New York papers.

CHAPTER V

THE story of the purchase of Alaska has been told many times. Official documents dealing with it are to be found in the *Proceedings of the Alaska Boundary Tribunal*, 7 vols., Washington, 1904; *House Executive Document 177*, 40th Congress, 2nd session; and Charles Sumner, *On the Cession of Alaska*, Washington, 1867—a reprint of his famous speech. For Secretary Seward's role there is also firsthand material in Frederick W. Seward's *Reminiscences of a Wartime Statesman and Diplomat*, New York, 1916, and *Seward at Washington as Senator and Secretary of State*, New York, 1891. The most comprehensive account of the entire transaction is Victor J. Farrar, *The Annexation of Russian America to the United States*, Washington, 1937. Among special articles dealing with this topic are the same author's "The Background of the Purchase of Alaska," *Washington Historical Quarterly*, Vol. 13, 1922, and "Joseph Lane McDonald and the Purchase of Alaska," *Washington Historical Quarterly*, Vol. 12, 1921; Thomas A. Bailey, "Why the United States Purchased Alaska," *Pacific Historical Review*, Vol. 3, 1934; James Morton Callahan, "The Alaska Purchase," *West Virginia University Studies*, Series 1, No. 2, 1908; William A. Dunning, "Paying for Alaska," *Political Science Quarterly*, Vol. 27, 1912; R. H. Luthin, "The Sale of Alaska," *Slavonic Review*, Vol. 16, 1937; and Hunter Miller, "Russian Opinion on the Cession of Alaska," *American Historical Review*, Vol. 48, 1943.

CHAPTER VI

THE basic material for our relations with Russia in the Far East are to be found in the appropriate annual volumes of *Papers Relating to Foreign Relations*, United States Department of State, and in contemporary records, including the digests of public opinion in the *Literary Digest*. There is also valuable material in such books and special articles as Andrew D. White, *Autobiography*, New York, 1905; Tyler Dennett, *John Hay*, New York, 1933, and the same author's *Roosevelt and the Russo-Japanese War*, New York, 1925; A. L. P. Dennis, *Adventures in American Diplomacy*, New York, 1928; Henry F. Pringle, *Theodore Roosevelt*, New York, 1931; Foster Rhea Dulles, *Forty Years of American-Japanese Relations*, New York, 1937; A. Whitney Griswold, *The Far Eastern Policy of the United States*, New York, 1938, and James K. Eyre, Jr., "Russia and the American Acquisition of the Philippine Islands," *Mississippi Valley Historical Review*, Vol. 28, 1942.

CHAPTERS VII-IX

THERE are extensive documentary sources for the period of the Russian Revolution and Allied intervention. The most important, and indispensable, include *Papers Relating to Foreign Relations, Russia, 1918*, 3 vols., *Russia, 1919*, and *Lansing Papers, 1914-20*, 2 vols.; Ray Stannard Baker, *Woodrow Wilson: Life and Letters*, Vols. 7 and 8, New York, 1939; Charles Seymour, *The Intimate Papers of Colonel House*, Boston, 1928; Robert Lansing, *War Memoirs*, New York, 1935; David R. Francis, *Russia from the American Embassy*, New York, 1921; and Elihu Root, *The Mission to Russia*, Cambridge, 1918. Among other contemporary records of Americans in Russia on official missions during these years attention should also be drawn to Edgar Sisson, *One Hundred Red Days*, New Haven, 1931; William C. Bullitt, *The Bullitt Mission to Russia*, New York, 1919; William Hard, *Raymond Robins' Own Story*, New York, 1920; William S. Graves, *America's Siberian Adventure*, New York, 1931; Carl W. Ackerman, *Trailing the Bolsheviki*, New York, 1919; and Ralph Albertson, *Fighting Without a War*, New York, 1920.

The most thorough treatment of these years among secondary sources, as already noted, is Frederick L. Schuman, *American Policy Toward Russia Since 1917*, New York, 1928, while a more recent authoritative account of one phase of the intervention program is L. I. Strakhovsky, *The Origins of American Intervention in North Russia*, Princeton, 1937, recently supplemented by the same author's *Intervention at Archangel*, Princeton, 1944. There is also some new material in Philip C. Jessup, *Elihu Root*, New York, 1938. A collection of documents now largely replaced by the official publications of the State Department is C. K. Cumming and Walter W. Pettit, *Russian-American Relations*, New York, 1920.

CHAPTER X

CONTEMPORARY newspapers and magazines, together with reports upon Congressional hearings, constitute the bulk of the material upon the period of the great Red scare. The author has made special use of the *Literary Digest*, the *Saturday Evening Post*, *Collier's*, the *New Republic*, the *Nation* and the *New York Times*. Interesting secondary sources would include, in

addition to F. L. Schuman, Frederick Lewis Allen, *Only Yesterday*, New York, 1931; Preston W. Slosson, *The Great Crusade and After*, New York, 1930; and Mark Sullivan, *Our Times*, Vol. 6, New York, 1935.

CHAPTERS XI-XII

AGAIN the most valuable material is that found in contemporary books, magazines and newspapers portraying the attitude of the American public toward Soviet Russia during the 1920's. Only the *Reader's Guide to Periodical Literature* can give an adequate idea of the hundreds of articles on Russia, but there is a helpful attempt to analyze public opinion in Meno Lovenstein, *American Opinion of Soviet Russia*, Washington, 1941. The official documents on recognition of the Soviet Union are limited to the Department of State release, *Establishment of Diplomatic Relations with the Union of Soviet Socialist Republics*, Washington, 1933. Two helpful articles which deal with the historical background of recognition rather than contemporary comment are Vera Micheles Dean, "American Policy Toward Russia," *Current History*, January 1933, and Malbone S. Graham, "Russian-American Relations, 1917-33: An Interpretation," *American Political Science Review*, Vol. 28, 1934.

CHAPTERS XIII-XV

FOR the period since 1933 the official documents may be most conveniently found in the collections of the World Peace Foundation, and in the two State Department series: *Press Releases*, 1929-39, and *Bulletin*, 1939-43. They are of course far from complete. The official *Peace and War*, issued by the State Department in 1942, and supplemented in 1943 with publication of the pertinent documents, almost completely neglects relations with Soviet Russia. There is some further documentary material in *The Public Papers and Addresses of Franklin D. Roosevelt*, 9 vols. to date, New York, 1938- . Absolutely invaluable is Joseph E. Davies' remarkable book, *Mission to Moscow*, New York, 1941. Reference may also be had upon our official relations with Russia between 1928 and 1931 to *Survey of American Foreign Relations*, 4 vols., New Haven, 1928-31, and since that date to the annual *The United States in World Affairs*, New York, 1932- . Both publications are issued, under different editors, by the Council on Foreign Relations.

Two lively and readable accounts of our foreign relations during these years, although treating only incidentally of Soviet Russia, are Joseph Alsop and Robert Kintner, *American White Paper*, New York, 1940, and Forrest Davis and Ernest K. Lindley, *How War Came*, New York, 1942. A brief study more directly related to relations with Russia is John L. Childs and George S. Counts, *America, Russia, and the Communist Party*, New York, 1943. The greater part of the material on recent years, however, must inevitably be found in contemporary newspapers and magazines. The *New York Times* has been used most extensively.

Note should also be made of five volumes on Soviet Russia's foreign relations: A. L. P. Dennis, *The Foreign Policies of Soviet Russia*, New York, 1924; Louis B. Fischer, *The Soviets in World Affairs*, London, 1930; Henry C. Wolfe, *The Imperial Soviets*, New York, 1940; T. A. Taracouzio, *War and Peace in Soviet Diplomacy*, New York, 1940; and, of far the greatest value for the very recent period, David J. Dallin, *Soviet Russia's Foreign Policy, 1939-1942*, New Haven, 1942. One documentary source on Russian policy is Maxim Litvinov, *Against Aggression*, New York, 1939. A biography of the Soviet statesman has also been recently published, Arthur Upham Pope, *Maxim Litvinov*, New York, 1943; and an interesting study of Lenin, Trotsky and Stalin is included in Edward Mead Earle, *Makers of Modern Strategy*, Princeton, 1943. Various articles dealing with Russian-American relations in the past few years may also be found in the *Russian Review* and *Soviet Russia Today*.

There remain finally to be noted a number of the many books describing wartime conditions in Russia which occasionally throw some light on the Soviet attitude toward the United States. In this category should perhaps be placed Wendell Willkie, *One World*, New York, 1943. Books by correspondents include Wallace Carroll, *We're in This with Russia*, Boston, 1942; Quentin Reynolds, *Only the Stars Are Neutral*, New York, 1942; Henry C. Cassidy, *Moscow Dateline*, Boston, 1943; James E. Brown, *Russia Fights*, New York, 1943; Walter Graebner, *Round Trip to Russia*, New York, 1943; and Larry Lesueur, *Twelve Days That Changed the World*, New York, 1943.

INDEX